EDUCATION IN FRANCE
1848–1870

Education in France
1848-1870

by R. D. ANDERSON

CLARENDON PRESS · OXFORD
1975

Oxford University Press, Ely House, London W. 1

GLASGOW NEW YORK TORONTO MELBOURNE WELLINGTON
CAPE TOWN IBADAN NAIROBI DAR ES SALAAM LUSAKA ADDIS ABABA
DELHI BOMBAY CALCUTTA MADRAS KARACHI LAHORE DACCA
KUALA LUMPUR SINGAPORE HONG KONG TOKYO

ISBN 0 19 827311 8

© *Oxford University Press 1975*

*Printed in Great Britain by
Billing & Sons Limited, Guildford and London*

Contents

0353865

Introduction

The history of education, a favourite field for the antiquarian or amateur approach, is of wider historical interest only when it is related to the context of a particular age and society, and when the historian knows what general questions it may contribute to answering. One obvious starting-point is the political context. The period of French history under study saw first the replacement of the July monarchy by the Second Republic, then the collapse of the Republic and the establishment of the Second Empire. We can learn something about the underlying nature of these regimes, and of the political creeds like liberalism and republicanism which they represented, by looking at their educational policies and ideals. Behind changes of regime, of course, lie shifts in the balance of social classes. But here a wider perspective is needed. Most historians of nineteenth-century France see a decisive break occurring around 1880, when the firm establishment of the Third Republic brought to its end an age dominated by the 'notables' or upper middle class, an age beginning either with the Revolution of 1789 or in 1830 when the liberal bourgeoisie finally beat off the aristocratic challenge to their ascendancy. The years around 1880 also marked an era in educational history, since the Third Republic celebrated its arrival with a series of major reforms; it is therefore with education in the 'age of the notables' that we shall be concerned.

Clearly, too, there are important questions to be asked about the 'bourgeois' nature of French society in the nineteenth century. How 'modern' or 'democratic' was it? What was the extent of social mobility, and how far was the famous principle of the 'career open to talents' turned into reality? These are matters intimately linked with the educational system. Historians who study them find themselves engaged in a common enterprise with sociologists, of whom several have recently turned their attention to French education in the nineteenth century. Vaughan and Archer, for example, have applied concepts derived from Weber to the comparative study of educational change in England and France, while French scholars like Pierre Bourdieu and Viviane Isambert-Jamati, following a tradition established by Durkheim, have emphasized the value systems implicit in education and the way in which it transmits knowledge and cultural patterns.

It might indeed be claimed that nineteenth-century France has a special significance for sociology, for it is on the historical model provided by the French Revolution that much sociological theory is based. This is obviously true of Marxism, but hardly less so of the idea of an advancing rationality bringing with it the phenomena which characterize modern industrial societies. Many sociological concepts have an implicit historical content which is not always acknowledged, but which is a legitimate concern of the historian. The society produced by the French Revolution would seem to have a paradigmatic quality: here if anywhere is the European model of a 'modern' society; here, in a society showing such features of modernity as the rise of a formalized bureaucracy and the movement from ascribed to achieved status, we would expect to find educational institutions which look forward to those of the modern industrial world. To some extent we do; but the picture is not a simple one, and as Vaughan and Archer point out, it was England with its archaic educational system, not France with its modern one, which industrialized more successfully.

The historian cannot ignore the theories and concepts suggested by the sociologist, for if they are valid they are tools for interpreting the past as well as the present. But conversely he is entitled to point out that generalization about the past is difficult, and that the possession of theoretical constructs can provide no short-cut out of the difficulties. With his instinct 'to complicate what appears too simple',[1] the historian will tend to insist on careful differentiation and discrimination, and will be suspicious of schematic polarizations or of over-simple views of education as the 'reflection' of a social system. With his awareness of the temporal context, and of change and discontinuity, he will not be led astray by superficial similarities; one often hears, for example, that French education is essentially the work of Napoleon—especially since 1968, with the implication that nothing much had changed in between—but profound changes lie behind the continuity of the institutional framework.

[1] L. Febvre, *Combats pour l'histoire* (1953), p. 208.

The first two chapters attempt to describe some of the specific realities of French education in the early nineteenth century, including those which were the product of the revolutionary and Napoleonic period. The educational system was not yet that of modern France—primary education was still neither free nor compulsory—but nevertheless France had a complex and in many ways advanced educational structure whose character and functioning one must seek to explain and understand.

The terms 'system' and 'structure' are perhaps misleading, for a basic point which must be made first of all is that there was no integrated educational system. To sensible men, it seemed obvious that 'in every civilized society, there are necessarily two classes of men', and that consequently 'there must be two complete systems of education, having nothing in common with each other'.[1] In France as elsewhere in nineteenth-century Europe, primary and secondary schools formed separate and self-contained sectors, one for the 'people', the other for the bourgeoisie. The social role of the schools, the values underlying the teaching, the place of religious education, the legal and administrative framework—all differed between the two. Another division was that based on sex, for boys' and girls' schools developed according to different rhythms—there were no lycées for girls until 1880—and were governed by different ideals, especially in the amount of influence allowed to the Church. The French educational 'system' therefore had four sub-systems, and within some of them things were further complicated by rivalry between state and Catholic schools. But all four sub-systems were controlled by the products of one of them: middle-class education for boys, the part of French education which enjoyed most prestige and which received the earliest and closest attention from the state.

---

[1] Destutt de Tracy, quoted in A. Prost, *Histoire de l'enseignement en France 1800–1967* (1968), p. 13.

CHAPTER ONE

Education, the state, and society

I. THE ROLE OF THE STATE

The centralization of French education under state control, perhaps its most familiar distinctive feature, was not applied uniformly to every part of the system. A public system of secondary education for boys was created a generation before serious attention was paid to the needs of the masses—the reverse of the pattern of state intervention in England. The orthodox view of secondary education was that 'this is the kind of education that has most importance for the State, because it alone forms and trains the enlightened classes of a nation'.[1] The state both provided schools and met some 20 per cent of their costs.[2] But the extension of central direction to the primary schools was a slow process still under way in our period.

State intervention was not a particularly ancient tradition. The idea that the general shape of education was a state responsibility and a matter for national legislation preceded the Revolution by only a few decades. It was the Church which superintended the numerous but ill-coordinated educational establishments of the ancien régime—the somnolent universities, the colleges for the upper and middle classes (generally run by religious orders), and the *petites écoles* which dispensed religious instruction and the elements of literacy to the children of the poor. The state had taken initiatives only with military and technical education. When the Revolution attacked the privileges of the Church, therefore, it destroyed the financial and corporate basis of the existing educational system. The universities disappeared, and colleges and village schools survived only precariously. Eventually the state was forced to step in to take the Church's place.

But what began as a matter of expediency soon became a matter of principle, and theoretical justifications for state action were elaborated. There was the principle of secularization, already

[1] C. Jourdain, *Le Budget de l'instruction publique* (1857), p. 283.
[2] Based on *Statistique de l'enseignement secondaire en 1865* (1868), Table 28.

proclaimed by the Enlightenment: education and the transmission of thought were activities too vital to society to be controlled by the Church, especially in a scientific age, and ought permanently to be kept out of its hands. This fitted in with the traditional 'Gallican' belief in subordinating the Church to state authority, a tradition re-emphasized by Napoleon and supported by the bureaucracy throughout the nineteenth century. There was the principle that education should form loyal citizens and patriots, applied in different senses but never abandoned by succeeding political regimes. Not least, there was the principle of national unity. It is easy to forget that in the early nineteenth century centralization was partly a response to the strength of centrifugal forces. The desire to use education to create a new national consciousness explains many nineteenth-century attitudes, especially the obsession with uniformity. In secondary education, the aim was to produce a homogeneous, nationally-minded educated class, and schools followed the same curriculum and examination programmes; the famous story of the minister of education looking at his watch was not so far from the truth. Local variations in the syllabus were looked on with suspicion, and this could stifle experiment and innovation. This also applied to the primary schools, where the concern for national unity was expressed in the teaching of the metric system (the 'national system', as it was called), and in the war waged on the *patois* and non-French languages which were spoken in the countryside in many areas well into the second half of the century.

Several plans for national systems of education were discussed during the years of revolution, but little was done until Napoleon created the 'University' in 1808. The University had no counterpart in other countries. It was both an administration through which the state ran its own schools and supervised private ones—this side of it became the ministry of public instruction in 1824—and the corporate body of state teachers in secondary and higher education. In its corporate aspect, the University is a prime example of how a body of teachers, controlling their own standards and recruitment through the examination system, can form a semi-autonomous force, a filter through which ideas and policies devised at the top had to pass before they reached the children in the classroom. A centralized system might seem to give the government unlimited power to change education, but in practice reforms could be modified or even sabotaged by the resistance of the teachers, and the autonomy of the University has in France acted as a counterweight to state control in the same kind of way as local autonomy in Britain. Educationally, the University was conservative, and was largely responsible for perpetuating the classical tradition in the lycées. Politically, it became a centre of moderate liberal ideas, and a refuge for free thought in times of reaction. Napoleon himself had conceived it as a kind of anti-clergy devoted to modern, secular ideas. In the early years, it turned out more Catholic than he intended, but its liberal tendencies became firmly established after 1830.

There was also an element of autonomy in the administrative side of the University. The permanent officials were few in number and mainly engaged on routine tasks. Policy was made, in the absence of a minister with strong ideas of his own, by a small group of advisers drawn from the higher reaches of the University, and in this way certain individuals could enjoy influence over a long period. Under the July monarchy, the centre of power was the Conseil royal, notoriously oligarchic and dominated by the philosopher Victor Cousin. At this time, leading figures in the University were also prominent in public life, and several of them—Guizot, Villemain, Cousin himself—served as minister of education. Not surprisingly, this was later looked back to as a golden age when the University was uniquely free from outside interference. Under the Second Empire, it suffered more from strong-willed ministers. But advisers of the same type as before—leading scientists, men of letters, professors at the Sorbonne and the faculty of law—continued to have an important policy-making role as inspectors-general.

Primary schools and primary teachers were felt to be only marginally part of the University, and the policy-making machinery was also geared to middle-class education. In the sixties, both higher and secondary education had eight inspectors-general, but primary education only four. This underlines the lack of central control in this sector. The pattern was much more like the English one than might at first appear, with the central state seeing its function as one of supervision and encouragement, and only gradually extending its direct intervention to improve standards and impose some uniformity. Under the ancien régime, the Church had licensed teachers, but the local secular authorities had been responsible for setting up schools and financing them. This situation continued in the nineteenth century: the state took over the Church's supervisory role, but the basic responsibility for primary education lay with the communes (village or town councils). Until after 1815, legislation on primary education did little more than sanction what communes chose to do, and the decisive step was the *loi Guizot* of 1833 which for the first time obliged every commune to have a school.

The local authorities—departments as well as communes—made a contribution to education which is often neglected, and not only in the primary field. Town councils ran 'municipal colleges' which supplemented the state's lycées, and they were to take the initiative in introducing new forms of technical school. A complete and logical local government system was one of the legacies of the Revolution, and while in this period the councils did not have much political independence they did have command over substantial funds, and could represent effectively the desires of middle-class parents and local business interests.

The government also preferred, as in England, to encourage primary education indirectly through collaboration with voluntary agencies. In a sense, the Catholic Church played the same role in France as the educational societies in England. Many local councils entrusted their schools to teaching orders on a contractual basis, and the larger orders—notably the Christian Brothers—trained their own teachers, worked out their own methods, and wrote their own textbooks. On the secular side, there was the Société pour l'instruction élémentaire, founded by liberals in 1815 to promote the Lancastrian system, and supported by several local societies. The lay societies normally confined themselves to encouraging education through publications and subsidies, but occasionally they ran schools themselves: until 1870, Lyons, the second city of France, ran none of its primary schools directly but entrusted some to religious orders and others to the lay Société d'instruction primaire du Rhône.[1]

One should therefore not exaggerate the centralization of French education. This was, after all, the age of *laissez-faire*, and although the liberal bourgeoisie were prepared to make large exceptions to

[1] M. Gontard, 'Une Bataille scolaire au XIXe siècle: l'affaire des écoles primaires laïques de Lyon (1869–1873)', *Cahiers d'histoire*, iii (1958), p. 270; cf. J. Simon, *L'École* (1865), pp. 392–3.

the doctrine of non-intervention in order to protect their interests against the Church, they remained firmly attached in principle to local and individual initiative. In fact, in 'centralized' France the state did not itself run a single primary school in 1848; even the training colleges for teachers were run by the departments. And while higher education was a monopoly of the state, its direct stake in secondary education was represented by just fifty-six lycées, fewer than one to each department.

2. SCHOOLS AND SOCIAL CLASS

The idea of secondary schools for the élite and primary schools for the masses had the virtue of simplicity, and did correspond to a rough division in society between privileged and unprivileged classes; the possession of a classical education was becoming, indeed, one of the accepted badges of middle-class status. But there were more than two social classes in nineteenth-century France, and before we can discuss 'middle-class' education or 'bourgeois' society some definitions are necessary. At the risk of oversimplification, those with a stake in secondary education may be divided into three groups. First, the old landed upper class, now mainly Catholic and legitimist in sentiment. Second, those elements in the middle class who had established their social dominance since 1789. These were the 'notables', the top stratum of the bourgeoisie, whose wealth was still based on landowning, the professions, and public service as much as on commerce and industry. This group may be called the 'liberal bourgeoisie'; but they were not always liberal in politics, and members of the same social group dominated French society under Napoleon III. As high officials, magistrates, or members of parliament, they controlled the decision-making machinery, and their values were reflected throughout our period in educational policy and the ideologies which lay behind it.

In time they were to give way to the third group, the 'middle middle class', distinguished from the upper until 1848 by not having the vote. They included most of those dependent on salaries and current income rather than inherited wealth: officials below the top level, all but a few lawyers and doctors, most businessmen, army officers, and members of the lesser professions like the secondary schoolteachers themselves. These men had normally had a secondary education, were anxious to give it to their sons in order to keep them out of the lower middle class of shop-keepers and white-collar workers, and could afford to do so. They obviously had a close affinity with the upper middle class whose ranks they were trying to join, and shared many of their values. But they might also feel frustrated at their exclusion from real influence, and this group provided many recruits to republicanism. When in power—briefly in 1848 and permanently under the Third Republic—they showed little desire for fundamental change in secondary education, but a real wish to broaden the basis of society by making primary education universal.

The first two of these social groups formed in many ways a single established, property-owning class, especially when seen from below. Their occupations and sources of wealth did not differ greatly. Nevertheless, there was a clear division between them in terms of status and of values, and conflict between the two groups lay behind most political and religious disputes in the first half of the century. Education became involved because the old landed class preferred Catholic schools for their sons. Disliking the work of the Revolution, and seeing the Church as sympathetic to their own ideals, they wanted to preserve their class identity in a changing world and insulate their children from the middle-class and materialistic spirit of the state lycées. The choice of school thus became one of the means by which men identified and defined a class allegiance which depended as much on ideology and family tradition as on more objective criteria.

The old upper class, though largely excluded from control of the levers of political power, retained both wealth and social prestige. In a sense, France did not have a single social hierarchy, but two, offering alternative roads to the top. The middle-class hierarchy was weighted towards power and employment by the state, and the state schools attracted those whose family tradition or individual ambition impelled them in this direction. The upper-class hierarchy was weighted towards status, and the Catholic schools opened the way to assimilation into the old aristocracy and perhaps to lucrative careers in the professions or private business. As the century went on, the top layers of the middle class were increasingly seduced by conservative values and by the attractions of Catholic education. Up to 1848, however, most of them remained attached to the lycées as a symbol and guarantee of the social conquests of 1789, and as a way of preserving the 'career open to talents' from the return of aristocratic privilege. The liberals in power resisted the Catholic campaign in the 1840s for the removal of legal restrictions on Church secondary schools; the campaign was to succeed in 1850, when alarm at the events of 1848 drove many liberals into the arms of the Church.

There was an important difference in this respect between French and English social history. In England, the professional class tended to identify itself from the start with the landed class, and to be assimilated into the latter by the development of the 'public' schools. This drove a wedge between the upper middle class, educated at public school and university, and the rest of the middle class. But in France the upper bourgeoisie had created its own schools embodying bourgeois values, and kept open its links with the social groups below it. The lycées offered the best education available, yet they also had moderate fees and thus had a democratic potential which went beyond narrow bourgeois interests. The result was the creation of a large class of educated men with a common feeling of 'middle-classness', and the easy assimilation of new elements in the middle class—especially commercial and industrial wealth—with the old upper middle class and its values. Sheldon Rothblatt has shown how in Victorian Cambridge the professional ideal evolved as a reworking of the University's traditional role of serving the landed class, and was used to mark its distance from the world of business. A similar ethic of professional and public service existed in France, but it was all the stronger because the University served the professional and official bourgeoisie from the start, and it was able to pervade the business class because the latter were welcome in the lycées and had no alternative educational system of their own.[1]

Consequently the question whether France had a 'modern' educational system does not admit of a simple answer. Official liberal ideology certainly stressed its meritocratic features, yet the reality seems far from the situation, supposedly characteristic of industrial societies, where education is the principal or even the only instrument of occupational selection and role allocation.

Napoleon's adviser Chaptal did indeed say that 'the principal goal of education ought to be to give everyone the knowledge

[1] S. Rothblatt, *The Revolution of the Dons* (1968), pp. 90–3. Cf. R. Anderson, 'Secondary Education in Mid Nineteenth-Century France: Some Social Aspects', *Past and Present*, no. 53 (1971), pp. 121–46.

necessary for him to fulfil the functions in society to which he is called'[1]—but that implied that it was not education itself that 'called' men to their positions. Another nineteenth-century view, expressed by the scientist and educational administrator Jean-Baptiste Dumas, was that 'alongside the wealth represented by landed property and transferable stocks, a new form of wealth has been established and developed: that whose capital consists in a solid and practical education, whose symbols and title-deeds are the degrees and diplomas which are its sanction and its reward. . . . Knowledge becomes then at all levels . . . a form of wealth and property of fixed value.'[2] Education became a new determinant of status, but did not replace the old ones.

One may suggest that the 'tightening bond between education and occupation in advanced industrial societies'[3] was at first apparent in France in only one occupational sector, but that as the years passed it did indeed tighten and spread to others. It was to public employments that the principle of merit was first applied. The secondary leaving examination, the baccalaureate, became a necessary qualification for many posts. But the full principle of recruitment by competitive examination applied only to a narrow range of jobs: the army and navy, which recruited their officers through the Polytechnique and other military schools; a few technical branches of the public service; and the University itself. 'Grandes écoles' like the Polytechnique or the École Normale, where a student's placing in both entry and passing-out examinations strongly influenced his chances of getting a desirable post, do indeed show the meritocratic principle in full flower; but this was not how most middle-class careers were recruited. Elsewhere in the public service, admission and promotion depended for the most part on influence, patronage, and demonstrated ability.

The really meritocratic feature of the French system was that it allowed a comparatively large number of young men to qualify to try their luck in middle-class careers, and to reach a point where their personal talent could become evident. For further progress, wealth and influence remained important. There were many middle-class occupations (and non-occupations) where the inheri-

[1] Quoted in L. P. Williams, 'Science, Education and Napoleon I', *Isis*, xlvii (1956), p. 371.

[2] *Journal général de l'instruction publique*, xxx (1861), pp. 382–3.

[3] A. H. Halsey in E. Hopper (ed.), *Readings in the Theory of Educational Systems* (1971), p. 263.

tance of land, property, or a business made paper qualifications unnecessary, and examinations were also of limited relevance for those looking for salaried positions in commerce and industry, where employers tended to believe in the virtues of learning on the job.

In other words, there was no single occupational hierarchy in France, but a set of different ones which attached varying importance to formal education. State employment was most closely linked with the state schools, and the lycées' teaching and outlook were geared to the occupations for which examination success was most useful. This had some significant consequences: the lycées appealed more to some social groups than others, especially to parents already in the public service and the propertyless but ambitious middle and lower reaches of the middle class; it was difficult for the lycées to adapt their teaching to the needs of less structured occupations, like business; and pupils of whatever background found themselves impelled by the links between schools, examinations, and state employment away from careers in commerce and industry and towards the occupations characteristic of the older upper bourgeoisie. The prestige which the law or the civil service enjoyed over more 'utilitarian' careers was often deplored by contemporaries, and has been seen by economic historians as one reason for France's economic 'retardation'.

Thus middle-class education was a very imperfect instrument of selection for middle-class careers. It was also unintegrated with primary education, and one cannot make sense of the French 'system' by a functional view which assumes that selection was its main task. France did not have an integrated educational ladder, or indeed any selection processes in the modern sense: at every level, public education was open to all who could pay the fees, and none were excluded on either social or academic grounds; on the other hand, there was no effective machinery for selecting and helping those of particular ability.

It is often assumed that in France 'state grants were provided for the most able pupils to proceed to secondary education'.[1] But except briefly after 1848 this was simply not the case. The state

[1] M. Vaughan and M. S. Archer, *Social Conflict and Educational Change in England and France 1789–1848* (1971), pp. 210, 214. Vaughan and Archer overstate the vertical integration of the French system, and consequently the contrast with England.

scholarships (*bourses*) created by Napoleon were not awarded on merit, but used to reward families which had served the state in some capacity, usually those of fairly high social status who had fallen on hard times. The typical *boursier* was the orphaned son of an officer rather than the poor but clever 'scholarship boy'. The number of *boursiers* was in any case declining: from 1842 to 1848 there were always over 1,900, but by 1865 there were only 1,588, giving some 300 vacancies to be awarded annually among 1,600 applicants.[1]

Local scholarships and private benevolence also helped some, as the case of the historian Ernest Lavisse shows. In the 1850s, his father's position as a fire-brigade officer got him a departmental scholarship at the college of Laon, but was too lowly to secure a state scholarship so that he could complete his studies at a lycée. Eventually he was offered reduced terms at a private boarding institution attached to a Paris lycée—one of several which looked out in this way for clever pupils to add lustre to their examination results—and so reached the École Normale.[2]

It was not these rather haphazard arrangements for helping individuals, but the relative cheapness and accessibility of secondary schools, which ensured that social mobility did occur through education. Every town of any size had some sort of secondary school which took day-boys at fees which even the lower reaches of the middle class might afford, though it was important for parents to take their chance early, as it was easier to enter the schools at the bottom than transfer to them later. The system was really one of self-selection imposed by parents' ability to pay, and a high proportion of pupils left before the end. Although in 1842 official statistics counted over 100,000 boys in secondary schools, only about 4,000 presented themselves annually for the baccalaureate, and those who passed faced the further hurdle of turning their qualification into a job.[3]

The absence of any overt machinery of exclusion, and the postponement of the weeding-out process to a late stage (a situation perceived by contemporaries as the 'overproduction' of

[1] Jourdain, *Le Budget de l'instruction publique*, Table 23; *Journal général de l'instruction publique*, xxxiv (1865), p. 110. For case studies of *boursiers*, see H. Duhaut, 'Le Lycée de Versailles (1815–1860)', *Revue de l'histoire de Versailles et de Seine-et-Oise*, xii (1910), pp. 216–22.

[2] E. Lavisse, *Souvenirs* (5th edn., n.d.), pp. 177–8.

[3] *Rapport au roi sur l'instruction secondaire* (1843), Table 27 and p. 62.

qualified men) suggest that France was nearer to the 'contest' than the 'sponsored' model of social mobility, to use Turner's helpful distinction.[1] Other 'contest' features are the emphasis on individual achievement, and on academic content rather than the cultivation of a life-style. On the other hand, the pre-existence of a well-defined élite, the way in which the schools passed on its values, and the non-vocational nature of classical education are nearer to the 'sponsored' model. Perhaps this is what would be expected in a society which was basically stable and traditional, but gradually being opened up by the new forces of competition and merit. The educational system itself was an important institutional embodiment of these individualist forces, and here the autonomy of the University came into play, for the teachers were themselves men of modest background who had risen through talent, and created an atmosphere in the schools which encouraged the repetition of the process.

How much social differentiation existed within each sector of education? The public nature of the system does seem to have restrained this, and it was one of the boasts of the University that in the classroom all distinctions of wealth and rank were ignored. No town outside Paris had more than one state secondary school, and it served the whole of the local middle class. Contemporary accounts suggest that mild social prejudice existed against the poorer pupils, but it was officially discouraged. The Catholic secondary schools were often more exclusive, and within the state system the better schools charged higher fees, creating a hierarchy which richer parents could exploit by sending their sons away, especially to the Paris lycées.

There was more scope for social discrimination in the primary sector. The law provided for only one type of school, open to all; but in practice the rich preferred to isolate their children from social contact with children of other classes, and sent them either to private schools or straight into the primary forms which existed in the secondary schools. But the primary schools still served a wide social range, and were not simply schools for the poor.

Local pressures for greater differentiation often existed. The local councils had to admit 'indigent' pupils free, but often seem to have separated free and fee-paying children, making the former

[1] R. H. Turner, 'Sponsored and Contest Mobility and the School System', in Hopper (ed.), *Readings in the Theory of Educational Systems*, pp. 71–90.

attend special charity schools. (This seems, however, to have been uncommon after 1848.[1]) The example of one town, the industrial centre of Mulhouse, shows how differentiation could evolve within the public system. In the 1830s, when the primary school was first opened, it mainly attracted middle-class children. By 1846 a reform commission was identifying four categories of pupils, each with different needs. After 1848, as more poor children came to use the school, the rich deserted it for private schools. In 1853, euphemistically named 'special classes' were created: they had higher fees, and the children in them arrived and left fifteen minutes later than the rest. In 1854, a new school, the École professionnelle, was opened to give primary education and a practical secondary education to the lower middle class. Since the town also had a classical college, Mulhouse had now achieved three complete and self-contained school systems.[2] But this was unusual. Separating children physically within schools and charging differential fees were of doubtful legality, and not practicable either in village schools or in the many large towns, including Paris, where the authorities had abolished fee-paying altogether. However, this example shows that the long-term tendency, as industrialization took hold and as the educational system itself expanded, was for education to become more stratified and more closely related to occupational patterns.

3. THE RELIGIOUS QUESTION

When contemporaries thought about the social purpose of education, they tended to be more concerned with its moral and intellectual influence on the individual and the consequent social effects than with the relation of education to occupation or social mobility. They took for granted the inequalities of wealth in their society, but they saw division of opinions as a grave social danger, and wanted to achieve 'moral unity' by creating a community living in harmony with common values. The elusive aim of 'moral unity', and the inclination among extremists of both left and right to use it as an excuse for forcing their own views on the nation, were part of the legacy of the Revolution, and help to explain why the control of education remained such a sensitive matter.

Religious conflict in the nineteenth century had its roots both

---

[1] See below, p. 162.

[2] R. Oberlé, *L'Enseignement à Mulhouse de 1798 à 1870* (1961), pp. 39, 47, 71–2.

in the intellectual divisions which began with the Enlightenment and hardened as science and reason made new conquests, and in the politico-legal conflict between Church and state which went back many centuries. The constitutional context was provided by Napoleon's Concordat of 1801, which restored the Church as a state-financed body, but imposed severe restrictions on many aspects of its life, notably the activities of religious orders. Napoleon's religious settlement also gave established status to the Protestant and Jewish faiths. France remained a basically Catholic country, with a Church that had not given up the idea of regaining the privileges of the ancien régime, but one where the state made forceful claims in the religious field, claims defended both by Gallican bureaucrats and by liberal politicians.

The actual issues in dispute were complex, and are worth summarizing for the sake of clarity. Here too, one may note, the dualities of the French system operated. The concern for ideological direction and national unity applied above all to the educated classes, and liberals were prepared to allow the Church an influence over primary education which they refused it over their own sons. Victor Cousin, who vigorously defended the rationalist philosophy of the lycées against clerical attacks, agreed that 'Christianity must be the foundation of the education of the people'.[1] And, of course, religious education was seen as peculiarly suitable for girls; at primary level religious orders played a dominant part in teaching girls, but their control of boys' schools was limited, and discouraged by liberal governments. Here official policy reflected public opinion, which saw religion as part of the female province of life, thought the influence of priests proper over women but unnatural over men, and reserved the luxury of independent thought for the stronger sex.

(i) *The place of religious instruction in schools*

Most people agreed that children should receive religious instruction; the issue was how far this should be given in public schools. Three points of view may be distinguished. The first was the republican ideal of the *école laïque*, as later established under the Third Republic. This held that religious teaching should be strictly excluded from the schools, and parents left to make

[1] Quoted in M. Gontard, *L'Enseignement primaire en France de la Révolution à la loi Guizot (1789–1833)* (1959), p. 483.

private arrangements as they chose. This secular system was put into force by the revolutionary legislation of 1792–5, and like their successors in the 1880s the republicans tried to work out a civic or lay morality, omitting all but the vaguest mention of God. The law of 1795, for example, prescribed the teaching of the 'elements of republican morality', later defined as the morality common to all ages, religions, and countries.[1]

This religious neutrality proved unpopular with parents, and when he came to power Napoleon abandoned *laïcité*, which went underground until 1848. In the University's secondary schools, he introduced a compromise. The ordinary school subjects were to be taught in a neutral spirit, so that no religious belief would be offended. But the syllabus included religious instruction as a subject by itself, and the lycées had chapels and chaplains. Protestant and Jewish parents could opt out and arrange for instruction in their own faith. This modified form of secularism was maintained in the lycées throughout our period. It was acceptable to the University, because it protected the lay character of its teaching and did not require teachers to be practising Catholics, and seems to have been acceptable to most Catholic parents, although it was attacked by the Church on the grounds that religion was not a separate subject but should be the inspiration behind all of the teaching.

This was the third point of view, and it was applied to the primary schools from the time of Napoleon. The *loi Guizot* of 1833 put 'moral and religious instruction' at the head of the subjects to be taught; the teachers themselves were responsible for this, and were therefore expected to be Catholics. In the primary sector, minorities were catered for by the principle of separate denominational schools: in 1840 there were 677 Protestant schools and 31 Jewish; there were also 2,052 'mixed' schools in places too small to have more than one school, though this practice was considered undesirable.[2] The only minority unprovided for were the freethinkers, and since the requirement to provide religious instruction applied to private as well as public schools they were effectively without rights. This system of 'confessional' primary education lasted until 1882.

---

[1] A. Aulard, *Napoléon Ier et le monopole universitaire* (1911), p. 6.
[2] M. Gontard, *Les Écoles primaires de la France bourgeoise (1833–1875)* (n.d.), p. 21.

(ii) *The Church and public education*

The Church continued to believe that education was an integral
part of its mission and that priests and members of religious orders
were better fitted than laymen to give it. Ideally, it would have
liked to see the schools subordinated to its own administrative
machinery, but failing that it sought to maximize its influence over
the state's schools. Here again, the politicians allowed in the
primary schools what they would not in the secondary. The lycées
and colleges were practically immune from interference by bishops
and priests, but in the village schools it was a different matter. The
loi Guizot gave the *curé* an official position as a member of the local
supervisory committee; he could enter the school whenever he
liked, and in practice, following the habits of the ancien régime, he
tended to look on it as part of his domain and to treat the teacher
as his subordinate. It is not surprising that personal conflict
between teacher and priest underlay many anticlerical disputes at
the local level.

Apart from the question of supervision, there was the issue of
the religious orders (*congrégations*) and their position in the public
schools. The law of 1833, endorsing an accepted practice, allowed
municipal councils to entrust their schools to a religious order
instead of a lay teacher. The most celebrated of the orders were the
Christian Brothers, founded by Jean-Baptiste de la Salle; they had
returned to France under Napoleon. Their contribution to
educational progress was important, but their influence was
limited to towns since they taught only in groups of three. Some
new orders for men were founded on the same model in the early
nineteenth century, but the real expansion was in orders of nuns,
who taught about half of all girls in our period.[1] The position of the
orders was a contentious issue throughout the nineteenth century,
but until the secularizing legislation of the Third Republic it was
in the public schools, not private ones, that they mostly worked.

(iii) *The question of private schools*

The right of the state to regulate private education was accepted
in France, but in general the University's 'monopoly' did not
prevent individuals from opening schools. The question became
a political one only if the Church sought to create its own system
of schools in rivalry with the state. As long as the Church had

---

[1] For figures, see below, p. 112.

influence over the state system, and the state schools were conducted in a Catholic spirit, this was unnecessary; but where these conditions were not met Catholics were prepared to devote much energy and money to creating schools where their own ideals could be preserved. By the 1840s, this was the situation in secondary education, since it seemed that the schools had escaped permanently from Catholic influence and that the tone of their teaching was increasingly secular. Hence the Catholic campaign for 'liberty of teaching' (*liberté d'enseignement*), whose connection with the social conflict between bourgeoisie and aristocracy has already been shown. The removal of the existing legal restrictions would mean above all the return of the Jesuits, and until 1848 that prospect was enough in itself to damn the proposal in liberal eyes.

The 'liberty' of primary education was not an issue. The liberals had no objection to Catholic primary schools, since they accepted the necessity of religious education at this level, and the Church had no need to open them when the public schools were so amenable to its influence. The principle of *liberté d'enseignement* was in fact incorporated into the *loi Guizot* for primary schools: anyone who met certain minimum requirements was free to open a school.

In 1848, therefore, the liveliest religious issue was the position of Catholic secondary schools. The position of the teaching orders was also potentially controversial, for further expansion, especially of the male orders, might well arouse anticlerical fears and provoke a reaction. The question of religious instruction in the schools, on the other hand, seemed to have been solved to everyone's satisfaction. The Revolution of 1848 was suddenly to reopen all these questions, and to prepare the way for the *loi Falloux* of 1850, which tipped the balance in favour of the Church.

CHAPTER TWO

The schools in 1848

1. MIDDLE-CLASS EDUCATION

We should beware of supposing that because some of the social implications of the school system were 'modern', what went on inside the schools was not highly traditional. The secondary curriculum in the nineteenth century derived directly, as many critics pointed out, from that originally worked out by the Jesuits. In the same way, the geographical pattern of secondary education under the ancien régime—a limited number of leading schools, with smaller schools in every town of any size feeding pupils into them and offering a more limited curriculum—was reproduced as the system recovered in the early nineteenth century. Legally, there were four types of school: the lycées (or 'royal colleges' before 1848); municipal colleges, housed and financed by town councils but with the teaching organized by the University; private schools, which might be run by priests or laymen; and the *petits séminaires* controlled by the bishops. In 1842 these shared the market as follows:[1]

	No. of schools	No. of pupils	Average size
Lycées	46	18,697	406
Municipal colleges	312	26,584	85
Private schools	1,016	43,195	43
Petits séminaires	127	c. 20,000	

There are no national figures for girls' schools, but we do have some for the Seine department (Paris area). In 1846 there were 266 *pensionnats* (lay boarding-schools) and 28 convents, with 13,487 and 1,600 pupils respectively, and about 2,000 girls attending courses for non-boarders; the total of about 17,000 was comparable with the 19,317 boys at secondary schools in the department in 1850.[2] Perhaps the surprising thing in these figures is the small

[1] *Rapport au roi sur l'enseignement secondaire* (1843), Table 26; cf. pp. 56–7.
[2] O. Gréard, *Éducation et instruction. Enseignement secondaire* (2nd edn., 1889), i, pp. 116–17, 122, 135 n.; Archives Nationales (A.N.), F^{17} 6839, unpublished statistical report for 1850, Table 19.

part played by convent schools, especially as it was said that only 8–10 of the 28 gave a serious secondary education. The normal girls' school was the small private school run by a lay mistress.

Boarding-schools were evidently preferred for girls, but in the lycées and colleges only 43 per cent and 46 per cent respectively were boarders. It had become usual for families to send their sons away if they could afford it, although the popularity of boarding was a nineteenth-century development rather than an old tradition. In deciding to make the lycées residential, Napoleon had faced the University with a paradox. Boarding goes naturally with an integrated approach to education which emphasizes character training and the personal influence of the teachers. But the University was never sympathetic to this approach, partly because of its conscious religious neutrality, partly because of the stress it laid on academic and intellectual achievement, an ethos more suited to the day school. The teachers refused to involve themselves in their pupils' personal lives, relations remained formal (professors addressed their classes as 'Messieurs'), and discipline was left to the *maîtres d'études*, an inferior grade of non-teaching employees. The discipline of the lycées was essentially negative and repressive, and this, combined with austere and uncomfortable physical conditions, made them more like barracks than anything else. The response of the pupils was to create a community life based on a continual conspiracy against the rules and the authorities, which sometimes broke out in open mutinies which were quelled only by calling in police and troops. The Catholic schools, which were willing to give positive moral training and see themselves as communities of teachers and pupils, made more of a success of boarding.

The lycées and colleges had forms for primary education, but secondary education proper started when Latin was begun in the seventh or eighth form, around the age of ten.[1] (One inheritance from the Jesuits was that the French schools, unlike their English counterparts, had separate annual forms, each with its own class-room and teacher.) In the early years, the staple diet of Latin, Greek, and French varied little. Greek received less attention than in Britain and Germany, but the study of the native language was a strong point of the French tradition, and was aided by the close

---

[1] The forms were numbered upwards as far as Second, above which came Rhetoric and Philosophy.

relation of Latin and French. The integration of classical and French teaching was a basic feature of the French system, for teachers believed that the study of the ancient world was 'an essential and almost indispensable element in the formation of the national spirit and the French genius. . . . Our destiny and our title of nobility is to be, by an uninterrupted succession, the sons and the heirs of antiquity.' And (for it is a Catholic teacher speaking) 'the French genius is like a great river fed by two tributaries: one descends from Calvary, the other from the Capitol!'[1] Thus the educated Frenchman could not understand his own language and culture without the mastery of Latin, and modern languages could never have the same educational value. So too translation and composition exercises in the classics had as their purpose the cultivation of French style. These exercises constituted a heavy load. Lavisse remembered himself as 'working always, for six years, writing Greek and Latin proses, Greek and Latin translations, French and Latin speeches, French and Latin essays, Latin verses . . .'[2] The *discours*, a speech put into the mouth of a fictional or historical character, was a French speciality; both speeches and essays were judged as exercises in style, and the content was often provided in advance in outline.

The other main exercise was studying literary texts, and again French had equal status with the classics. The French authors studied were invariably those of the *grand siècle*, the seventeenth century, with the addition of Voltaire. This was the most classical as well as the greatest age of French literature, and could be integrated by the teachers into their concept of a classical education as later authors could not. In the classroom, the emphasis was on style and expression; the texts were gone through in detail, and the teacher expounded the finer points. What the poet, orator, or historian was actually saying was too often passed over, especially as the classical authors were usually studied only in collections of extracts.

The concern for style therefore ran right through classical education, and can be linked with some characteristics of the French intellectual tradition: a sense of discrimination and propriety, a sensitivity to nuances of feeling and expression became the marks of a literary education. It also encouraged what Pierre

[1] L. Lecuyer, *Du beau et de son rôle dans l'éducation* (1856), p. 28.
[2] Lavisse, *Souvenirs*, p. 212.

Bourdieu (in an essay discussing how education forms national habits of thought and unconscious cultural 'master-patterns') calls 'the cult of brilliance and distinguished performance'.[1] The prizes in the University went to those who wrote the most elegant Latin proses. On the other hand, the baccalaureate, passing which was the purpose of secondary education for most pupils and parents, was mainly a test of the memory. It was still basically an oral examination, the questions being chosen by lot from a 'programme'. In the 1840s the programme contained no fewer than 500 questions. Fortoul reduced them to 146, and Duruy in 1864 abolished the programme altogether; both reformers also strengthened the written element in the examination. But the key to success, as with the competitive examinations which were also part of the system, remained intensive cramming rather than literary taste.

The 'formalism' or 'verbalism' of the University's tradition had its critics at the time, who attacked it for caring more about form than content, more about elegance than truth, more about cultivating taste than turning out men with independent and vigorous minds. A literary education, it was said, was fully appreciated only by a small élite, and became a sterile routine for the rest. There was much to justify these criticisms, for the schools certainly did little to encourage true self-expression or originality. What mattered was (to use the words which constantly recur) the 'imitation' of the supreme 'models' handed down from the past.

The final year centred on philosophy. If that subject had been taught with the aim of sharpening the critical spirit, it might have balanced the conformism of classical education. But in the 1840s the philosophy taught was the 'eclecticism' of Victor Cousin, which had become a major component of the University's distinctive intellectual outlook. It was a form of deism, or natural religion based on reason; it was commonly called 'spiritualism', best translated as anti-materialism. Cousin's philosophy asserted the existence of certain higher ethical values, identified in the University's mind with the humane values instilled by the classics. The philosophy was 'eclectic' because Cousin thought he was distilling the essence of all the great philosophies of the past, so arriving at the fundamental truths which all mankind accepted: 'the spirituality of the soul, the liberty of man, the law of duty, the distinction

---

[1] In M. F. D. Young (ed.), *Knowledge and Control. New Directions for the Sociology of Education* (1971), p. 201.

between vice and virtue and merit and demerit, and divine
providence, full of justice and goodness'.[1] Cousin claimed that it
was compatible with Catholicism, and formed a 'lay' philosophy
suited to the University's mission of creating national unity among
men of all creeds;[2] Catholics denied this, and denounced it as
atheistical. In the classroom, the philosophy tended to be little
more than the demonstration of orthodox and conventional
truths—'the exposition of a few commonplaces verified by
M. Cousin', as Edmond About recalled.[3]

Philosophy was not the only non-literary subject taught in the
schools. History was the best-established, because it fitted in well
with classical education. Modern languages and elementary science,
however, though compulsory, were not highly regarded, and
tended to be fitted into odd corners of the timetable. More will be
said in chapter four about the development of science for pupils
with specialized needs, and about the way in which many schools
were developing non-classical education at a lower level. However,
the dominance of the classics was not seriously challenged, and the
traditional literary teaching formed the trunk on to which any new
developments had to be grafted.

The survival in a flourishing state of this traditional form of
education demands some explanation. It had not gone unchallenged at the time of the Revolution: theorists like Turgot and
Condorcet had wished to make secondary education scientific and
vocational, and the first new schools to be created, the *écoles
centrales* of 1795, had a radically new syllabus based on the natural
sciences. Yet these schools failed, and when Napoleon substituted
the lycées for the *écoles centrales* in 1802 he made a partial return
to the traditional curriculum; the reversion to tradition was
completed in 1809. There were some non-academic reasons for
the failure of the *écoles centrales*: parents disliked the absence of
religious instruction and the unstructured syllabus, which allowed
them to pick and choose between subjects. But why did science
not make more appeal to middle-class parents?

Durkheim, who suggested that secondary education in the
nineteenth century was dominated by the conflict between the

[1] J. Barthélemy Saint-Hilaire, *M. Victor Cousin, sa vie et sa correspondance*
(1895), i, p. 466.
[2] *Oeuvres de M. Victor Cousin. Cinquième série. Instruction publique* (1850), ii,
pp. 134–5.
[3] E. About, *Le Progrès* (1864), p. 389.

ideals of the *écoles centrales* and those of the old colleges, related
the educational tradition founded by the Jesuits to the values of
the Renaissance aristocracy. The stress on general culture rather
than vocationalism seems to fit in with this, and the encouragement
of individual brilliance might be explained as part of the aristocratic concept of 'prowess'.[1] Some theorists have seen the adoption
of 'aristocratic' and old-fashioned values by the nineteenth-
century bourgeoisie (which can easily be exaggerated) as one
reason for France's lack of economic dynamism.

However, the cult of individual achievement can equally well be
related to the 'bourgeois' ethos of competition which was certainly a feature of the age (in France, said Cousin, we would hold
a competition among babes in arms to find the best dribbler).[2] The
fact is that traditional French education seemed to adapt itself
effortlessly to the consequences of the Revolution (as it did to the
advent of the Third Republic), remaining general and non-
vocational. One wonders therefore whether Weber's 'struggle of
the "specialized type of man" against the older type of "cultivated
man" '[3] is really the key to understanding educational change in
this period.

One explanation may be that secondary education under the
ancien régime was not particularly 'aristocratic'. Recent research
suggests that the Jesuit colleges had a remarkably wide social
recruitment,[4] and there is a case for saying that the social role of
secondary education did not change radically between the seventeenth century and the 1930s. Cournot observed in 1864 that
historically classical education in France represented the social
aspirations of the bourgeoisie,[5] and it may be that even in the
eighteenth century it stood for the principle of merit and talent
against privilege. Two of the most 'meritocratic' institutions of the
University date, as Bourdieu and Passeron point out, from the
ancien régime: the *agrégation* (a competitive examination for
recruiting teachers, 1766), and the *concours général* (a prize
competition between the Paris lycées, 1747).[6]

---

[1] Cf. Jesse R. Pitts in S. Hoffmann and others, *France: Change and Tradition*
(1963), pp. 241 ff.   [2] E. Bersot, *Questions d'enseignement* (1880), p. 223.
[3] Vaughan and Archer, *Social Conflict and Educational Change*, pp. 18–19.
[4] F. de Dainville, 'Collèges et fréquentation scolaire au XVIIe siècle',
Population, xii (1957), pp. 467–94.
[5] A. Cournot, *Des institutions d'instruction publique en France* (1864), pp. 43–5.
[6] P. Bourdieu and J.-C. Passeron, *La Reproduction* (1970), p. 182 n.

It is also evident that social groups or individuals whose wealth is new and status insecure will be attracted by the legitimating force of traditional forms of education; the point has already been made that the accessibility of the French schools encouraged the new middle class to assimilate with the old. In any case, it is easy to see why large numbers of parents had no quarrel with classical education. They were concerned about their sons' careers, and paper qualifications were more necessary than before. But this did not yet mean that the schools had to prepare for specific jobs. There were very few 'scientific' careers available. The chief one was the army, which demanded a mathematical preparation (this was given in the lycées, their main concession to specialization). But medicine, for example, demanded no scientific qualifications from entrants to the faculties, where specialization began. The general assumption was that families aiming at professional or official careers could afford to put off vocational training until after the secondary stage. A general classical education was still seen as the best qualification for entry to any career. Thus as long as the needs of the wealthy upper middle class were put first, the ideal of a single form of education producing one type of cultivated man could be preserved more or less intact, and was valued because it maintained the cultural homogeneity of the educated class. As we have seen, the upper middle class did dominate policy-making, though secondary education itself reached a much wider group, and tension between the leisurely traditional ideal and the more urgent vocational needs of the lower ranks of the middle class underlay many of the problems of educational reform.

Finally, the classics survived because of the sheer weight of tradition and teaching experience behind them, which the *écoles centrales* had no time to build up. When Napoleon created the University, he naturally turned to men who had taught in the old colleges, and they continued to teach what they knew; and once established, the University became a powerful vested interest. Besides, the arguments deployed in defence of the classics were not unimpressive. Given the feeling that secondary education should be general rather than vocational, it was easy to dismiss subjects like science or modern languages just because they were practical, 'utilitarian', and needed only by men in certain careers.

Perhaps the strongest card played by defenders of the classics was the claim that they were a unique instrument of moral as well as intellectual education. Unlike science, which 'desiccated' the mind, a literary education cultivated the pupil's imagination, sensibility, and moral sense as well as his reason and judgement. Classical civilization had given uniquely perfect expression to the ideals of truth, beauty, and virtue. In the works of the classical authors, the highest truths were stated, and the noblest moral lessons taught, in the most beautiful language; here were models of thought and conduct as well as of style. The teaching sought to appeal to the pupil's heart as well as his head, in the hope that enthusiasm for truth and virtue would be awakened by admiration for beauty of expression, and would be absorbed unconsciously through prolonged contact with the great writers of the past. The method was intended to appeal emotionally to the impressionable adolescent, so that the memory of a more noble and elevated world of ideals would survive even when Latin and Greek were forgotten to give guidance and inspiration amid the materialism and self-interest of adult life.

This pedagogic ideal, whose aim was to isolate the pupil from the real world and make him live for a time in an idealized, heroic classical world, a 'pedagogic universe' carefully created for the purpose, was inherited from the ancien régime.[1] It was codified in Rollin's *Traité des études* of 1726, which remained the University's bible. There is no doubt that this coherent tradition, which made the classics a complete and rounded education in themselves, gave immense strength to the teachers' resistance to criticism. In particular, they were not worried by charges that their teaching was out of touch with the spirit of the age, because that was, in a sense, its whole point.

The survival of the classics was also helped by the relationship which had developed in France between secondary and higher education. The principle was that general education was concentrated in the lycées and confined to them (hence the inclusion of subjects like philosophy), so that secondary education produced the complete educated man. Higher education was vocational, and consisted of specialized professional schools rather than universities in the British or German sense. They were of two kinds: the *grandes écoles* founded to train men for state service and recruited by competitive examination, of which the École Polytechnique,

[1] G. Snyders, *La Pédagogie en France aux XVIIe et XVIIIe siècles* (1965), *passim.*

founded in 1794, was the model; and the faculties. There were
faculties of letters, science, theology, law, and medicine, but only
the last two, devoted purely to professional training, had a
significant number of students.

One of the *grandes écoles*, the École Normale Supérieure, was
a vital part of the University. Its main function was to train
teachers, and its graduates formed an élite who usually got the best
posts—in the top forms and in the big Paris lycées—and who often
went on to become professors in the faculties of letters and science.
But in the absence of true universities, the École Normale also
became the target of many others who wanted to pursue scientific
or literary studies at a higher level, and *normaliens* were prominent
in many fields of intellectual and public life. The intensive training
given in the school tended to give them a distinctive stamp: the
esprit normalien was a kind of distillation of the University's ethos—
high intellectual seriousness, combined with a concern for precise
expression and literary elegance, and often masked by irony. The
liberalism and tolerance of the University were also inculcated by
the school, and brought it into conflict with repressive political
regimes.

The *grandes écoles* were in many ways glorified lycées: residential, involving hard work in a competitive atmosphere within
rigorous time limits, and governed by strict discipline. But in the
faculties, things went to the other extreme. The faculties were
purely teaching and examining bodies, with no residential
accommodation or control over students' private lives. Studies
could be prolonged indefinitely, and examinations taken annually
without attending courses. Medicine, requiring clinical work in
hospitals, was more serious than law, which was the favourite
choice of the sons of the rich, aiming at careers in politics or
diplomacy, or wishing to sample the pleasures of an idle life in
Paris for a few years before settling down. They were probably
outnumbered, however, by ambitious, hardworking and con-
ventionally minded students intent on acquiring their professional
qualifications. For middle-class education—secondary and higher
—was on the whole a solid and serious affair, valued by parents
because they knew that the University was efficient in its task of
preparing for the examinations which were indispensable in a
society where wealth and position had to be competitively acquired
and tenaciously defended.

Because of this efficiency, the system, established in outline under Napoleon, did not change in any essential way in our period, though the number of pupils and institutions expanded. The intellectual level of the middle classes seemed satisfactory, and the standard of professional competence in nineteenth-century France was high. The army, the law, medicine, the civil service, the University itself, became professions with a deeply rooted sense of common identity and common standards, and their training was one reason for this. At the highest level, the scientific and technical training available was second to none, and the achievements of French engineers show that France did not lag behind the demands of the age. The Polytechnique, though still basically a military school, produced a succession of distinguished engineers who built France's railways and extended French enterprise around the world, and it was the centre around 1830 of the Saint-Simonian cult, which so well represented the self-confidence, vision, and professional consciousness of the new technocratic élite. At a rather lower level, scientific and practical education was perhaps less satisfactory. But only in the 1860s did the feeling arise that France was slipping behind other nations and that a major overhaul of middle-class education might be required.

2. PRIMARY EDUCATION

As we have seen, the state was slow to act to improve primary education, and for many years it continued along traditional lines. At a time when most village schools were taught by one teacher for the whole of his career, changes had literally to await the passing of a generation, and many archaic practices lingered on, defying the condemnation of inspectors and the circulars of reforming ministers. When introducing his law in 1833, Guizot sent special inspectors to visit every school in France, and their reports painted a dark picture, largely confirmed by modern research, of the wretched material state of the schools, the poverty of the teachers, the apathy of parents and local notables, the backwardness of methods, and the neglect of moral and religious education.[1] Some villages still relied on migrant teachers, traditionally drawn from certain mountainous areas, and hired for the season.[2]

[1] P. Lorain, *Tableau de l'instruction primaire en France* (1837).
[2] Gontard, *L'Enseignement primaire en France de la Révolution à la loi Guizot*, pp. 355, 541–2.

The ancien régime was still alive, and the *instituteur* (the new term introduced by the Revolution) was only slowly replacing the *maître d'école*.

It was to improving the quality of the teachers that the efforts of the central government were first directed. A significant step was the creation in 1816 of the *brevet de capacité*, a teachers' certificate which in future all would have to possess, though members of religious orders were exempt on production of a 'letter of obedience' from their superiors. This privilege, confined to female orders after 1830, became a standing grievance with anticlericals. The Restoration governments acted in other ways to encourage education, but the Revolution of 1830 accelerated progress, for the liberals of the July monarchy believed firmly in the need to bring morality, enlightenment, and 'moral dignity' to the masses. Guizot's law of 1833 was the real turning-point.

The basic provision of the *loi Guizot* was that every commune was obliged to maintain a public school, though education was neither compulsory on parents nor free. Free admission was to be given to poor children, and in practice this came to be interpreted generously. Communes had to provide a schoolhouse, where the teacher lived as well as taught, and to pay the teacher a small fixed salary. But the bulk of his income would come, as before, from the fees paid by families, and so would vary according to the size of the school and the prosperity of the area. Where local resources were insufficient, the state accepted the need to give aid, and so committed itself to a substantial and continuing subsidy.

Raising the status of the teacher was one of Guizot's principal aims. Each department had to maintain an *école normale* to train teachers: these schools were to make a vital contribution not only to raising standards, but also to creating a sense among teachers that they belonged to a profession and a public service. By 1847, there were 76 *écoles normales* for boys (47 of which had existed before 1833), but only 10 for girls, for one of the weaknesses of the *loi Guizot* was that it applied only to boys' schools. Some of its provisions were extended to girls in 1836, but they did not include an obligation on communes to set up a separate girls' school. The development of girls' education, and the condition and status of women teachers, tended always to lag behind in this way. This was despite the fact that opinion was hostile to mixed education, seeing moral danger in the mingling of the sexes and the teaching of girls by men. Most village schools were in fact mixed schools (with partitions down the middle of the classroom, if official instructions were observed), but for fifty years after 1833 much of the effort of educational development went into the creation wherever possible of separate provision for girls.

Another weakness of the law was that, like the legislation of the Restoration, it relied on the voluntary efforts of local notables to organize and develop education, both in the communes and through committees set up to supervise schools over a wider area. This conformed with liberal ideas, but did not work out well. The notables were often indifferent or hostile to the spread of popular education, and in the long run only stimulus from the centre could overcome this apathy; the appointment of full-time inspectors of primary education in 1835 was an important step along this road.

Whatever its weaknesses, the law did begin to put schools within the reach of all, and provided a mechanism for continual expansion and improvement. Every year, trained teachers replaced untrained ones. Every year, the number of communes without a school fell (5,667 in 1837, 2,690 in 1850, out of 36,000–37,000). The numbers of pupils rose as follows:

	Boys	Girls	Total
1832	n.a.	n.a.	1,937,582
1837	1,579,888	1,110,147	2,690,035
1847	2,176,079	1,354,056	3,530,135
1863	2,265,756	2,070,612	4,336,368
1866	2,343,781	2,172,186	4,515,967

The literacy statistics tell a similar story: in 1832, 53 per cent of conscripts were illiterate; by 1848 the figure was 40 per cent.[1] In 1848 the effects of the *loi Guizot* were still working themselves out, and the need was to enforce it fully and fill in the gaps rather than go beyond it. The *loi Falloux* of 1850 in fact re-enacted the law of 1833 with only minor changes, and it remained the legal foundation of primary education throughout our period.

The official regulations of 1834 defined three 'divisions' in primary education, covering the age-groups six to eight, eight to

---

[1] *Statistique comparée de l'enseignement primaire (1829–1877)*, pp. cx–cxi; C. M. Cipolla, *Literacy and Development in the West* (1969), Table 25. Cf. below, pp. 158–9.

ten, and ten upwards. Before this, however, a child might attend a
salle d'asile. As their name indicates, these were originally intended
for children whose mothers were working, and were found mainly
in towns and industrial centres; they gave a simple nursery-type
education. Beginning as an initiative of private charity, the *salles
d'asile* were officially recognized and encouraged from 1837. Local
councils could provide public *salles d'asile*, and a teachers' certificate and a system of inspection (giving women their first foothold
in the educational administration) were created. In 1847, a school
for training teachers was opened in Paris, directed by one of the
pioneers of the movement, Marie Pape-Carpantier.

'In all the divisions', said the regulations, 'moral and religious
instruction will come first.' It occupied a good deal of time, and
was based on the catechism with additional exercises: reading
religious works aloud and reciting prayers in the first division,
sacred history in the second, 'Christian doctrine' in the third.
Reading-books and copybooks were also of a pious or moralizing
kind, a crucifix was part of the official mural decor along with the
map of France and a portrait or bust of the reigning monarch, and
on Sundays and feast days the children were conducted to church
in a body. The teacher therefore had no chance of neglecting this
part of his duties.

Reading was the branch of education which received most
attention, but once children had learnt to read there was little
effort to encourage the habit. The reading matter was un-
interesting—the religious orders were especially criticized for
teaching reading out of religious manuals which were meaningless
to children—and French literature was not approached in even the
most elementary way. Time was, however, spent on exercises in
reading Latin (so that the church services could be followed) and
manuscript documents. Peasant parents attached special importance to the latter, and complained if their children were not taught
to decipher old leases and deeds. The same rather old-fashioned
approach was applied to writing, where three styles had to be
mastered, though this was still valuable for those seeking jobs as
clerks. The 1834 regulations were progressive in laying down the
simultaneous teaching of reading and writing, against the older
practice of teaching them in succession.

The arithmetic taught did not go beyond vulgar and decimal
fractions and the metric system. The only other compulsory subject

was the 'elements of the French language'—spelling and grammar. Other subjects—drawing, singing, history, and geography—were optional. Thus the education given was little more than a training in basic skills, and perhaps could aim no higher when the training of the teachers was itself so limited. When more advanced subjects were taught, like grammar or history, learning by heart was the method usually resorted to.

Official instructions did not lay down the methods to be used, partly because this was a controversial question. The Lancastrian system, whereby one man taught a large school indirectly through monitors, was borrowed from England under the name of the 'mutual method', and at first aroused great enthusiasm. It was, however, associated with political liberalism and opposed by Catholics. Though enjoying new favour after the 1830 Revolution, it gradually died out as its defects became clearer and as the supply of trained adult teachers increased. But in 1848 it was still in use in a modified form in many towns, including Paris.

The rival 'simultaneous' method was that pioneered by the Christian Brothers and used by other religious orders. It involved the class being taught as one unit by a single teacher, and implied the division of the school into separate classes. The 'divisions' of Guizot's regulations were based on this practice. Schools run on the 'simultaneous' method still had only two or three classes, containing children of different ages, but it did make possible the use of oral exposition in teaching and work based on common books and exercises. The need for uniform textbooks was in fact a problem: the Christian Brothers produced their own, but in other schools the idea was only gradually accepted. Parents disliked the expense, and were in the habit of sending their children to school with books handed down in the family. By 1848, the simultaneous method was recognized as the most efficient; but in one-teacher schools, which were the vast majority, it could be applied only imperfectly, the teacher taking one group while the other read or wrote on its own. This was still an advance on the older 'individual' method, in which each child was called up to the teacher's desk separately to recite his reading or produce his exercise. But this method, the only one practicable in many ill-equipped rural schools, was certainly still widely used.

Inadequacy of method and irregular attendance meant that the number of children on the school rolls was a poor indication of the effectiveness of primary education. The tradition was that it ended with a child's first communion, and the majority left at ten or eleven, especially in the countryside. Even if basic literacy had been achieved, there was no guarantee that it would survive without practice, and the higher literacy statistics of urban areas are related to the townsman's more frequent need to read and write as well as to the provision of schools. In the countryside, learning might be traditionally respected, and encouraged by Church and state, but its use was less obvious. One weakness of primary education, often pointed out by critics, was that it seemed divorced from the daily life which the child knew. There was no practical teaching relevant to farming, no elementary science to explain familiar phenomena, no study of local history or geography. Within its narrow limits, primary education like secondary stressed the abstract and general rather than the particular and useful.

The men who created the system in any case attached more importance to its moral than its intellectual functions. The moral atmosphere of the schools was meant to inculcate the values which the middle class thought suitable for the poor, and many of the attitudes taught were 'deferential'—respect for superiors, acceptance of inequality, Christian resignation. To say that the school was designed as an instrument of social control is a platitude; it did not always work as the designers intended. It worked best where the social structure favoured it, as in the still semi-feudal west, where the priest dominated the school and the landlord stood behind the priest, or in some industrial towns where factory-owners were establishing a new feudality. But many of the 'bourgeois' virtues which were taught—thrift, temperance, the dignity of work, self-respect—were not so different from the democratic ideals of 1848, and could well awaken the spirit of independence among peasant farmers and artisans, especially as the teachers themselves were sympathetic to that spirit.

Perhaps there were good reasons for not stimulating the ambitions of children too much, for the school leaver had very limited prospects. The majority took up unskilled work, or joined in the work of the family farm, as they would have done in the summer even while at school. For others, there were some ways forward, though they were fewer for girls than boys, and did not normally include going on to a secondary school. First, there was apprenticeship, usually begun around the age of fourteen. The apprenticeship system, however, was in decline, and was only gradually being replaced by various forms of technical education for workers.[1] For those who wanted to continue full-time education, there were the 'higher primary schools' created by Guizot (following German precedents) for 'the laborious classes who, in the towns, have to deal with the needs and tastes of a more complex, rich, and demanding civilization'.[2] The law of 1833 required towns with a population over 6,000 to maintain a school of this type. The subjects taught included geometry and its applications to drawing and surveying, elementary science, and history and geography. There was no manual training, and the bias was towards commerce and the needs of the lower middle class rather than industry. By 1850, there were 436 higher primary schools for boys, with 27,159 pupils, and 271 for girls.[3] These figures were not large in relation to the potential demand, and in fact the schools were considered a failure and were abolished by the *loi Falloux*. Those who wanted this sort of education preferred to seek it in the secondary sector.

A third way forward was the *école normale*. Schoolmasters tended to encourage their best pupils to become teachers themselves, and the *école normale* offered both further general education and the prospect of a secure and non-manual job. It will be noted that since the *écoles normales* took their pupils from the primary schools most primary teachers had no experience of secondary education. This illustrates the self-contained nature of each sector, and the mental barriers between them. *Professeurs* and *instituteurs* had different intellectual backgrounds and values, corresponding to their different social origins: in 1846 75 per cent of primary teachers were said to be sons of peasants, the rest sons of artisans; but only 16 per cent of secondary teachers in 1842 came from peasant families, the rest belonging to the urban lower middle class (26 per cent artisans) or the middle class proper.[4] *Professeurs* were suspicious of the *esprit primaire*, supposedly hostile to disinterested study and culture, while *instituteurs* thought the secondary schools exclusive and élitist.

[1] See below, pp. 84, 86.

[2] F. Guizot, *Mémoires pour servir à l'histoire de mon temps* (1858–67), iii, p. 65.

[3] *Statistique comparée de l'enseignement primaire (1829–1877)*, Table 16.

[4] Gontard, *Les Écoles primaires de la France bourgeoise*, p. 49; P. Gerbod, *La Condition universitaire en France au XIXe siècle* (1965), p. 110.

The secondary teachers had had a strong professional sense since the foundation of the University, but the achievement of the same thing by the *instituteurs* was a long struggle. Even after the *loi Guizot*, there was no career structure and no minimum salary. Many teachers lived in poverty, yet were cut off by their education and their white-collar status from the villagers from whose class they had sprung. The position of the lay woman teacher, facing a wall of prejudice, and paid an exiguous salary, was even worse, though a teacher's marriage often helped solve the problem. The teacher was still not a state official, but depended on a contract with the commune, and had to defer to the mayor and local notables.

The teacher also found himself regarded as the subordinate of the priest. As well as teaching religion in the school, he was often required to act as *chantre* (leading the singing at church services) and to ring the bells, serve at mass, and attend at weddings and funerals. These traditional obligations would be included in the contract, and the central administration did not disapprove of them; church music was taught in the *écoles normales* by way of preparation. The evidence is that increasing numbers of teachers resented this role, and saw themselves rather than the priest as the true source of enlightenment in the countryside. But until 1848 they had to keep their resentment to themselves, for they were unlikely to get the backing of the municipal council or the educational administration in any quarrel with the priest. A more agreeable task performed by most rural teachers was acting as *secrétaire de mairie*, clerk of the municipal council. They learnt at the *école normale* how to keep the registers of births and deaths, and how to survey land in case they were called in as arbiters in boundary disputes. This is a pointer to the respect and influence which the teacher could gain in a small community, especially in the early days when he would be one of the few literate men in the village. This sort of satisfaction was denied to the urban teacher, who was just one of the crowd of minor officials, but who was also free from the oppressive presence of mayor and *curé* and from the intellectual isolation of his rural colleague.

The development of professionalism was tied up with the growth of government intervention. The more education became a national service, the more dignity and independence of local influences the teacher could achieve. On the other hand, he then became more subject to the caprices of the bureaucracy. The secondary teachers, dependent on being moved for their promotion, already experienced this, and found that the state took an active interest in their private lives. The teacher was expected to maintain a front of decorum and sobriety; attendance at cafés, smoking in public, and other forms of conspicuous enjoyment were frowned on, and the teacher's choice of newspaper, his friends, his marriage, and his churchgoing habits were all things which might be noted in his file and influence his career. This sort of discipline was normal for public officials at the time, but teachers were in a particularly sensitive position because parents needed to be assured of their respectability and Catholic critics were on the watch for any lapses.

The government's view of the primary teacher's task was outlined by Guizot in a circular sent to every teacher after the new law was passed. Primary education, he said, had a vital role in preserving order and social stability and forming good citizens; 'faith in Providence, the sacredness of duty, submission to paternal authority, and the respect due to the law, to the ruler and to the rights of all, such are the sentiments which [the teacher] will endeavour to develop.' This sense of mission, it was hoped, would reconcile him to his monotonous and poorly-paid task. 'A profound feeling of the moral importance of his labours must sustain and inspire him, and the austere pleasure of having served mankind and contributed secretly to the public good must become the just salary paid only by his conscience. It is his glory . . . to exhaust himself in sacrifices which are hardly realized by those who profit from them, to work for men and to expect his reward only from God.'[1]

Instilling these attitudes was one of the functions of the *écoles normales*, in which the same elevated moral tone prevailed. Some were strongly Catholic in atmosphere, while others seem to have had a left-wing slant which foreshadowed the combination of militant anticlericalism and moral earnestness which typefied these schools under the Third Republic. One such was the school at Évreux, whose first director, Arsène Meunier, was a republican and anticlerical later prominent in the events of 1848. After a stormy career at Évreux, Meunier went to Paris and founded the first journal for teachers, the *Écho des instituteurs* (1845), itself an

[1] Quoted in Gontard, *Les Écoles primaires de la France bourgeoise*, pp. 4–5.

important indication of the growth of professional feeling.[1] Meunier was fiercely hostile to the religious orders: he contrasted the lay teacher, 'a man of his time, who understands progress and makes himself its most active agent', with the *frères ignorantins* who wanted to stifle the intelligence, enslave the soul, and instil into pupils the ideas of the thirteenth century.[2]

Events were to show that the teachers had now become a force to be reckoned with. Though lacking the institutional autonomy of the University, the primary teachers lent weight in the same way to the liberal and democratic tendencies in French society. The desire of the authorities to have the children of the poor brought up to obedience and religious orthodoxy might fail unless the teachers themselves believed in this programme; the strength of the middle-class reaction against the teachers after 1848 was partly due to a new awareness of their potential influence, and to a feeling of being let down by previously faithful auxiliaries.

There was thus potential conflict between governments and teachers; governments had also to consider public opinion, which meant the parents and local notables, whose political and religious views were generally far more conservative than the teachers'. If a liberal government backed the teachers, it risked driving parents into the arms of the Church and provoking a political reaction against state schools. If a conservative one tried to please the parents by treating the teachers with a strong hand, it risked killing the idealism which kept the educational machine going. The Second Republic fell into the first trap, Napoleon III into the second.

[1] J. Vidalenc, *Le Département de l'Eure sous la monarchie constitutionnelle 1814–1848* (1952), pp. 584, 596–9, 601–2.

[2] L.-A. Meunier, *De l'enseignement congréganiste* (1845), pp. 38, 41, 73.

CHAPTER THREE

The politics of education 1848-52

I. THE SECOND REPUBLIC

The revolution of 1848 was a real revolution, which temporarily shook the dominance of the 'notables' and brought to power a set of men with quite different ideas. As an introduction to this, it may be helpful to outline the three main sets of ideas on education current at the time, which corresponded roughly to the three upper- and middle-class groups described in chapter one. The first ideology was the conservative and Catholic one. This envisaged a society ordered according to a hierarchy determined by inheritance and tradition, with a landed class dominating paternalistically a basically rural society. In such a society, education was likely to be a disruptive force, whether it was that which helped the urban middle class to push their way forward, or the popular education which encouraged the poor to ask questions and to have opinions of their own. Conservatives felt no compulsion to take the initiative in extending education; but if it was to develop, it was best that it should do so under the aegis of the Church, which knew how to impart sound instruction without loosening the bonds of deference. The state, in this view, should withdraw as far as possible from the direct provision of education—an idea also held by some middle-class theorists who believed in economic liberalism.

The second set of attitudes was that of the liberal bourgeoisie. They too saw society as a hierarchy, but one open to the power of money and merit. The middle class, they thought, governed not by hereditary right but because they were the educated and productive class, and education was accepted as a determinant and regulator of social status, one so important that doctrinaire liberalism was ignored in order to maintain state education for the middle class. The liberals were aware that education was a disruptive force, but they thought that leaving the masses in ignorance was more dangerous than a controlled social mobility (*déclassement*) which would act as a safety-valve for social pressures. In a liberal society, moreover, it was necessary that individuals should be able to escape their hereditary lot. A primary education which was available to all but neither free nor compulsory matched the liberal vision of a society in which the individual could win a higher place through self-help, sacrifice, and responsibility.

The liberals too knew that education allowed men to read newspapers and form political opinions, but they were readier than the conservatives to gamble on this turning out well, perhaps because they had more confidence that men could be intellectually persuaded to accept an unequal society. 'To enlighten the masses', wrote a liberal newspaper in 1833, 'is to make them better and happier, and to associate them through their intelligence and their understanding of their own interest with this great machine of society, where even the humblest has his place but where too the humblest can aspire to any position.'[1] Thus they encouraged primary education, but with the emphasis on 'moralization' and on limiting its extent. Guizot himself said that 'the tendency to widen . . . universal primary instruction does not deserve legal encouragement; the purpose of laws is to provide for what is necessary, not to go ahead of what may become possible, and their mission is to regulate social forces, not to excite them indiscriminately.'[2] Since Guizot refused as prime minister before 1848 to extend the franchise, the idea of 'educating our masters' was evidently not yet part of liberal thinking.

The third set of attitudes, that of the republicans, differed from the other two in starting from the needs of the masses rather than those of the governing class. Universal primary education would be the foundation of a national education system, and was seen as the central social reform of the Republic, the cure for all social ills. The new minister of education in 1848 was an old campaigner in the cause of popular education, Hippolyte Carnot (son of the revolutionary leader). Carnot had been influenced in his youth by the doctrines of Saint-Simon, which he combined with the democratic republican tradition. Two Saint-Simonian friends, Jean Reynaud and Édouard Charton, became Carnot's main

[1] Quoted in Gontard, *L'Enseignement primaire en France de la Révolution à la loi Guizot*, p. 454.
[2] Guizot, *Mémoires*, iii, p. 66.

advisers, and he bypassed the old guard of the University by creating a 'high commission for scientific and literary studies' to work out policies. It included scientists, philosophers (Quinet and Renouvier), liberal philanthropists, and educational experts of left-wing views, including Arsène Meunier, whose writings are a good guide to the ideas behind the new policy.

When men like Carnot and Meunier looked at education as it had developed, they found much to dismay them, and might well feel that the promise of 1789 had been betrayed. The education of the masses had been neglected, and used to teach submission to social and religious authority, rather than to produce free men worthy to be citizens of the Republic. The idea of a common education for all had been forgotten, and instead there was one form of education for the privileged and another for the helots. 'On one side, the rich, for whom alone the banquet of civilization is served; on the other, the poor, who have to be happy to pick up a few crumbs.'[1] The first task for democrats was to break down this barrier—perhaps, indeed, it was the main task if their political ends were to be achieved. For 'the greatest cause of inequality among men is not wealth, it is education. . . . The democratic principle is so strong among us that hardly anything remains besides the ignorance of the so-called inferior classes to stop their fusion with the others. Destroy that ignorance, and you have solved the problem of equality.'[2]

The introduction of universal education was therefore Carnot's first priority, and he prepared a parliamentary bill which made primary education free and compulsory for both boys and girls. Great improvements were to be made in the position of the teachers, with payment by the state instead of the local councils, four salary grades so that a career structure was established, and retirement pensions. The school programme would include 'all that is necessary to the development of the man and the citizen as far as is conceivable in the present conditions of French civilization'; the main addition to Guizot's list was 'elementary notions of the phenomena of nature and of the principal facts of agriculture and industry'. Another aim was to 'make the whole of France as republican in heart and mind as it is today in its institutions', and

---

[1] L.-A. Meunier, *Lutte du principe clérical et du principe laïque dans l'enseignement* (1861), p. 352, and cf. pp. 195–6.
[2] Ibid., pp. 340–1.

the schools were to develop the sentiments of liberty, equality, and fraternity.[1]

Religious instruction, however, lost its place at the head of the list of subjects, and was to be given separately by priests or ministers, not the teacher. Inspired by the brief mood of fraternity which followed the revolution, Carnot expected the co-operation of the Church, and—unlike Arsène Meunier—was not hostile to religion as such. Carnot also intended to preserve complete freedom for private schools, though he asserted the rights of the state by abolishing the 'letter of obedience' for nuns.

When Carnot's bill was presented to Parliament, the minister was already on the way out, and he did not have time to elaborate his plans for the other sectors of education. His central idea was that secondary and higher education should be opened up to all by turning the state scholarships into a 'generous and regular system of state adoption' of the best pupils in the primary schools, so that talent would be discovered and advanced wherever it existed, and the revolutionary principle of equal access to office would become a reality at last.[2] Carnot justified this not only on grounds of justice for the individual, but because choosing the most able would make the social machine more efficient. Here he showed his Saint-Simonian belief that in a modern society the function of education should be to discover the 'aptitudes' of men and direct them towards the 'vocation' which they could best fill. Another Saint-Simonian touch was Carnot's enthusiasm for the Polytechnique, one of whose founders was his father: he saw his scholarship scheme as a vast extension of the competitive principle for which the school stood.

He also intended to give the Polytechnique a new rival, the École d'Administration, one of the most interesting of the Second Republic's ideas. This was to be a 'grande école' for the civil and diplomatic services, and its aim was not only to make these into professions with a proper training, but also to extend the merit principle into fields where patronage and political favour were still all-important. The École d'Administration was opened in 1848, but died the following year in the new political climate. Its memory remained, and helped to inspire the École libre des Sciences

[1] Gontard, *Les Écoles primaires de la France bourgeoise*, pp. 71–2.
[2] H. Carnot, *Le Ministère de l'instruction publique et des cultes depuis le 24 février jusqu'au 5 juillet 1848* (1848), pp. 21, 47.

Politiques of 1871 and the École nationale d'Administration of 1946.

Carnot's scholarship policy was very partially carried out later in 1848 when half the existing *bourses* in the lycées were thrown open to competitive examination. This was the only major change affecting secondary education. An indication of what the republicans might have done if they had remained in power is given by Meunier's plan for an integrated system of education running 'from the *salle d'asile* to the faculties'. All children would attend a common school until the age of twelve, and would have the chance to stay at school until they were eighteen, education being free at all levels. But the secondary schools would be of two kinds: the traditional type preparing for the learned professions, now recruited by competitive examination and with a modernized syllabus, but still teaching Latin; and *écoles professionnelles* preparing for industry, agriculture, and other practical professions, in which theoretical and manual teaching would be combined.[1] The aim was to give equal opportunity of access to a form of education which remained privileged, but the ideas were radical enough for their day. The Third Republic was not to go so far; and one may detect a split as early as 1848 between the republican left, of whom Meunier was typical, and the orthodox leadership, most of whom were themselves products of classical education and wanted to make primary education universal but leave the secondary system intact.

The Second Republic saw a rapid reaction against the idealism and fraternity of February 1848, a reaction which deepened with every turn of events, and which was based on the alarm of the propertied classes at the threatening forces which seemed to have been unleashed. This reaction was soon directed against the schoolteachers, who were blamed for acting as village demagogues and stirring up popular feeling. Conservatives began to turn to the Church and to religious education to 'save society'. Carnot gave a weapon to his opponents by using the schoolteachers to influence opinion in the election campaign of April 1848. The teachers, as agents of the Republic in every village, seemed the obvious counter to the influence of the landlords and priests; Carnot sent them 'manuals of civic instruction' which they were to distribute and comment on. Although only a minority of teachers became

[1] Meunier, *Lutte du principe clérical*, pp. 447–9, 486 ff.

republican militants, there seems little doubt that most *instituteurs* welcomed the Republic with some enthusiasm. It was a regime whose ideals and aspirations were close to their own, and which promised to give them a new sense of dignity, to back them in their struggles with the *curé*, and to bring them more concrete rewards than the satisfaction of duty well done. But these early hopes were followed by bitter disillusion, and even the teachers who had not been politically active were to pay a heavy price for 1848.[1]

The elections produced a republican majority, but over the next months social tension increased, culminating in the working-class rising in Paris in June. After the 'June days', all radical schemes came under suspicion, and Carnot himself was forced to resign in July. For a time, moderate republican views still prevailed, and Parliament began to consider a watered-down version of Carnot's bill for primary schools: education would be compulsory, but no longer free, and 'moral, religious and civic instruction' appeared at the head of the programme, though the dogmatic part of religion was to be taught separately by the priests. The election of Louis-Napoleon as President of the Republic in December 1848 doomed even this project.

Political and legislative changes in nineteenth-century France tended to come about through the alternate application of rival programmes, rather than through the gradual evolution of a consensus, with the consequence that the programmes became fixed and timeless. So it was in 1848. The republican plans for education, though largely abortive, were significant because they represented a tradition handed down intact from the time of the Revolution ('the laws of primary education are all traced out for us in the immortal declarations of our fathers', said Carnot[2]) and which survived to appear again in more propitious times. In 1850, Edgar Quinet published *L'Enseignement du peuple*, a classic statement of the republican position. But for the time being the way was open for the return of another tradition—or rather, as it turned out, for the coalescence of the formerly rival programmes of bourgeois liberals and conservatives.

---

[1] Cf. P. Lévêque, 'Sur quelques instituteurs "rouges" de la Seconde République', *Annales de Bourgogne*, xxxvii (1965), pp. 289–300.

[2] P. Carnot, *Hippolyte Carnot et le ministère de l'instruction publique de la IIe République* (1948), p. 43.

2. THE LOI FALLOUX

Louis-Napoleon, though elected by universal suffrage and relying ultimately on the votes of the peasants, found his political allies in the anti-republican 'party of order' which brought together Catholics and Orleanist liberals. The support of the Catholics was especially important, and Napoleon seems to have given definite promises about educational policy to their political leaders like Montalembert. After his election, he appointed one of this party, Armand de Falloux, as minister of education. For the changes which the Catholics wanted to see, nothing less than a comprehensive law would suffice. This was to be the *loi Falloux*, and the minister began by appointing an 'extraparliamentary commission' to prepare a bill, since until new elections in 1849 Parliament itself was more republican than the government and continued to work on its own project. This commission included representatives of the two parties who were now uneasy political allies, and was charged with working out a new compromise between the interests of religion and those of the state and the University. On the Catholic side, it included Montalembert, bishop Dupanloup, and Catholic journalists and intellectuals like Augustin Cochin, Armand de Melun, and Henri de Riancey. On the liberal side were the leaders of the University—Cousin, Saint-Marc Girardin, and the director of the École Normale, Paul-François Dubois.

The chairman was the liberal politician Adolphe Thiers. Under the July monarchy, Thiers had vigorously defended the University against Catholic attacks. But now his opinion had changed. He believed—and in this he was typical of the bourgeoisie which he represented—that dissension within the property-owning class was a luxury which could no longer be indulged in now that the precipice had opened up before its feet. In the discussions of the commission, of which a verbatim account has survived, the atmosphere of fear and class hatred is palpable. Thiers himself expressed his willingness to abandon primary education to the Church and his hostility to the schoolteachers with a brutality which shocked the other members of the commission.

The commission started from the idea that the events of 1848 were due to the subversion of society by evil forces—'le mal'—which had caused the people to turn away from the natural path

of duty and obedience. The chief agents of these forces were the
teachers, whose real inclinations had been revealed by the policies
of Carnot—'thirty-seven thousand socialists and communists,
veritable *anticurés* in every commune'.[1] The remedies—since a
complete transfer of the schools to the Church was impracticable—
were to encourage the growth of the Catholic orders at the expense
of the lay teachers, to crush the pretensions of the latter, and to
limit the scope of what was taught. Religion was called on to save
society, and the Church was ready to respond to the call. The
choice, in Montalembert's formula, was between socialism and
catechism.[2]

Thus in the debates preceding the law primary education was
the main interest, and the issue of liberty for secondary education,
which had aroused so much passion before 1848, was relatively
ignored. Liberty for private schools was now granted as part of
the compromise. But the liberals refused to sacrifice the state's
own secondary schools to the Church, and defended the secondary
teachers against accusations that they too had contributed to 'le
mal'. The schools which their own sons attended would continue
to be free from clerical interference. The liberals also defended the
rights of the state when the new administrative machinery of the
law was devised, and ensured both that the state retained some
rights over private education and that the Church's influence over
the public schools was limited. The bill which emerged was thus a
compromise, not a Catholic triumph, and was indeed attacked by
Catholic intransigents like Louis Veuillot. It also disappointed true
liberals, for it was a share-out of authority on a new basis between
Church and state rather than a real liberalization. But then, as
Thiers said, 'with absolute liberty, what right would you have to
prevent Raspail or Proudhon from teaching?'[3]

The bill prepared by the commission was submitted to Parliament in 1849, and eventually passed in 1850. The debates were
long and wide-ranging. The left naturally denounced the bill as a
surrender to the Church, while the government intervened on
various points to protect the interests of the state. But the *loi
Falloux* in its final form differed only in detail from what had been

[1] Thiers, quoted in Gontard, *Les Écoles primaires de la France bourgeoise*, p. 85.
[2] Ibid., p. 111.
[3] *La Commission extraparlementaire de 1849. Texte intégral inédit des procès-
verbaux* (1937), p. 189.

agreed in the commission. Its provisions can be grouped under four headings.

(i) *The primary teachers*

The aim of the authors of the *loi Falloux* was to encourage communes to entrust their schools to religious orders instead of lay teachers. But this had also been possible under the law of 1833, and had been the custom in many places for as long as public education had been organized. There was thus no change in the law.[1] What mattered was how far Catholics dominated local councils, and how the central administration used its supervisory powers; in both respects, conditions were to favour the orders for a decade after the law, and their influence was to increase greatly.

The provision of the law most directly aimed at the lay teachers concerned the *écoles normales*. These had come under special attack from conservatives. It was they, it was said, which encouraged the teacher in a spirit of defiance towards religion, and which turned him into a demagogue by giving him knowledge and social ambitions which were frustrated by the realities of his humble task. The law therefore dropped the obligation on departments to maintain an *école normale*, allowing a system of pupil-teachers in model schools instead. In fact, only four departments took this course, for Louis-Napoleon's government, alarmed at the possible drying up of the supply of teachers, did its best to keep the *écoles normales* in existence. But in 1851 new regulations for the schools showed what spirit they were now to be conducted in. The age of entry was raised from sixteen to eighteen, entry examinations were replaced by inquiries into the conduct and morality of the candidates, the syllabus was cut down, and religion dominated life even more than before. These measures were effective for a time in destroying the liberal tendencies which the schools had developed under the July monarchy.[2]

In 1849–50 many of the teachers who had been politically active were purged, the government introducing a special law in 1850 giving prefects absolute powers of discipline over teachers

---

[1] The law of 1850 was much maligned, and one will often read that it allowed schools to be run by religious orders, put religion at the head of the syllabus, etc., when these things went back to 1833 and before.

[2] M. Gontard, *La Question des écoles normales primaires de la Révolution de 1789 à la loi de 1879* (1962), pp. 76–9.

for six months. Some 3,000 to 4,000 were dismissed or punished in other ways.[1] Those who were left, however, found that the *loi Falloux* improved the teacher's material lot even if it limited his intellectual independence. For the first time, a minimum salary was laid down (600 francs a year) and a proper pension system was promised. Since many communes could not make the teacher's income up to the minimum out of their own resources, the result was that more public money was channelled in the form of subsidies to the poorer areas.

(ii) *Primary education*

Much of the *loi Falloux* was simply a re-enactment of previous legislation, including for example the right of the poor to exemption from fees, and the right to open private schools. The list of school subjects was the same as in 1833, with religious and moral instruction again coming first. An important change, however, was that the higher primary schools as such were abolished, as was the special *brevet de capacité* for teachers in them. The subjects formerly taught were now listed as optional subjects in primary schools, and this gave legal sanction for carrying on the existing schools, but there was no obligation or incentive to found new ones. The higher primary schools had not been an entire success, but to abolish them without replacement was a step backwards. They were a casualty of prejudice against *déclassement*, and of the obscurantist mood expressed by Thiers in 1849: 'Reading, writing, and reckoning, that is all that should be taught; as for the rest, it is superfluous.'[2]

The law was more generous to girls' schools. Most provisions of the law applied equally to boys and girls (though not the minimum salary for teachers), and one of the basic ideas of the *loi Guizot* was for the first time partially extended to girls. In future, communes would be obliged to maintain a separate girls' school unless their population was under 800. Founding such a school would usually mean the transfer of the girls from a mixed school with a lay teacher to a girls' school run by a teaching order, and this was the main reason for the provision. As a corollary, the 'letter of obedience' was re-established.

[1] Gontard, *Les Écoles primaires de la France bourgeoise*, p. 107.
[2] *La Commission extraparlementaire de 1849*, p. 31.

(iii) *Private secondary schools*

The law introduced 'liberty of teaching' for secondary education by extending to it the system which had been worked out for primary education in 1833. Anyone who was adequately qualified— in this case, who had five years teaching experience and the baccalaureate or an equivalent—could open a school. The process of authorization was in the hands of the University, and it retained powers of inspection and discipline, but the 'monopoly' was gone.

What the law left unsaid was as important as what it said. It did not, for example, repeat the restrictions imposed in 1828 on the development of the bishops' *petits séminaires* as ordinary secondary schools, and these were now free to expand. Nor did it mention the Jesuits, whose return was the most important consequence of the law in the secondary field. The law also abolished, by not re-enacting, all the restrictions which the University had previously imposed on what private schools could teach: only schools with special permission had been able to teach the full course, and this had been enforced by making candidates for the baccalaureate produce a 'certificate of studies' attesting that they had attended the final forms in a state school or an authorized private school. The 'certificate of studies' was abolished in 1849 and not revived. But the state retained control of the baccalaureate itself and of the other degrees awarded by the faculties, and this gave it indirect influence over what private schools taught. Higher education remained the monopoly of the University.

The public secondary schools were unaffected by the *loi Falloux*, with one exception. This was that municipal councils were allowed to withdraw their colleges from the University and transfer them to private teachers. As with primary schools, Catholic influence in local politics worked to the advantage of the Church. The number of municipal colleges fell from 307 in 1850 to 232 in 1859, most of those lost being replaced by Catholic schools.[1] This part of the law was naturally resented by the University, for it deprived many teachers of their jobs.

(iv) *Administrative machinery*

These rather technical sections of the law (see the Appendix for further details) were much debated, and were the first to be

[1] J. Maurain, *La Politique ecclésiastique du Second Empire de 1852 à 1869* (1930), pp. 140–1.

changed. The aim was to introduce representatives of the Church and other 'live forces of society' into the supervision of education at all levels. The main change was that the 'academies', the units of local educational administration, were reduced from regional to departmental size. This made it easier for the bishops to exercise influence, and in the academy the University's representative, the rector, shared power with a *conseil académique*, which included the bishop. The same principle was applied to the new central council of the University, the Conseil supérieur, which was very different from the old Conseil royal. The *universitaires* were outnumbered by bishops, magistrates, and members of the learned academies which formed the Institute. There were also representatives of private education: the Conseil supérieur had ultimate responsibility for the legal supervision of private teachers and for examination programmes, and its composition was seen as an important safeguard of educational liberty. The University itself felt that the influence given to outsiders destroyed its autonomy; it noted that the law carefully avoided using the word University, and feared that the work of Napoleon had been overturned.

Although based on a short-lived political alliance, the *loi Falloux* proved a lasting compromise. Its basic provisions survived minor changes, and there was no legislation of comparable scope until 1880. In primary education, the law was to lead to a great expansion of the teaching orders, and in secondary education to the opening of many new Catholic schools. Yet, as the law itself recognized, there could be no real return to the ancien régime. The *loi Falloux* intensified the religious orientation of education, and provided the University with new competition, but it did not fundamentally threaten the dominance of education by the secularized state.

3. THE COUP D'ÉTAT AND THE MINISTRY OF FORTOUL

'Of all my uncle's institutions', Louis-Napoleon is reputed to have said of the University, 'it is the one which I understand the least.'[1] In his book *Des idées napoléoniennes*, Louis-Napoleon had duly described and praised Napoleon I's educational work. But once he had achieved supreme power himself he took little interest in the subject, and was content to leave policy to his ministers. This freedom of action allowed the ministers to impose their own

[1] A. Mourier, *Notes et souvenirs d'un universitaire, 1827–1889* (1889), p. 79.

ideas on education, but it also reflected the low priority given to education under the Second Empire. It was looked on as a dull and technical affair, was ignored by the leading political figures, and was starved of funds. The ministers of education were not men of political weight, and on several occasions they found themselves unable to persuade their colleagues or the Emperor to adopt the plans which they had elaborated.

Napoleon III's first minister of education was Hippolyte Fortoul, an interesting if unadmirable figure. In the thirties, he had made a career as a man of letters and art critic, and had had republican views and close links with the Saint-Simonian movement, though with the literary and romantic side of it rather than the industrial and scientific one. In 1841 he had entered the University and taught at the faculties of Toulouse and Aix with some success. In 1848 he was still thought republican enough to be asked by Carnot, Reynaud, and Charton to join them at the ministry of education.[1] He refused, as he now had parliamentary ambitions. He was elected in 1849, and quickly undeceived his old friends, voting with the right and attaching himself to the followers of Louis-Napoleon. He spoke once or twice on higher education, but not on the *loi Falloux*. In October 1851 the Prince-President rewarded his loyalty by making him minister of marine, and after the *coup d'état* in December he became minister of education and religious affairs. He was the only *universitaire*, almost the only intellectual, in Louis-Napoleon's entourage.

Fortoul's Bonapartism was the fruit of ambition and cynicism rather than of conviction, but once he had decided to break with his past he entered fully into the spirit of the new regime. He was of authoritarian personal temper, intolerant of criticism and dogmatic in applying his ideas; he displayed these qualities in office, and became the most unpopular minister that the University knew in the nineteenth century. For many years afterwards, judgements of Fortoul's work were influenced by the memory of the teachers' hostility to him. He was seen, rightly enough, as the instrument of political reaction; he was also seen as a clerical, but this was not really the case. The survival of his private papers makes it possible to understand Fortoul's policies better, though hardly to rehabilitate him.

[1] P. Raphaël, 'Fortoul et la Seconde République, d'après des documents inédits', *La Révolution de 1848*, xxvii (1930–1), pp. 189, 198–209.

The situation after the *coup d'état* was not an easy one. The University was suspect to Louis-Napoleon as a centre of liberalism and a rallying-point for opposition. At the same time, he had incurred new obligations to the Catholic party, and might need to make further concessions to them. For some time, Louis-Napoleon's intentions were in doubt—his habit was to listen enigmatically to advice from many quarters before making up his mind. To Montalembert, Parisis, and other Catholic leaders he floated the idea of dismantling the University altogether and handing education over to the Church, but they proved un-enthusiastic.[1] In the end, Napoleon decided to preserve the University. His own instincts were against giving the clergy power outside the spiritual sphere, and no doubt like other rulers he realized the value of the University as an instrument of the state's power.

Fortoul later claimed that it was he who had 'saved' the University, and it is possible from various sources to reconstruct the outline of a bargain between the minister and Louis-Napoleon. The University would survive. In return, Fortoul promised to purge it of political opposition and to modernize its teaching—for one of Napoleon's objections to the University was that it was out of touch with the spirit of the age. Fortoul was given a free hand provided that he did not embarrass the government politically or demand additional expenditure.[2]

Fortoul's own papers are not enlightening on this period. He claims that the month of December 'was devoted by the minister to personal meditation on the measures demanded by the state of society'.[3] In fact, once the political situation became clear, he began to prepare a comprehensive piece of legislation which would replace the *loi Falloux* and reform every aspect of education. This proposed *loi Fortoul* met political difficulties, and could not be

---

[1] P. de la Gorce, *Histoire du Second Empire* (1894–1905), ii, p. 141; É. Lecanuet, *Montalembert* (1895–1902), iii, p. 46; C. Guillemant, *Pierre-Louis Parisis* (1916–25), iii, p. 486 n. 1; N. F. L. Besson, *Vie de Son Éminence Monseigneur le cardinal Mathieu, archevêque de Besançon* (1882), ii, pp. 24–6.

[2] F. Buisson, *Dictionnaire de pédagogie et d'instruction primaire*, first part (1882–7), article Fortoul; A. Cournot, *Souvenirs (1760–1860)* (1913), pp. 223–4; M. du Camp, *Paris: ses organes, ses fonctions et sa vie dans la seconde moitié du XIXe siècle* (1869–75), v, pp. 128–30.

[3] Fortoul papers, A.N. 246 AP 17, folder 1. Fortoul arranged his papers to form a comprehensive record of his ministry, with commentary. The work was cut short by Fortoul's death.

enacted as a whole, but major parts of it appeared piecemeal in a
series of laws and decrees over the next few years. It included, for
example, the reform of secondary education which was to be
known as bifurcation; important changes in the administration and
financing of primary schools; the reinforcement of the minister's
disciplinary powers in the University; and reforms in higher
education, including the creation of new faculties. Among the
proposals not carried out were the dissolution and reconstitution
of the École Normale, and the withdrawal of the municipal colleges
from the University, leaving town councils to decide their future.
One reason for the dropping of the latter may have been the
campaign against it run by the *Revue de l'instruction publique*, the
organ of the liberal *universitaires*, which tried valiantly to maintain
a critical attitude for a year or so after the *coup d'état*.

The most controversial of Fortoul's proposals amounted to the
repeal of the *loi Falloux*: private schools would have again needed
special authorization. Fortoul proposed to make this acceptable to
the Church by handing the power to authorize schools run by
priests to the bishops, while keeping it in state hands for lay
schools. It was the political implications of this which eventually
prevented Fortoul's 'organic law' from being accepted, but it
reached an advanced state of discussion. The first full version was
drawn up in January 1852, and Fortoul entered on long negotiations
with Parisis, leader of the ultramontane party among the bishops.
Parisis was eventually won over, and expressed strong regret when
he heard the scheme was to be withdrawn, contrasting the simple
principle of sharing authority between Church and state with
'the complications and contradictions, I will venture to say the
deceits and dangers of the law of 15 March 1850'. He took the view
that 'since our teaching rights, which are part of the very essence
of our apostolic mission, are formally reserved and recognized, we
do not have to concern ourselves with whether liberty for all is
possible and preferable today or not'.[1] It is unlikely that all the
bishops shared this view; Sibour, for example, the moderate
archbishop of Paris, protested against the reintroduction of
arbitrary authorization when shown a copy of the project.[2]

Nevertheless, Louis-Napoleon was on the point of signing the

[1] Fortoul papers, A.N. 246 AP 18, Parisis to Fortoul, 3 June 1852; Parisis to
Louis-Napoleon, 21 Feb. 1852 (copy).

[2] Fortoul papers, A.N. 246 AP 17, folder 2, comments of Sibour on draft plan.

bill in March when a delay in transmitting documents allowed him to have second thoughts. The more urgent parts were then detached and enacted separately. The remainder was submitted to the Conseil d'État, and again nearly got through in May; last-minute hesitations by Napoleon then caused a postponement which proved permanent. It was, it seems, the hostility of the magistrates and officials on the Conseil d'État to the reduction of state influence involved in Fortoul's project which eventually swayed the balance.[1]

If Fortoul's 'organic law' had passed, his policies would have had much greater coherence. As it was, he was allowed to enact the purely educational parts of his plans, but had to accept a political compromise. From 1852, the relations between Church and state and between government and University assumed the form that they were to retain until the Italian war caused a reorientation of the Empire's policies in 1859–60. During the authoritarian Empire, the government put the defence of order and religion at the centre of its claim to support, and Fortoul was to prove adept at the rhetoric of reaction. But alliance with the Church did not preclude vigorous defence of the rights of the state, and this too was reflected in Fortoul's policies.[2]

The principles of the *loi Falloux* were now not questioned, and there was no attempt to impede the opening of Catholic secondary schools or the transfer of primary schools to religious orders. But the rights of inspection and discipline which the law gave the University were not neglected, and the lycées, the schools most directly affected by Catholic competition, were actively defended. Fortoul was alarmed at the drop in numbers which followed the *loi Falloux*, and sought to bring pupils back to the schools by various improvements, including the syllabus reform discussed in the next chapter. The hand of the state was also strengthened by changes in the administrative machinery in 1852 and 1854. The law of 1854, in particular, restored the 'regional' academies and made the rectors once more powerful officials. Fortoul took the opportunity to get rid of many clerical officials appointed after 1850. The new rectors were conservative and Catholic, but they

[1] The various versions of the project and related documents are in A.N. 246 AP 17–18. One version is printed in L. Liard, *L'Enseignement supérieur en France 1789–1893* (1888–94), ii, pp. 448–63. Cf. Cournot, *Souvenirs*, pp. 227–9.
[2] See below, pp. 122–4.

were mostly distinguished members of the University, and firm defenders of its rights.[1] Thus the University began to re-emerge as an independent force—and the fact that the word 'University' was freely used again was an advance in itself. But the University 'saved' by Fortoul was to be a new University, purged, Catholic, and submissive.

In 1852, Fortoul had taken powers to discipline the University by abolishing the legal safeguards which had previously protected the secondary teachers from the kind of purge applied to the *instituteurs* since 1849. Some teachers were dismissed, and others resigned rather than take the oath of loyalty which was now demanded of all public servants. The men involved were not numerous, but they were distinguished, and harm was done to the University by this episode; to have been a martyr of 1852 was later a title to honour.[2] Those teachers who remained found, like the *instituteurs*, that they were expected more than ever to be submissive to authority and to behave as models of respectability. Outward deference to religion was expected, and Fortoul recommended that teachers, 'even the professors of mathematics', should be urged to attend mass.[3] Another aspect of the policy was Fortoul's celebrated circular on beards. This pointed out that 'now that calm is returning to men's minds and order to society, it is important that the last traces of anarchy should disappear'. It was therefore not to be tolerated 'that teachers should appear before their pupils carelessly dressed, or let their beards grow, thus adopting manners in their external appearance that are hardly compatible with the gravity of the professorate'.[4]

There was a point behind this. Fortoul had decided that the best way to defend the University from its enemies was to give them no pretext for attacking it. After dissidents had been purged or disciplined, it was necessary to show that the University was thoroughly moral, respectable, and Catholic. This was also the best way of competing with the Catholic schools, for Fortoul wanted the lycées to regain the rich clientele which had been deserting them since 1850. He argued that parents had lost

---

[1] A.N. F^{17} 2754, comments on the new rectors, 1854.
[2] Cf. Gerbod, *La Condition universitaire*, pp. 256 ff., 296–304, 331–4.
[3] Fortoul papers, A.N. 246 AP 21, meeting of officials, 6 Oct. 1855.
[4] Circular of 20 Mar. 1852. (Official decrees, etc., are cited thus by date only, as they are available in various collections. See Bibliography, section II A.)

confidence in the University because it seemed irreligious, and that confidence would return if the Christian character of the University were stressed. The teachers' liberty of conscience was to be sacrificed to the prejudices of the right-thinking middle class, a class which had swung sharply away from liberalism since the days of Victor Cousin's University.

The new spirit was symbolized by an annual religious service, the Fête des Écoles; in the Pantheon, now reconsecrated as a church, representatives of the clergy and the University gathered to celebrate their reconciliation with each other and the union of learning and faith. In the lycées, religious instruction was strengthened, although it still occupied only one hour a week, and the rights of Jews and Protestants were not affected. When issuing a circular on the subjects and methods of teaching in 1854, Fortoul stressed that moral education was as important as intellectual, and claimed that the University was now well equipped to give both.[1]

In 1852–3, a number of speeches by Fortoul and his officials elaborated the theme of the 'new' or 'regenerated' University. The new University was distinguished by its moral and religious character, and by the way in which, while faithful to its literary traditions, it had adapted its teaching to meet the needs of a scientific and industrial age. As Fortoul said when laying a foundation stone for the new Sorbonne (a symbolic gesture only— rebuilding had to await the Third Republic), it was to unite 'the faith of the times of St Louis, the taste of the age of Louis XIV, and the enlightenment of the Napoleonic era'.[2]

Adapting the University's teaching to the needs of the Napoleonic era meant, above all, the reform of the secondary curriculum. It has already been suggested that this reform was promised to Napoleon as part of the price for saving the University. The other political motive was the desire to 'strike a great blow to restore the fortunes of the state schools'[3] by concentrating on a side of education where the University was strong and the Catholic schools were weak. Exploiting the University's experience in scientific education and its supply of trained teachers was in fact

[1] Instruction of 15 Nov. 1854.
[2] *Journal général de l'instruction publique*, xxiv (1855), p. 439.
[3] C. Jourdain, *Rapport sur l'organisation et les progrès de l'instruction publique* (1867), p. 131.

more sensible than trying to challenge the Catholics on their own ground of religion and morality.

Thus a new interest in scientific education was one result of Louis-Napoleon's seizure of power, though it had come about in a rather devious way. It was one of the few positive developments of this period, which was generally one of intellectual repression and educational stagnation. The Second Empire's reliance on universal suffrage did not prevent it from neglecting primary education throughout the 1850s. It was a decade when the government was deliberately promoting economic development, but little of this activity spilled over into education. Only fumbling initiatives were taken in the field of technical education, while Fortoul's reform of the lycées was based on ideas developed within the University before 1848 rather than on any new Saint-Simonian inspiration. And as we shall see, this reform largely failed because it was forced on a University already hostile to the government on political and intellectual grounds.

CHAPTER FOUR

The reform of secondary education

I. THE PROBLEM OF REFORM

The position of classical education was so strong that no reform which did not leave it more or less unchanged for those who wanted it was practical politics. The most that could be done was to provide a modern alternative. Two sorts of alternative could be envisaged: a full secondary education based on modern subjects but equal in status to the traditional curriculum; and a shorter, more practical type of education aimed at a rather different social class. A demand probably existed for both of them, but governments tended not to distinguish clearly between these different demands, and to concentrate on developing only one of the alternatives: Fortoul's reforms in 1852 concentrated on the first, Duruy's in 1865 on the second.

Both forms of modern education existed in embryo in the University. Although the integrated classical curriculum was still considered the norm, higher scientific education had developed within the lycées to prepare boys for the entrance examinations of the government's *grandes écoles*. There were special mathematical forms—Elementary Mathematics, preparing for Saint-Cyr, and Special Mathematics, organized only in the larger schools and preparing for the Polytechnique and École Normale—which candidates entered before completing the normal course. Some non-scientific subjects, including philosophy, continued to be studied. The scientific teaching itself was strongly mathematical, reflecting the specialized demands of the military schools, and Napoleon I's belief in science as mainly a tool for engineers and artillery officers—he had abolished the much broader scientific education, with the emphasis on the natural sciences, offered in the *écoles centrales*.

This scientific education, though limited in purpose, was serious and advanced. It ensured that the schools had a corps of science teachers, whose training was one function of the University's higher scientific institutions. And the number of pupils involved was considerable, for military careers had a strong appeal, and the prestige of the *grandes écoles* meant that there were always more candidates than places. In 1850 there were 3,266 competitors for 449 places, and it was the army which attracted most:[1]

	Candidates	Admissions
École Normale	184	30
École Polytechnique	664	90
Saint-Cyr	1,783	270
Naval school	553	44
State forestry school	82	15

As Prost points out, a large section of the French upper class received a scientific rather than a literary training throughout the nineteenth century.[2]

Thus the intending specialist was well provided for in the lycées. But the idea that science should be a part of general education was slow to develop. Some elementary mathematics was taught in the lower forms, but physics, chemistry, and natural history, though never entirely neglected, were squeezed into odd corners of the syllabus. Between 1840 and 1847, under the regulations introduced when Cousin was minister, they were taught only at the end of the course, in the Philosophy form. This arose from the notion that science was a difficult and even dangerous subject, to be approached only when the mind had been properly formed by the classics; it meant that the many pupils who left the course before the end learnt no science at all.

The University's traditions in fact made it difficult to fit new subjects in—and science was competing for time with other novelties like history and modern languages. The syllabus was dominated by the leisurely classical course, with its two-hour classes taught by a single form teacher. It was difficult for specialist teachers to find a foothold, and the modern idea of 'periods' of equal length devoted to different subjects was not accepted. The University also clung to the principle that all educated Frenchmen should share a common culture, and was opposed to allowing pupils a choice of subjects. What happened, therefore, was that new subjects were added without the time

[1] A.N. F17 6839, unpublished statistical report for 1850, Table 20.
[2] Prost, *Histoire de l'enseignement en France*, p. 58.

allocated to the classics being cut down, and it is not surprising that complaints about overwork and dangers to health began to be heard.

The second alternative to the classics appeared in the form of the 'special courses' which lycées and colleges began to organize from the thirties. These were shorter courses, usually taught by less qualified staff, which concentrated on modern subjects, often with a commercial bias. They were aimed at those who could not hope to complete a full secondary education, and because they did not teach Latin they were open to boys from the primary schools. There was little difference between the special courses and Guizot's higher primary schools, and the former were often more successful because of the prestige of the secondary school. In many towns, the college and higher primary school shared the same building and were officially combined; the division between primary and secondary sectors was not as sharp in practice as in theory. Although these courses opened up new educational opportunities, they really had the conservative aim of diverting lower-middle-class pupils away from the classics. In the absence of any alternative, it was common for pupils to follow the classical courses for a few years and then leave, but conservatives thought this dangerous, as learning Latin aroused unhealthy ambitions and stimulated the desire for *déclassement*. The development of modern education was often justified as a way of relieving pressure on the overcrowded liberal professions, and many *universitaires* welcomed a form of education that would remove unsuitable pupils from their classical forms, provided that it remained of inferior status.

In the last years of the July monarchy, there was a good deal of discussion in the higher University administration of how to provide a 'bifurcation'[1] within the schools, either by building on the special courses or by adapting the scientific education given for the *grandes écoles*. As early as 1834, in a report on German schools, Cousin had outlined a plan remarkably similar to the 'bifurcation' introduced by Fortoul in 1852, but he had done nothing about it when in power.[2] The immediate origin of Fortoul's policy lay in a report presented in 1847 to the reforming minister

[1] The first use of the term which I have found is by Charles Giraud, a member of the Conseil royal, in *Séances et travaux de l'Académie des sciences morales et politiques*, ix (1846), p. 247.

[2] V. Cousin, *État de l'instruction secondaire dans le royaume de Prusse pendant l'année 1831* (1834), p. 34.

Salvandy by the faculty of science of Paris. Its author was the dean of the faculty, the chemist Jean-Baptiste Dumas. Over the next twenty years, Dumas was to dominate reform within the University, and as Fortoul's chief adviser he devised the reforms of 1852.

Dumas's report began by regretting the abandonment of 'the tradition of a wide scientific education which was set in movement, with some excesses perhaps, in the *écoles centrales*', and called on the University to take up the task again, to meet the needs of the 'agricultural, commercial, and industrial classes' who were now as important as the liberal professions, and to respond to 'the progress accomplished by the human intellect, as well as the positive interests of modern civilization'.[1] It proposed action to improve scientific education at every level. In the lycées, preparation for the *grandes écoles* was to be made more efficient, so that the University would not lose ground to private cramming schools. For non-specialists, science was to be taught as an integral part of education throughout the school, and it was recognized that some of the classical programme would have to be sacrificed to allow this. For those aiming at scientific professions, there would be new 'scientific colleges'; pupils would follow the lower forms of the ordinary schools before entering these colleges, which would be parallel with the higher classical forms and of equal status. Their teaching would be based on the natural sciences rather than on the 'minute and sterile study of pure mathematics', and in what amounted to a powerful plea for the independent intellectual validity of scientific education the report saw them preparing boys for the administration, medicine, and the armed forces as well as for industry and agriculture.

Perhaps the most interesting proposals were those for 'intermediate' education, which was to be based on the higher primary schools. Here flexibility and recognition of the diversity of needs were the keynote. At one end, intermediate education might approach the teaching of the colleges, and use the same school in small towns. At the other, it would be integrated with technical and adult education. Even the primary schools were not forgotten —the report proposed the teaching of practical subjects like hygiene, natural history, and meteorology.

The comprehensive and coherent nature of the 'Dumas plan' was striking. Unfortunately, most of the later attempts to apply

[1] Report of 6 Apr. 1847.

some of its ideas fell down because they chose to concentrate on one or two parts in isolation. The first of these attempts was Salvandy's reform of the lycées in 1847. This had two parts. In the ordinary course, science teaching was spread out over all the forms as recommended by Dumas, though this was done chiefly by extending mathematics—the natural sciences still did not begin until Rhetoric. The second innovation was that special education (*enseignement spécial*) was to be organized in every school according to an official programme. In form, this was a development of the existing 'special courses', but the programme was that proposed by Dumas for his 'scientific colleges'. The three-year course would include mathematics and science, history and geography, Latin, French, and modern languages. Pupils would enter it from the fourth form of the normal course, where they would already have started Latin and Greek. Official documents stressed that the new education was to be of equal status with the classics.[1]

The new 'special education' was therefore very different from the old courses, and largely irrelevant to those who used them. It still left unsatisfied the demand for intermediate education, Dumas's proposals for which were not taken up by Salvandy. In any case, the reform of 1847 was soon overtaken by events. The programmes, though reissued in 1848 and 1849, seem to have remained a dead letter, the courses going on much as before. The reform did, however, stimulate the creation of these courses where they had not previously existed.

As we have seen, none of the events of the Second Republic had much effect on the life of the lycées. Carnot's pronouncements on the future of the classics were vague, though he showed his awareness of the problem of reform by appointing a commission to look into the overloading of pupils and its effects on health. A new regulation on gymnastics and military training showed the same concern.[2] In October 1848, as a last gesture of republicanism, the study of the Revolution and Empire was added to the history course, which had previously stopped at 1789.[3] In 1850, the question of reforming the syllabus of the lycées was raised in the

---

[1] *Arrêté* of 5 Mar. 1847, circular of 6 Aug. 1847. Cf. L. Trénard, 'L'Enseignement secondaire sous la Monarchie de Juillet: les réformes de Salvandy', *Revue d'histoire moderne et contemporaine*, xii (1965), pp. 120–3.

[2] Carnot, *Le Ministère de l'instruction publique*, pp. 21–2, 46–50.

[3] *Arrêté* of 8 Oct. 1848.

new Conseil supérieur, but nothing came of it.[1] When Fortoul became minister, therefore, the starting-point for a reformer was still the Dumas report of 1847 and the partially abortive changes made by Salvandy.

2. THE DEMAND FOR REFORM

The fact that the modernization of the lycées was being contemplated at the end of the July monarchy reflected the growing pressure of public opinion. It is probably true to say that this pressure came from writers and groups of intellectuals rather than parents. For even if there was a latent demand for a more modern education, it was difficult for parents to avoid choosing the classics when they presented such obvious social advantages or to conceive a real alternative before it had been developed in concrete form. Nor did much pressure come from within the University—except as we have seen from its scientists. The average teacher hardly questioned the virtues of classical education, and teachers were not much given in any case to thinking about educational problems. It is significant, for example, that the radical review *La Liberté de penser*, run from 1847 to 1851 by a brilliant group of young *normaliens*, virtually ignored questions of educational reform, and was in no way hostile to the classical tradition. Reforming the lycées, therefore, inevitably meant imposing the ideas of outsiders on a reluctant teaching body.

Within the University, the administrators, who had more contact with the world outside, were more conscious than the teachers of the need to move with the times. Saint-Marc Girardin, liberal man of letters and colleague of Cousin on the Conseil royal, argued in 1847 that it was better to introduce moderate reform than to risk by obstinacy a more radical reform which would replace the dominance of classics by the dominance of science.[2] The philosopher Cournot, a high official under Fortoul, saw the swing away from the classics to more practical subjects as an inevitable result of social changes since the Revolution and of the materialistic 'spirit of the age'. Governments could modify such tendencies, but not in the long run resist them.[3]

---

[1] A.N. F^{17} 12950, Conseil supérieur, 13–14 Aug. 1850.
[2] Saint-Marc Girardin, *De l'instruction intermédiaire et de ses rapports avec l'instruction secondaire* (1847), p. 75.
[3] Cournot, *Des institutions d'instruction publique*, pp. 43–7.

It was the spokesmen for the social and economic tendencies identified by Cournot who were in fact the chief advocates of science. But the relation between educational debate and politics was not always straightforward. Not all the friends of political progress were critics of the classics, nor were all champions of the sciences men of the left—as the coincidence in 1852 of reform and reaction shows. There was a whole set of conservative arguments for teaching science, and some of them were used in Dumas's report of 1847. The classics, it was said, could be politically dangerous because the ideal world which they depicted was very different from the real world; young men who left school might be shocked by the contrast, and tempted by utopian ideas of remodelling society. The makers of the French Revolution, after all, had been inspired by classical examples. The sciences, on the other hand, were practical, down-to-earth subjects which kept boys firmly in touch with reality and turned their minds to useful activities. The arguments about *déclassement* also came in here: giving more weight to the sciences would encourage interest in careers in industry and commerce rather than the liberal professions.

Conversely, many liberals and republicans continued to see the classics as a source of humane values, and to suspect science because it lacked a moral dimension. The republican opposition before 1848, although it included some scientists like Arago and Raspail, was not generally hostile to the traditional system.[1] The severest criticisms came not from the political liberals, but from the liberal economists, organized around the *Journal des Économistes*. In 1850, one of their leaders, Frédéric Bastiat, claimed in a book called *Baccalauréat et socialisme* that the classics were at the origin of the recent social upheavals: socialism was an invention of the ancient world, and a direct line led from Plato to 1848. However exaggerated this thesis, it attacked the University at a sensitive spot by undermining the claim that the classics had a unique moral value. What had men of the nineteenth century, who lived by honest work, to learn from a civilization based on slavery, plunder, and conquest? There was a parallel between Bastiat's ideas and those of the *abbé* Gaume, whose *Le Ver rongeur* (1851) attacked the study of the 'pagan' classics, and also blamed it for

[1] G. Weill, 'Les Républicains et l'enseignement sous Louis-Philippe', *Revue internationale de l'enseignement*, xxxviii (1899), pp. 38–9.

the growth of modern revolutionary ideas. Both books appealed
to the reactionary mood of the period, and Gaume's book caused
great controversy among Catholic teachers.

Gaume's remedy was the replacement of the pagan classics by
the Christian ones—the Fathers of the Church. Bastiat, however,
along with other members of the liberal school like Michel
Chevalier, Adolphe Blanqui, and Frédéric Passy, wanted to see a
modern education centred on science, modern languages (for they
were strong internationalists), and economics. The economists
were, of course, opposed to state intervention, and cited the
fossilization of classical education in the hands of the University
as an example of the evil effects of monopoly. In many ways, they
took over ideas first popularized by the Saint-Simonians. They
declared that society had moved into a new industrial era, a
'scientific civilization'.[1] In the new age, the great task was to
liberate the productive energies of man, and the intellect was a
form of capital which should be exploited to give the maximum
return. We should not be afraid, said Chevalier, of making
education 'utilitarian'; the useful is good, first because it *is* useful,
and second because it tends to 'bring the mind down to earth
instead of wandering in the clouds, a region where purely classical
education too often transports it'.[2]

Chevalier also pointed out that since the Revolution a new
industrial and commercial middle class had arisen, which had a
right to an education suited to its needs. Most arguments for
scientific education used this idea of new classes, variously called
the *classes moyennes*, the 'intermediate' classes, or the 'industrial,
commercial, and agricultural classes'. But there was much confusion about their identity. To the historian, two distinct groups
seem to be involved. First, there were the upper ranks of the
industrial and commercial class, the members of which could
afford to send their sons to the lycée and for whom it was natural
to seek integration into the older bourgeoisie and to establish a
family stake in the traditional professions. Second, there was the
true 'intermediate' class of clerks, shopkeepers, minor officials,
schoolteachers, factory foremen, salesmen, and so on, who could
not afford a full education and wanted something more relevant to

[1] F. Passy, *De l'instruction secondaire en France* (1846), p. 48.
[2] M. Chevalier, *De l'instruction secondaire à l'occasion du rapport au roi de
M. Villemain* (1843), p. 27.

their ambitions for their children. But these were frequently confused, partly because of the contemporary tendency to think in terms of occupational groups (the rich merchant, the clerk, and the village shopkeeper were all classified as in 'commerce') rather than stratification by wealth. There was a tendency to talk as if a new form of education should serve the *whole* of the 'industrial and commercial class', and that just as 'liberal education' suited the 'liberal professions', so something more practical was needed by the new professions. But if this form of education was inferior in status to the classics, as was almost inevitable, it would in fact fail to attract those who could afford something better. These semantic problems hampered the efforts of reformers for many years.

But critics were right to relate the need for reform to the changing balance of occupations within the middle class, and they pointed out the paradox that in an age of economic progress secondary education remained what it had been in an aristocratic and 'feudal' society. 'With a few exceptions, we teach our children what was taught in the Middle Ages, when France was covered with monasteries and the University in thrall to scholasticism.'[1] Auguste Comte put the same point in a more theoretical way, seeing literary education as a relic of the 'metaphysical' age, which was about to give way to the positive age in which education would be based wholly on science.[2] Comte's personal influence was still limited to a handful of disciples, but he stood for a very general mood, constantly growing in strength, of faith in science, progress, and the benefits of material civilization. This faith was very apparent in Dumas's 1847 report. It was shared by a good part of the middle class, and although the events of 1848 destroyed some of the optimism, one form of reaction to those events was the feeling that it was time to turn to the development of industry and the creation of prosperity instead of the sterilities of politics. This mood was encouraged and exploited by the government of Napoleon III.

3. BIFURCATION

One of Fortoul's earliest and most significant decisions was the

[1] Adolphe Blanqui in *Séances et travaux de l'Académie des sciences morales et politiques*, ix (1846), p. 229.
[2] A. Comte, *Oeuvres choisies* (ed. H. Gouhier, n.d.), pp. 86–8, 132 ff., 262–4.

choice of Jean-Baptiste Dumas as his principal aide. Since 1847, Dumas had taken to public life, and was active in various ways in furthering the progress of industry; he served as minister of commerce in 1850–1. Unlike the liberal *universitaires* of the July monarchy, Dumas had no strong political commitment, and as a good technocrat served different regimes without question. He was, we are told, a born committee chairman,[1] and there were few committees appointed by Fortoul of which he was not a member. He, Fortoul, and the astronomer Le Verrier—famous as the discoverer of Neptune, but apparently a man of limited administrative ability—formed a 'triumvirate' which worked out the new policies.

Fortoul's other appointments to the Conseil supérieur and to posts as inspector-general tended to bring forward scientists and scientifically minded philosophers like Cournot and Ravaisson. As in other fields, the coming of the Second Empire meant the destruction of vested interests—in this case, of the Cousinian old guard—and chances for new men. But the new men were still members of the University rather than outsiders, and the Saint-Simonian bankers and economists who helped to form the Second Empire's commercial and industrial policy had little say in education. Michel Chevalier, for example, was on the Conseil supérieur in 1852, but dropped the next year; there was a personal enmity between him and Dumas which dated from the latter's days at the ministry of commerce.

The reform of 1852, called 'bifurcation', was largely the work of Dumas, and represented a second attempt to apply the ideas of the 1847 report. As the name suggests, it consisted of dividing the higher forms (above the fourth) into two sections, one scientific and one 'literary'. The scientific sections were based on, and replaced, the mathematical classes which had prepared for the government schools. They thus offered a real choice between two sorts of full secondary education, leading to qualifications of equal status. This was a more radical reform than Salvandy's 'special education', which had offered a shorter and inevitably inferior alternative to the classics but left the traditional course unchanged.

Under the system of bifurcation, every boy had to choose (at about the age of fourteen) between the two sections. In the literary

[1] D. Nisard, *Souvenirs et notes biographiques* (1888), ii, p. 266.

section, the classics remained the staple fare, and led to the *baccalauréat ès-lettres* and to the usual careers of law, teaching, and public service. The science section led to a new *baccalauréat ès-sciences*, which was needed for entry to the faculties of medicine and for the government schools. The examination programmes of the latter were harmonized with the baccalaureate programme, and the class of Special Mathematics was retained in the larger schools for those attempting the more difficult examinations.

Neither section was narrowly specialized, and the two sections of each form met for common teaching in certain subjects—history and geography, French, modern languages, and some Latin. In the separate classes, the scientific section studied mathematics and science, while the classicists did more Latin, Greek, and general science. At the end of the course, the two sections were reunited in the Philosophy form (now renamed Logic). These arrangements were ingenious, but demanded a flexibility of method which the University hardly possessed—splitting the teaching of Latin was especially awkward.

The syllabus of the science sections was virtually identical with that proposed for the 'scientific colleges' in Dumas's 1847 report. But the idea of teaching some subjects in common was a new one, and although present from the first in Fortoul's plans it seems to have been given more weight than originally intended in order to counter criticisms. The version of the plan submitted to the Conseil supérieur in March 1852 said only that the two sections 'may have some points in common',[1] and when it was unveiled to the public the impression was given that the sections would be purely specialized. This attracted much criticism in the press,[2] as it seemed that the utilitarian spirit had triumphed and that the University's tradition of an integrated syllabus had been abandoned. The legitimist *L'Assemblée nationale*, for example, regretted that 'For the first time in French society, those who intend to go into high positions in commerce and industry, the administration, science, medicine, or the learned professions . . . will be dispensed or rather excluded from the noble studies which for centuries have cultivated and fortified the French genius.'[3] Fortoul replied by

[1] Fortoul papers, A.N. 246 AP 18.

[2] Cf. P. Raphaël, 'Fortoul, Sainte-Beuve et Cucheval-Clarigny', *La Révolution de 1848*, xxvii (1930), pp. 43–8.

[3] 18 Apr. 1852, copy in A.N. F17 68781.

issuing a circular which stressed the importance of the common teaching and claimed that both sections would give a truly liberal education, though combining the cultivation of the imaginative and reasoning faculties in different proportions.[1] He also pointed out that a split already existed because of the development of mathematical specialization, and bifurcation was an improvement because it forced the specialists to study other subjects as well. In the same way, Dumas argued that the old system had been leading to a 'trifurcation' (the classical course, preparation for the *grandes écoles*, and 'practical' education), but the reform averted the danger that 'the nation would find itself permanently divided into irreconcilable castes'.[2]

All the same, some of Fortoul's pronouncements had a Saint-Simonian ring. Justifying the reform in a report of 1853, he criticized the old system for failing to take account of the 'diversity of vocations'; the University had neglected the development of the 'particular aptitudes of individuals', concentrating on turning out 'a certain universal type of cultured elegance' instead of fashioning 'diverse instruments for the different functions of society and the state'.[3] But Fortoul himself was a literary man, and in the debates on the plan among officials and in the Conseil supérieur he supported those who insisted on strengthening the elements taught in common, especially the literary subjects in the scientific sections; according to Cournot, Dumas and Le Verrier were at first against this, but were eventually won over by Cournot himself.[4] Fortoul was anxious that his plan should not be seen as an attack on the classics. He thought the current of the age was running with science, and in 1855 he told his officials 'we must preach the cause of letters, for the cause of the sciences can look after itself'.[5] In a letter to Silvestre de Sacy of the *Journal des Débats* (in which he also argued the case for bifurcation as a weapon against the Catholic schools) he claimed to have 'saved' the classics as he had saved the University. 'I found Latin and Greek lost; I tried to

---

[1] Circular of 22 May 1852. Cf. speech in *Journal général de l'instruction publique*, xxi (1852), pp. 628–9, and report of *commission mixte*, 23 July 1852.

[2] Speech in *Journal général*, xxii (1853), pp. 797–800.

[3] Report to Emperor, 19 Sept. 1853.

[4] Cournot, *Des institutions d'instruction publique*, p. 341 n. and *Souvenirs*, p. 229. Cf. A.N. F[17] 12950, Conseil supérieur, 15, 23, 30, 31 Mar. 1852; F[17] 6878[1], Fortoul's working papers for meetings of council.

[5] Fortoul papers, A.N. 246 AP 21, meeting of officials, 6 Oct. 1855.

save them, as far as I could, by linking them with scientific education.'[1]

Whether or not the classics were in danger, the reform of 1852 certainly marked an important step forward for scientific education. The scientific sections provided for the first time a balanced modern education which was an attractive alternative to the classics. Scientific and non-scientific subjects shared the time equally, and were arranged so that even those who did not complete the course had studied something of everything. The details were worked out by a commission of experts, in whose report the hand of Dumas may be detected.[2]

The scientific sections were meant to unite several functions. First, they took over the business of preparation for the government schools. There was no fundamental change here, but some technical problems were neatly solved: the programmes of the different examinations were co-ordinated for the first time, and the baccalaureate became compulsory for entry, so that unsuccessful candidates still had a useful qualification.

Second, the scientific sections were to lead to the faculties of medicine. This was a controversial reform, first proposed in Dumas's 1847 report. The traditional view was that doctors should receive the normal classical education, and start scientific studies only in the faculty. The arguments used to justify this were typical of those used to defend the classics in general: the doctor's duties were human as much as scientific, and only the classics could develop the moral sense; without a literary and philosophical training, medical students were liable to the dangers of materialism and scepticism. And behind this lay the feeling that if doctors did not have a 'liberal' education their hard-won bourgeois status would be threatened.[3] This part of Fortoul's reform was openly criticized in 1852, and persistent pressure from the medical profession succeeded in getting it reversed in 1858, when the literary replaced the scientific baccalaureate as the qualification for entry to the faculties.[4]

[1] Fortoul papers, A.N. 246 AP 16, Fortoul to de Sacy, 16 Sept. 1852.
[2] Report of *commission mixte*, 23 July 1852; cf. *arrêté* and programmes of 30 Aug. 1852.
[3] A. Bonnet, *Du décret du dix avril dans ses rapports avec l'éducation du médecin* (1852), *passim*.
[4] Decree of 23 Aug. 1858. For the pressure, see A.N. F17 4346, table of wishes of *conseils académiques*, Nov. 1856 (Paris, Lyons); F17 1640, monthly

The scientific sections were also designed to lead to practical careers in industry, commerce, and agriculture. The programmes gave as much weight to the natural sciences as to mathematics, and insisted on teaching them in a practical spirit. The new scientific baccalaureate would thus produce 'generations vigorously prepared for the battles of production' instead of those 'careerless *bacheliers* embittered by their impotence' who were the fatal product of the old system.[1] A related theme much stressed in official pronouncements was that the new plan offered an education attractive to the commercial and industrial classes. These classes, it was said, had been tempted to skimp on their sons' education because the classics were irrelevant to their needs. But now an education was available which combined usefulness and the cultural and moral benefits of literary education. The reform therefore both met the legitimate needs of these classes and offered to assimilate them to the educated élite. As we shall see, the popularity of the scientific sections in the industrial areas suggests that there was something in this argument.

Fortoul hoped that the organization of the scientific sections would allow the special courses—'veritable colonies of illiterate barbarians'[2]—to be abolished. He talked of doing so as late as 1855, but was dissuaded by his officials.[3] If the special courses had disappeared, their lower-middle-class customers would have left the schools, for the scientific sections could not meet their needs. One of the weaknesses of the reform was a failure to look closely enough at just who the 'industrial and commercial classes' were and what they needed, and Fortoul himself had a mania for administrative symmetry which made his plan inflexible. In fact, the special courses survived, with inferior status and *ad hoc* programmes, to become the basis of the reform which succeeded bifurcation.

For the reform of 1852 did not last long. It failed primarily because of the hostility of the teachers, who were able to bring

---

reports of rectors, Paris, Dec. 1857; F^{17} 4350, minutes of *conseils académiques*, Paris, Dec. 1857 (filed under Aix, 1858).

[1] Report of *commission mixte*, 23 July 1852. Cf. speeches of Dumas and Le Verrier in *Journal général de l'instruction publique*, xxii (1853), p. 542, xxiii (1854), p. 538.

[2] Fortoul papers, A.N. 246 AP 16, Fortoul to de Sacy, 16 Sept. 1852; cf. circular of 18 Apr. 1855.

[3] Fortoul papers, A.N. 246 AP 20, meeting of officials, 3 Oct. 1855.

pressure on the administration to have it first modified and then
abolished. It was difficult enough at the best of times to make a
success of a reform which seemed to threaten the position of the
classics and which demanded complex changes in teaching
arrangements. It was impossible at a time when—even apart from
strictly political repression—Fortoul was introducing numerous
disciplinary measures which made the teacher's daily task more
burdensome and in some cases affected his career prospects and
income.[1] Bifurcation deserved a better fate, for it was a serious,
intelligent, and logical attempt to solve real problems, and it made
innovations of permanent value in the content and method of
teaching.

4. HISTORY, PHILOSOPHY, SCIENCE, AND ART

'Bifurcation' was basically a reform of the structure of secondary
education; but by moving away from the idea of grafting auxiliary
subjects on to a classical trunk towards a balanced curriculum, it
also involved some rethinking of what was taught. Fortoul's ideas
were codified in a set of 'general instructions' on methods in 1854,
the first of its kind. The least change was in the teaching of the
classical languages, especially in the early stages; by the time
pupils entered the scientific section, they had already done four
years of Latin and three of Greek. If Fortoul had been prepared
to prune some of the traditional exercises, room might have been
found for modern subjects without the need for a bifurcation, but
the storm which later ministers raised about their heads when they
attempted this shows that he was prudent to avoid it. His one new
idea was a course in the 'comparative grammar' of Latin, Greek,
and French, intended to take account of the new science of philology, but rather above the heads of the fourth-form pupils to
whom it was given.

He also made changes in the texts prescribed for reading. As a
concession to Catholic feeling, some of the 'Christian classics'
were added, as recommended by Gaume, and Pascal was excluded
and Voltaire censored: the position of these two authors in the
syllabus was always a good test of the political temperature. Though
this appears reactionary, Fortoul could easily have gone further,
for his correspondence with Parisis shows the kind of pressures
which existed. In 1854, the bishop complained that the bacca-

[1] Cf. Gerbod, *La Condition universitaire*, pp. 309 ff.

laureate programme included books which were on the Index—
Voltaire's historical works, and Descartes' *Discourse on Method*.
Fortoul countered this by suggesting that Parisis should himself
prepare expurgated editions, but the complaints continued—by
1856 Montesquieu was under attack.[1] Fortoul's resistance to
extreme demands helps us to understand his claim that by
insisting on an outward show of religious conformity he was preserving the essential traditions of the University from its enemies.

History was the subject most closely allied with the classics,
and was in a state of transition at the time. The traditional reliance
on the ancient historians had encouraged a personalized, moralistic
approach, and like the classics generally historical teaching had
presented an idealized moral world—the world of Corneille or
David—which displayed the heroic virtues of patriotism, duty, and
self-sacrifice, and taught direct moral lessons. But a more scientific
approach was gaining ground, largely through the textbooks of the
future minister of education, Victor Duruy, then teaching in a
Paris lycée. Although Duruy's textbooks had come under official
suspicion because of his liberal views—in 1851 he was reprimanded
for preferring Athens to Sparta—he states in his memoirs that
Fortoul asked him to draw up the new history programme.[2] The
1854 instructions were forward-looking in condemning the
memorization of facts and dates and recommending teaching the
broad outlines of national development and political change. The
main alteration in the teaching was chronological: before 1852,
it started with the Old Testament in the lowest forms and ran
through to 1815; now modern history was brought in earlier, and
French history up to 1815 had been covered by the end of the
fourth form. The general result was to give more importance to the
history of France, and the subject's role as a stimulus to patriotism
was emphasized. Geography, taught at this time simply as an
annexe of history, followed the same pattern.

History was a potentially controversial subject. In an outburst
at a meeting in 1855, Fortoul attacked the school of history led by
Michelet and represented by the École Normale. These historians
had a weakness for abstract generalization and speculation—
things which Fortoul thought had no place in schools. He preferred

[1] Fortoul papers, A.N. 246 AP 24, Parisis to Fortoul, 10 May 1854, 16 Jan.
1855, 8 Jan., 1 Mar. 1856, and Fortoul to Parisis, 22 Jan., 18 May 1855.
[2] V. Duruy, *Notes et souvenirs (1811–1894)* (2nd edn., 1902), i, pp. 71–9.

the scholars of the École des Chartes, who kept strictly to the facts, and he suggested recruiting teachers from this purer source. In any case, such a sensitive subject should be kept under minute supervision.[1] But this reactionary language, though typical enough of Fortoul, does not seem to have had any effect on the plans drawn up by his officials, and it is perhaps an exaggeration to say that he 'dismantled the teaching of history'.[2]

Modern languages remained a neglected part of the University's teaching. They were one of the subjects studied by both sections, and were included in the scientific baccalaureate—their first foothold in that examination. Candidates for the government schools, at least, had an incentive to take them seriously: the army required German and the navy English (no doubt with the potential enemy in mind). The 1854 instructions included sensible remarks on the need to teach the languages in a practical way and to concentrate on the spoken language. But the real obstacle to improvement was the quality of the teachers, who were usually expatriates, and who generally had lower status and salaries than other teachers. A step forward had been taken in 1848 with the creation of a special *agrégation* for modern languages, but Fortoul went back on this when he reduced the number of *agrégations* to two, in letters and science. This also affected the specialist teaching of history and philosophy.

Fortoul's treatment of philosophy did much to earn him a bad reputation in the memory of the University. The subject was renamed Logic—which was held to indicate a narrowing of approach and a surrender to Catholic opinion—and the effect of Fortoul's reforms was to lessen its importance in the syllabus. In private, Fortoul himself said that the University should adopt a purely Christian philosophy, the philosophy of Bossuet, in order to regain the confidence of parents in the soundness of its teaching.[3] But, as with his remarks on history, what was actually done reflected the views of his advisers.

The context of Fortoul's reforms was reaction against the philosophy of Cousin, whose personal influence in the University was destroyed by the *coup d'état* of 1851. Cousin had been

---

[1] Fortoul papers, A.N. 246 AP 21, 6 Oct. 1855.
[2] P. Gerbod, 'La Place de l'histoire dans l'enseignement secondaire de 1802 à 1880', *L'Information historique*, xxvii (1965), p. 128.
[3] Fortoul papers, A.N. 246 AP 21, 6 Oct. 1855.

bitterly attacked by the Catholics in the 1840s, but he also had his critics within the University, including for example the young *normaliens* led by Taine. Two of these critics were among Fortoul's officials: Ravaisson, a spiritualist and forerunner of Bergson, who believed that Cousin had denied him a career in the University;[1] and Cournot, neo-Kantian, mathematician, and severe critic of the outdated 'scholasticism' of Cousin. Remarks in Cournot's books suggest that he strongly influenced, if he was not entirely responsible for, the 'logic' programme of 1852. As with Dumas and the sciences, the destruction of the 'old University coteries'[2] allowed new men whose ideas had previously been ignored to come to the fore.

Logic was one of the traditional divisions of philosophical teaching, and it has commonly been supposed that Fortoul's reform simply meant concentrating on this branch of the subject to the exclusion of the others. In fact this was not so. The ground covered remained the same as in Cousin's syllabus, but the new name was meant to indicate a new emphasis on intellectual methods thought appropriate to a subject studied in common by the two sections. Its purpose was 'expounding the operations of the understanding and applying the principles of the art of thinking to the study of the sciences and of letters'.[3]

In the 1852 programme, each term of the year had a theme. In the first term, this was the human mind (the 'psychology' of the old system) and the nature and use of language (an innovation). In the second, it was intellectual method—the old 'logic', but with a new emphasis on the methods of scientific inquiry. In the third term, the rules of method were applied to the study of the moral order: free will, the spirituality and immortality of the soul, the existence and providence of God, the moral law and its sanctions were successively demonstrated. This corresponded to the ethics and 'theodicy' (natural religion) of Cousin. For the literary section, these lessons were supplemented by the study of texts—Plato, Aristotle, Cicero, Augustine, Bacon, Descartes, Pascal, the 'Logique de Port-Royal', Malebranche, Bossuet, Fénelon, Leibniz, and Euler.

Behind the headings of the new programme, most of the old

[1] F. Ravaisson, *Testament philosophique et fragments* (n.d.), pp. 21–3.
[2] Cournot, *Souvenirs*, p. 230.
[3] Decree of 10 Apr. 1852.

survived, and in editions of textbooks published before and after
1852 only minor changes were needed.[1] The main innovations—
the study of language and scientific method—give the syllabus a
distinctly modern look. These were the two subjects in which
Cournot expressed a special interest when discussing philosophical
education in 1864, and this is what suggests that he had a hand in
the 1852 programme.[2]

Whatever the spirit behind the programme, it was not that of
orthodox Catholicism. Only 'natural' religion was taught, and
moral and religious truths were approached through the operations
of the human reason. It was something that such a programme
could be maintained at all in the atmosphere of the 1850s, when
many conservatives thought philosophy should be removed
altogether from the schools. An insight into this atmosphere is
given by the discussion in the Conseil impérial of the section of
the 1854 instructions relating to logic. The original draft recommended the 'Socratic' method of teaching by interrogation. But,
said the committee, 'Who can foresee where this dialogue . . . on
the most delicate and formidable subjects will stop?' To ensure
that discussion remained strictly within the bounds of the programme, 'direct teaching' was recommended instead.[3]

But if the programme of philosophy remained as extensive as
before, there is no doubt that in practice its teaching suffered
under Fortoul. Questions on the subject occupied a smaller place
than before in the baccalaureate, and for various reasons it was
easier after 1852 for boys to take the baccalaureate without having
attended the Logic form at all. The numbers in these forms fell
heavily: in the Paris lycées, there were 500 pupils in Philosophy
in 1847, but only 98 in Logic in 1858, 75 in 1859.[4] The teaching
itself was inhibited by Fortoul's hostility to 'speculation', and
teachers found it safer to take refuge in a narrowly dogmatic
approach.[5]

The sciences were, of course, the subject which benefited most

---

[1] For example: C. Bénard, *Manuel d'études pour la préparation au baccalauréat
ès lettres . . . Philosophie* (1850), and *Manuel d'études pour la préparation au
baccalauréat ès lettres . . . Logique* (1852).

[2] Cournot, *Des institutions d'instruction publique*, pp. 120–9.

[3] A.N. F¹⁷ 12956, Conseil impérial, 15 July 1854.

[4] A.N. F¹⁷ 4352, report of *inspecteur d'académie* Bouillet to *conseil académique*
of Paris, June 1859.

[5] Cf. Lavisse, *Souvenirs*, pp. 252–3.

from the 1852 reform, and by it secured an accepted place in the schools which they were not to lose again. Up to the point of bifurcation, science still meant mathematics. In the higher forms, the non-scientists now had regular scientific teaching: geometry and physics in the third form, chemistry and 'cosmography' (a mixture of astronomy and geography) in the second, natural history (zoology, botany, and geology) in Rhetoric. But the standards achieved were not very high. The non-specialists' mathematical education, for example, only touched on algebra, and did not cover trigonometry or the use of logarithms.

In the scientific sections, the time was shared between mathematics and the natural sciences, and one new subject, mechanics, was introduced into the programme with the needs of industry in mind. The requirements of the government schools were thus not allowed to dominate the syllabus, and both the commission of experts in 1852 and the instructions of 1854 put great emphasis on teaching science in a practical manner. Teaching was to begin with observation and description, to move from the concrete to the abstract, to avoid arid theorizing. The everyday applications of the sciences were to be pointed out, and schools were urged to organize visits to factories, botanical excursions, and practical exercises such as surveying. There was no mention, however, of laboratory work. Schools possessed apparatus which the teacher used for demonstration when teaching physics and chemistry, but as far as one can tell laboratories did not exist. These official instructions, though no doubt far from completely carried out, were a notable departure from the academic and anti-utilitarian traditions of French teaching.

Another subject to which attention was paid in 1852 was art. This was a special interest of Dumas, whose report in 1847 had recommended teaching drawing in the 'intermediate' schools so that public taste would be improved and the artistic standards of French industry maintained. The superiority of French industry, and its ability to export, were held to rest on taste, design, and craftsmanship. The London Exhibition of 1851 brought this question to the attention of public opinion, and Dumas, a commissioner at the Exhibition, warned that France might lose her competitive position if she did not improve her art education.[1]

[1] *Bulletin de la Société d'encouragement pour l'industrie nationale*, l (1851), pp. 278–80, li (1852), pp. 301-2, 404–11. Dumas was president of this society.

It was natural, given Dumas's interest in the question, that these ideas should have some influence on the reform of the lycées. In the commission of scientific experts in 1852, 'those members . . . who represented industrial interests' stressed the importance of taste, 'an ornament of our civilization, an immense capital for our manufactures'. For France, taste 'takes the place of the coalfields of England and the great natural resources of Russia and the United States'.[1] The commission used this as an argument for teaching literature in the science sections—what better way to cultivate taste?—but they also recommended two classes a week in drawing. *Dessin linéaire* (ornamental, technical, and architectural drawing) was to be added to the freehand *dessin d'imitation* which had always been taught as an extra in the lycées.

Fortoul, himself a former art critic, also took up the theme of industrial competition and the need for art education in his public pronouncements,[2] and he set up a committee to reform the teaching of *dessin d'imitation*. The presence of Ingres, Delacroix, and other artists lent the committee prestige, but its report was written by the philosopher Ravaisson. Most of the recommendations followed academic orthodoxy, but the committee also noted the needs of industry, and proposed the study of the design of 'the objects which serve for the most ordinary usages of life'. As for style, the report declared (as was fitting in a University document) that Greece provided the supreme models of beauty, but that Roman, Oriental, medieval, and Renaissance art might also be drawn on— an eclecticism typical of Second Empire taste.[3] The recommendations of this committee were put into effect by Fortoul. But the real place to improve art education was in the training of designers and craftsmen, not in the lycées—an example of the misconception of objectives that was one of the weaknesses of Fortoul's reforms. In Britain, the Great Exhibition stimulated the growth of technical education, but that was a field neglected by Fortoul.

A fundamental weakness of all Fortoul's recommendations on teaching was that they reflected an anti-intellectual spirit. He wanted to cut subjects down to their essentials, and to discourage 'abstraction' and 'speculation'. Thus the recommendations on the

[1] Report of *commission mixte*, 23 July 1852.
[2] Report to Emperor, 19 Sept. 1853, speech in *Journal général de l'instruction publique*, xxi (1852), pp. 417–19.
[3] Report of committee, 29 Dec. 1853, and *arrêté* of same date.

need to make science or history more concrete were based on the idea that 'historical and philosophical discussions are hardly suitable for children. . . . In the lycées, the lessons should be dogmatic and purely elementary. It is in a higher region, and before another audience, that teaching can originate in free inquiry.'[1] To ensure that teachers kept in line, they had to keep a daily journal which was inspected by their superiors. Thus, claimed Fortoul, the reforms were 'achieved in advance, and as it were minute by minute'.[2] Even in the 'higher regions', the same spirit was applied to the École Normale, which in future was to concentrate strictly on preparing for 'the laborious and modest conditions of the art of teaching', instead of pursuing learning for its own sake. It is easy to see how this offended the spirit of the University, and how a man who used this language and so clumsily wielded the weapons of authority was incapable of invoking its willing co-operation in his reforms.

[1] Report accompanying decree of 10 Apr. 1852.
[2] Report to Emperor, 19 Sept. 1853.

CHAPTER FIVE

Education in the 1850s

1. DEMOCRATIC DESPOT?

The government of the Emperor has nothing to fear from the progress of enlightenment; the more equally primary education is distributed, the more the people will be in a position to understand and appreciate the benefits of the regime under which we are living, and to increase by their active intelligence the moral and material forces of France.[1]

Thus Fortoul in an official circular of 1854. One might indeed expect that a regime which rested on the mass support of the peasantry and which claimed to protect the interests of the industrial workers would use the expansion of primary education both to improve the condition and to gain the support of those classes. Yet in fact education came low in the government's list of priorities, and the primary schools were neglected throughout the 1850s. Napoleon III himself showed no interest in them, and Fortoul's policy was dominated by the desire to save money and to appease the fears of the propertied classes. The resources devoted to education are a good test of the true ideals of modern governments, for it is a public service of an expensive and unglamorous kind. The Second Empire does not come well out of this test, preferring to spend its money on warfare and on public projects which brought more concrete rewards of prestige and profit.

The main fact in the history of the primary schools in the 1850s is the growth of the religious orders and the increasing proportion of children taught by them. Of educational innovation in the true sense there was little. During Fortoul's ministry, the paucity of legislation in this field contrasts forcibly with the attention lavished on the lycées. Fortoul himself, as a man of letters, found more to interest him in the reform of the faculties or the reorganization of the Imperial Library than in the education of the masses.

If the plans drawn up by Fortoul in 1852 had gone through, there would have been a drastic reduction in state spending on primary education. His plans reached the stage where budget

[1] Circular of 3 Feb. 1854.

estimates for 1853 based on them were submitted to Parliament, only to be withdrawn hastily when the project proved abortive. The total education budget would have fallen from 22,454,767 francs in 1852 to 19,940,313. It seems that Fortoul was under pressure from the finance minister to reduce expenditure, but it was he who chose to make primary education suffer. The general state subsidy to poor communes was to be abolished (saving 3,560,000 francs), and the expenditure transferred to local taxation. The inspectors of primary education were to be suppressed and their functions shared between other officials (saving 624,333 francs)—a notably retrograde step. And the amount spent on teachers' salaries was to be reduced. This was actually carried out in 1853: Fortoul got round the minimum salary of 600 francs prescribed by the *loi Falloux* by creating a new grade of 'assistant' teachers (*suppléants*) paid only 400 or 500; since *suppléants* could be in charge of schools in small communes, the effect was to worsen the position of younger teachers, though the new scale also included supplementary payments which could bring the minimum up to 800 francs after ten years' service, thus going part of the way to creating a proper career structure. The other parts of Fortoul's proposed budget showed the priority given to middle-class education: nearly 200,000 francs were to be spent on creating new faculties, and over 700,000 on converting colleges into lycées so that every department had a lycée.[1]

Fortoul succeeded in stabilizing the cost of primary education throughout the fifties: the amount spent from central funds in 1852 (6,131,391 francs) was not reached again until 1860; by 1869 it was to be over 12,000,000.[2] One contributing factor was that Fortoul was hostile to free education, and in 1853 (though this was not in his 1852 plan) he changed the rules on remission of fees. Formerly all children certified as indigent by the local authority were admitted free. It was now said that this had been abused, and in future the prefect was to fix in advance the numbers to be admitted free to each school.[3] This quota does not seem in fact to have much reduced the proportion of free pupils.[4]

[1] Draft budgets in Fortoul papers, A.N. 246 AP 17, folder 7. Decree of 31 Dec. 1853 on teachers' salaries, and earlier versions in A.N. 246 AP 17–18 (in one draft teachers' salaries were to start at 300 francs).

[2] C. Nicolas, *Les Budgets de la France depuis le commencement du XIXe siècle* (1882), Table 22, Annexe.

[3] Decree of 31 Dec. 1853.   [4] See below, p. 162.

Anticlericalism as well as parsimony lay behind this move. The refusal of the Christian Brothers to accept fees was one reason for their popularity, and limiting exemptions was one of the government's weapons against them. In 1855, Fortoul reported that negotiations about this with Frère Philippe, Superior of the order, had failed. He instructed his officials to apply the new regulations so that the order was forced into submission, and expressed his determination to resist the domination of education by the orders. His attitude to free education was in any case that it was 'one of those chimaeras which can lead many minds astray and which recall the worst days'. He also thought it was time to abolish the practice of admitting all children free adopted in Paris, Lyons, and other large towns.[1]

Fortoul's conservatism appeared too in a discussion of scholarships. The question arose whether scholarships for the lycées should be given to the sons of primary teachers. No, said Fortoul. Some may benefit from it, but to the majority classical education will simply give 'tastes of luxury, insupportable pretensions of mind, and ideas above their station (*des sentiments au-dessus de leur condition*)'. The *boursiers*, he claimed, were already the most troublesome element in the lycées because of their origins—they were 'brutes', 'animals', and it was a crime to launch them into society. It was good, no doubt, that talented individuals should get on, but this should be through their own efforts. To encourage these efforts too much might weaken the springs of action, 'for it is often in proportion to the obstacles that it meets in society that human energy develops'. Some of Fortoul's officials—notably Nisard and Ravaisson—protested against this, and said that it was a duty of government to promote the national welfare by seeking out talent at all levels of society, but the mood was against them. Fortoul even claimed that the Conseil d'État had demanded the complete abolition of scholarships, and that he had saved them with difficulty.[2]

In fact, one of Fortoul's earliest reforms had been to abolish the open competition for half the state scholarships which had somehow survived since 1848. From 1852 onwards they were again entirely in the gift of the government, and awarded on political grounds. There was an examination, but it was a qualifying not a

[1] Fortoul papers, A.N. 246 AP 20, meeting of officials, 5 and 2 Oct. 1855.
[2] Fortoul papers, A.N. 246 AP 21, meeting of officials, 10 Oct. 1855.

competitive one, and Fortoul explained that 'I am not disturbed if the level of the examination is fixed rather low; otherwise there would be difficulties in getting through candidates who while not completely ready are nevertheless fitted to profit from the benefits and favours of authority.'[1]

The coming of the Second Empire, then, did not bring any new spirit into the administration of primary education, and certainly not a more democratic one. Almost the only important positive measure was a new set of regulations for the *salles d'asile*, which had been put under the special protection of the Empress Eugénie and a committee of Bonapartist ladies.[2] Otherwise the government contented itself with expressing enlightened sentiments in public circulars to officials. At this time the regime had no intention of challenging the prejudices of the conservative middle class, which saw no great urgency in the development of popular education and wanted it to be given on the cheap.

The atmosphere lightened somewhat, however, when Fortoul died in 1856 and was replaced by Gustave Rouland. Rouland was a magistrate from Normandy, and was typical of an important group of ministers and officials with the same background and attitudes. In religious affairs he was Catholic but Gallican, in social policy conservative but intelligent. He put order before liberty, but saw progress and paternalistic social reform as one of the best guarantees of continuing order. In his speeches, a more liberal Bonapartism than Fortoul's is expressed, with the emphasis on the Emperor's concern for the working classes, solidarity between the classes, 'imperial democracy, which governs equally for all', and the ideology of self-help.[3]

In 1857, Rouland issued instructions on the teaching of the different primary subjects, stressing the need for a simple and practical approach.[4] In 1858, a series of welcome improvements to teachers' salaries began—the *suppléants* disappeared in 1860.[5] But Rouland's most interesting initiative was an essay competition among schoolteachers on the theme of 'the needs of primary education in a rural commune, from the triple point of view of the school, the pupils and the master'.[6] Nearly 6,000 essays were

[1] Ibid., and cf. decree of 7 Feb. 1852.   [2] Decree of 21 Mar. 1855.
[3] G. Rouland, *Discours et réquisitoires de M. Rouland* (1863), ii, p. 59.
[4] Circular of 20 Aug. 1857.
[5] Decrees of 20 July 1858, 29 Dec. 1860, 19 Apr. 1862.
[6] *Arrêté* of 12 Dec. 1860.

submitted, in which the teachers expressed their complaints and their wishes. The inquiry revealed much about the material conditions in which education was carried on and the standards which it achieved. But what came out most strongly was the poverty endured by the teachers, and their resentment at their subordination to the clergy.[1] For a decade, the teachers had had to work in the atmosphere of suspicion and hostility generated by the *loi Falloux*. The administration had given them little support in this situation, and had added new burdens of its own—the teachers found themselves used as auxiliaries of the prefect in elections and plebiscites. But by 1860, the situation was changing. Political crisis was once more setting Church and state at odds, and evolution towards the 'liberal Empire' was about to begin. Rouland was able to give a new direction to the Second Empire's educational policy.

2. THE QUESTION OF ENSEIGNEMENT PROFESSIONNEL

The use of the term *enseignement professionnel* is an example of the ambiguities of terminology which often confused the discussion of educational reform. It meant literally 'vocational' education, but was more often used to refer to a form of general education. In its basic sense—specialized training for a particular job—it corresponded to what came in the 1860s to be called technical education. Vocational education in this sense was already organized by the state at various levels—it included, for example, the professional faculties and *grandes écoles* at one end of the scale, and the government's three agricultural and three veterinary schools at the other. The state was also already involved in industrial education through the *écoles d'arts et métiers* at Châlons-sur-Marne, Angers, and Aix. Originally intended to train skilled workers, these had come to supply industry with well-qualified men who became engineers or managers, but they still took their pupils from the artisan and working class rather than from the secondary schools. The state also had a traditional responsibility for mining, and ran three schools: the élite École des Mines at Paris, a school for mining engineers at Saint-Étienne, and a school to train miners as 'maîtres-mineurs' at Alès. All these schools were sometimes referred to as part of *enseignement professionnel*, but the

[1] See Gontard, *Les Écoles primaires de la France bourgeoise*, pp. 149–53.

idea that they might form part of a co-ordinated system of specialized education was slow to develop.

The term *enseignement professionnel* was much more commonly used to mean a sort of education which, though modern and directed towards the practical needs of industry or commerce, remained general rather than purely vocational. In this sense it resembled higher primary education, and it was in fact the higher primary school founded by the municipality of Paris in 1839, and later called the École Turgot, which became the model most frequently appealed to by proponents of *enseignement professionnel*. Its director, Pierre-Philibert Pompée, became one of the chief experts on the question. He played an active part in the educational work of the Second Republic, but resigned on political grounds in 1852 and opened a private school of the same type at Ivry in the Paris suburbs.

Pompée distinguished his sort of *enseignement professionnel* clearly from education designed for workers. It was, he insisted, a form of true secondary education (he disapproved of the term 'higher primary'), intended for the 'middle class (*classe moyenne*), the class which has grown most in importance since the French Revolution'.[1] He wanted to see this type of education organized on a national scale in 'French colleges', parallel to and more numerous than the 'Latin colleges' which would remain for the minority of 'individuals whose destiny is to direct the others'. Pompée's ideas were more radical than, say, Guizot's because he would have liked to abolish the distinction between primary and secondary education so that all children started off in common classes. He compared the ideal educational system to a railway train: all the passengers start together, but get out at different stations along the way and change at junctions for branch lines.[2]

The École Turgot was very successful at meeting the needs of the lower middle and artisan classes in Paris, and its pupils went into commerce and industry in a rough proportion of two to one. In 1848, its courses lasted four years and there were 309 pupils. In 1856 a fifth year was added, and by 1861 the numbers were over 600; they were to rise to 834 by 1870.[3] The programme included

[1] P.-P. Pompée, *Études sur l'éducation professionnelle en France* (1863), p. 6.

[2] Ibid., pp. 273–5. Cf. *Enquête sur l'enseignement professionnel* (1864–5), i, pp. 79–80 (evidence of Pompée).

[3] O. Gréard, *Éducation et instruction. Enseignement primaire* (1887), pp. 151 ff., 368–9.

science, 'graphic arts', history and geography, and modern languages. There was no specialization or vocational training—all boys followed the same syllabus.[1]

This *enseignement professionnel* was not very different from the special courses of the colleges, but Pompée claimed that his methods were totally different from those of the University. Pompée was an educational pioneer—he admired Pestalozzi and helped to popularize his work in France. His principle was to start with what was concrete and familiar to the child, and to work from that to the abstract. His methods at Turgot and Ivry included the study of collections of practical objects (contemporary progressive opinion always laid much stress on this and on the formation of 'technological museums'), scientific experiments, and visits to factories and workshops.[2]

These ideas were also relevant to a type of *enseignement professionnel* with which Pompée was not himself directly concerned: technical training for artisans and skilled workers. The mechanization of industry was causing both a demand for new skills and the breakdown of the traditional apprenticeship system. Despite the attempts of the legislature to reinforce it in a law of 1851, apprenticeship did not become customary in the new factories,[3] and the feeling grew that full-time training was needed instead. At the same time, even *enseignement professionnel* for workers was thought to need an element of generality, so that it was not reduced to simply teaching manual skills. 'The idea of associating manual work with the cultivation of the intelligence in the education of the laborious classes . . . marks the point of departure for industrial education,'[4] wrote Alphonse Audiganne in an article published in 1851.

In this article Audiganne surveyed what vocational education for workers actually existed in 1851, and found that it was most developed in the industrial north and east, least in the west. In the major towns, part-time instruction was usually available in schools of drawing (*écoles de dessin*, especially developed in the north) and in evening courses on various practical subjects like chemistry. These courses, which were attended by both adult and younger

---

[1] *Enquête sur l'enseignement professionnel*, i, pp. 14–17.

[2] Ibid., i, pp. 72–3.

[3] J.-P. Guinot, *Formation professionnelle et travailleurs qualifiés depuis 1789* (n.d.), pp. 114–19.

[4] *Revue des Deux Mondes*, new period, x (1851), p. 864.

workers, might be organized by the municipal councils, or by philanthropic societies sponsored by employers like the Société industrielle at Mulhouse and the Société philomathique at Bordeaux. But true industrial schools were much less common— Audiganne cited examples at Dieppe (for girls, teaching sewing and lacemaking), Lyons, Strasbourg, Nancy, Nîmes, and Le Puy. The schools which he most approved of were those where the instruction was closely related to the specializations required by local industry and linked with apprenticeship. Schools of this kind normally had workshops and gave a craft training; this inclusion of 'manual work' distinguished them from Pompée's type of school for the lower middle class. The question of manual work became one of the chief points of controversy among the propagandists for *enseignement professionnel*, and it was also one of the concerns of socialist educational theorists. Both Fourier and Proudhon, for example, believed that manual and intellectual education should go together and wanted to see the 'union of school and workshop', which would mean in practice manual work for all in the schools.[1]

A related idea, the 'union of theory and practice', is found in Michel Chevalier and other writers inspired by Saint-Simonian ideas. Today, they argued, industry is no longer based on empirical practice but on scientific knowledge, and there can be no progress without a constant interchange between science and industry. To ensure this, the men who direct industry and work in it must have theoretical as well as practical knowledge, and their education must combine the two.[2] Auguste Comte saw this combination as the basis of a new class linking the pure scientists and the actual directors of industry, the class of '*engineers*, whose special function is to organize the relations of theory and practice'.[3] In these ideas lay the germ of an over-all theory of technical education, uniting in fruitful interaction the training of hand and of brain.

The other main dispute among the proponents of *enseignement professionnel* was whether it should be organized by the state or left to local initiative. Opinion on the whole favoured the latter. The needs of industry and commerce, it was said, varied from town to town, and if the schools were to succeed their teaching would

[1] G. Duveau, *La Pensée ouvrière sur l'éducation pendant la Seconde République et le Second Empire* (n.d.), pp. 144, 148, 155, 159.

[2] M. Chevalier, *De la nécessité de fonder l'enseignement professionnel* (1846), *passim*.

[3] Comte, *Oeuvres choisies*, p. 106.

need to vary. Central control would mean uniformity, and would alienate the local industrialists whose support was vital. Reformers especially feared the dead hand of the University, and thought that its academic methods would be fatal in dealing with an education which needed a practical and useful bias.

In the 1850s, local initiative achieved more than state action. In one town after another, *écoles professionnelles* appeared, claiming to give a general preparation for industry and commerce. Some of these schools were obviously of near-secondary status, and aimed at the lower middle class, others were more geared to the needs of workers. An example of the first type was the *école professionnelle* opened at Grenoble in 1851, and developed from the municipal higher primary school. The course lasted four years, and included scientific and commercial subjects. Fees were charged, and boarders taken as well as day-boys, although the municipal council offered some scholarships. There was no manual work in this school, and it was indeed denounced on these grounds as not being a true *école professionnelle* by a rival private teacher.[1]

On the other hand, manual work was a feature of schools founded at Rouen in 1850 and at Orléans in 1851 (as a development of the higher primary school). The school at Orléans also gave agricultural teaching, and it was reported in 1855 that pupils went in about equal proportions into commerce, agriculture, and industry. But despite the manual work, this school was evidently stimulating white-collar ambitions, for no fewer than 60 of 240 school-leavers since 1851 had gone on to the *école normale*.[2] Another town where an *école professionnelle* was based on the higher primary school was Nantes; in 1853, it was flourishing, giving courses based on mathematics and chemistry to nearly 200 pupils, though later it declined.[3] Nantes also had an active Société industrielle which ran evening courses, and a private school, the Institution Livet, which specialized in manual work.[4]

Little encouragement for these initiatives came from Parliament

[1] C. Bertrand, *Lettres sur la fondation d'un véritable enseignement professionnel à créer à Grenoble* (1857), pp. 6, 11–13, 34–5, 38–9; G. Perrin and L.-J. Veyron, *Notice historique sur l'École professionnelle Vaucanson* (1889), pp. 12 ff.

[2] *Cinquantenaire de l'École primaire supérieure et professionnelle de Rouen* (1900), pp. 82–91; A.N. F¹⁷ 11708, report of *inspecteur d'académie* of Loiret, 10 Jan. 1855.

[3] *Enquête sur l'enseignement professionnel*, i, pp. 323–4.

[4] E. Livet, *L'Institution Livet et l'enseignement dans la seconde moitié du XIXe siècle* (1905), pp. 52–4, 58–9.

or from governments. In 1848, Pompée was a member of Carnot's advisory commission, and tried to incorporate a national scheme for *enseignement professionnel* into his proposed legislation.[1] A similar plan was drawn up by the teachers at the Conservatoire des arts et métiers, an institution which made an important contribution to adult education in Paris; its director, General Morin, was one of Fortoul's advisers on the reform of the lycées in 1852, and will be met with again in the sixties.[2] These suggestions came to nothing, although the republicans did succeed in carrying out a reform of the state agricultural schools.

In the debates on the *loi Falloux*, *enseignement professionnel* was hardly mentioned. An attempt to raise the question in the 'extra-parliamentary commission' merely called forth a prejudiced outburst from Thiers: 'it is the kind of establishment which I detest and despise most of all. The *écoles professionnelles*, inspired by a detestable spirit, will be good for nothing but turning their pupils into little Americans . . .'[3] In the parliamentary debate, an attempt was made to include *enseignement professionnel* in the law, but this 'Lasteyrie–Wolowski amendment' was rejected after Parieu, the minister of education, had argued that it was only a subdivision of secondary education. The only mention of *enseignement profession-nel* in the law was in a clause dealing with the qualifications required of private teachers.

Parieu does seem nevertheless to have contemplated some action. In June 1850 he set up a commission to look into the whole question of *enseignement professionnel*. It discussed various matters of principle, and heard expert witnesses, including Pompée.[4] But this commission never produced a report, and its work evidently lapsed when Parieu left the ministry. Equally abortive were the plans attributed to the ministers of commerce Schneider in 1851[5] and Persigny in 1852.[6] Thus Fortoul had an opportunity to make a fresh start in this field unhampered by previous policies. The next section tells how he mishandled this opportunity.

[1] Pompée, *Études sur l'éducation professionnelle*, pp. 231–4.
[2] The teachers' plan is printed in *Enquête sur l'enseignement professionnel*, ii, pp. 663–71.
[3] *La Commission extraparlementaire de 1849*, p. 194.
[4] Pompée, *Études sur l'éducation professionnelle*, pp. 263–81. Papers of the commission in A.N. F[17] 6891.
[5] A. Audiganne, *Les Populations ouvrières et les industries de la France* (2nd edn., 1860), ii, p. 371 n. 1.
[6] *Revue de l'instruction publique*, x (1852), p. 2262.

3. FORTOUL AND TECHNICAL EDUCATION

Technical education or *enseignement professionnel* had no place in the plans originally drawn up by Fortoul in 1852, although as we have seen the interest of Fortoul and Dumas in the question of art education did have some effect on the lycées. Yet in 1853–4 Fortoul founded three *écoles professionnelles*. This was the result of his meeting with César Fichet, director of a private industrial school at Menars, near Blois. Fichet had published a pamphlet on *enseignement professionnel* in 1847, and in 1852 submitted a memorandum on it to the Emperor—it was presumably this which aroused the government's interest in him.[1] Fichet's ideas were interesting, but somewhat confused—and the 1847 pamphlet bore distinct marks of crankiness. It included the Saint-Simonian ideas of allocating children to social functions according to their aptitudes and the need to unite theory and practice. In 1852, Fichet's memorandum stressed themes well calculated to appeal to the government—the need for a more moral and religious spirit among employers, and the dangers to French industry of foreign rivalry.

It was the employing class, the sons of merchants and manufacturers, who interested Fichet. The reform of 1852 had sought to attract them to the lycées, but Fichet condemned this for giving them the ambition to enter the professions. Instead the 'jeune maître' should be brought up from the start in the atmosphere of the industrial world, in a school which would teach him to understand and contribute to industrial progress.[2] Fichet's most original idea was that manual work in the workshops should be a part of industrial education even at this level. He believed that there could be a generalized manual training distinct from apprenticeship to particular crafts, which would give an understanding of the practical side of industry, and train the hand and eye along with the brain. Manual work would produce the 'théoriciens-praticiens' whom modern industry needed, and would create harmony between master and man. It was also a discipline of general

---

[1] C. Fichet, *Mémoire sur l'apprentissage et sur l'éducation industrielle* (1847), and *Mémoire sur l'enseignement professionnel, suivi d'un plan d'instruction industrielle rédigé en 1852* (n.d.). Cf. printed and MS. versions of latter in A.N. F¹⁷ 11708, which is the general source for what follows.

[2] Fichet, *Mémoire sur l'apprentissage*, pp. 20, 27–8.

educational value: in the words of Fichet's disciple Denniée, 'The *écoles professionnelles* should be industrial Lycées in which the teaching of Greek and Latin is replaced by the practice of the workshop.'[1]

Fortoul met Fichet in July 1853, after reading his memoir, and told him that he intended to create four schools, on a regional basis; Fichet was to be responsible for organizing them. In August, an article in the official teachers' journal revealed the plan to the public, announcing that 'a decisive step has just been taken in the progress of the reorganization of our general system of education'. It referred to Fichet's achievements at Menars, and said that the minister 'has judged him worthy to be associated with his plans; he has called him to Paris, given him his instructions and charged him with organizing establishments analogous to the *école professionnelle* at Menars' in different parts of France—the first would be at Toulon. *Enseignement professionnel*, defined as the 'education which through enlightening practice by theory prepares for the professions of agriculture, commerce, and industry', was designed for the 'classe intermédiaire'. The lycées existed for the liberal professions, the primary schools were adequate for the workers; the *écoles professionnelles* would fill the gap, and it was suggested that they would replace the higher primary schools. There was the usual confusion here about who the 'intermediate' classes were. Nor was it clear how manual work would be relevant to commerce and agriculture.[2]

After this, the government seemed to lose interest in the project. No legislation followed, and the schools were only occasionally mentioned in official publications and speeches. Fichet himself, however, thought that the schools were to be organized on a grand scale by the state and that he was to be a salaried official with a recognized status. He drew up elaborate administrative schemes, giving himself extensive powers, and wrote several times to urge the definitive 'organization' of the schools. When these demands were ignored, he styled himself the 'organizer' or 'director general' of the *écoles professionnelles*, and even after Fortoul had dispensed with his services in 1854, he carried out unasked-for inspections and sent unwanted reports. For Fortoul soon realized that he had fallen into the hands of a charlatan, and Fichet became an em-

[1] A.N. F17 11708, Denniée to Rouland, 27 Sept. 1856.
[2] *Journal général de l'instruction publique*, xxii (1853), pp. 539–40.

D

barrassment when his vanity and incompetence alienated the local
authorities with whom he had to deal.

Three of the projected schools were founded, at Toulon for the
south, Mulhouse for the east, and Lille for the north. Fichet
renamed his school at Menars 'École impériale professionnelle du
Centre', but an attempt to provide a school for the west at Rouen
failed. Only the school at Mulhouse was a success, for reasons which
illustrate the defects of the others. It was in the hands of an
exceptionally able director, L. L. Bader; it had the moral and
financial support of the municipal authorities; it sought the
co-operation of local industrialists, and adapted its programme to
meet their needs.[1] Above all, Fichet was, in Fortoul's own words
'ousted, shown the door. I authorized his exclusion, and it is only
since his departure that things have taken a reasonable turn.'[2]
Fichet had offended the local notables by his officiousness, and
played no real part in the organization of the school. This school at
Mulhouse was to flourish in the sixties, with its workshops and
manual work, and to be a frequently cited model in discussions of
enseignement professionnel.

The schools at Lille and Toulon failed partly because of the
character of their directors. At Toulon, Fortoul chose a primary
teacher, A. Jaume, who had recommended himself to the authorities by publishing a fervently Bonapartist *Histoire des classes
laborieuses.* At Lille, the director was a pupil of Fichet, Victor
Denniée, who had himself published a pamphlet on industrial
education. Both men were led astray by Fichet, who led them to
believe that the government would act in their support and imposed
on them his own authority as 'organizer'. This paralysed their
initiative, and led them to accept commitments beyond their
means.[3] Both schools eventually faced bankruptcy, but the government refused to accept responsibility for their debts, on the ground
that they were legally private schools.

In fact the schools had started with a state subsidy to cover
salaries, but Fortoul's intention had been that municipal councils
should meet most of the running expenses. He was not, however,
prepared to do what was needed to get their support: to respect
local opinion, to build on existing local initiatives, to gain the

[1] Cf. Oberlé, *L'Enseignement à Mulhouse*, pp. 173 ff.
[2] Fortoul papers, A.N. 246 AP 21, meeting of officials, 8 Oct. 1855.
[3] See especially A.N. F[17] 11708, memoir submitted by Denniée, 22 May 1856.

goodwill of employers. At Lille, for example, local opinion wanted a state *école d'arts et métiers*. The *école professionnelle* did not offer a practical enough training to meet this need, and merely threatened the interests of the existing higher primary school and the 'écoles académiques' (evening courses for workers), both run by the municipality.[1] Only pressure from the prefect, who saw political dividends in the scheme, secured a municipal subsidy.[2] Denniée's personality, and the failure of the school to live up to its ambitious promises, completed the disillusion of the council. The story was similar at Toulon, and both councils withdrew their subsidies as the failure of the schools became apparent.

Flexibility in the programmes would also have been necessary to gain local acceptance. But Fichet insisted on imposing, in every detail, the syllabus of his own school at Menars. This covered five years, with manual work in the last three; there was also a general 'modern' education, including French, modern languages, history, science, book-keeping, and technical drawing. The resources available were quite inadequate for teaching this programme, even though Jaume at Toulon combined the functions of 'professor of French, English, Italian, and arbori-culture'.[3]

While local officials gave warnings about the position of the schools, and Jaume and Denniée sent agonized appeals for money, Fortoul vacillated. In 1855, he acknowledged the failings of Fichet, but claimed that he was still very interested in this branch of education.[4] In 1856, there was a sudden burst of energy, and even after Fortoul's death the responsible officials were urged once more to give their support to the schools.[5] But the true situation was eventually realized. The school at Toulon was allowed to close in 1857. It had not been unsuccessful, with some 100 pupils in 1855 and 1856; but they had been drawn from the working class, and so unable to pay the fees needed to keep the school going.[6] Jaume

[1] A.N. F^{17} 11708, Fichet to Pillet, 7 Dec. 1853. Cf. P. Pierrard, *La Vie ouvrière à Lille sous le Second Empire* (1965), p. 354.
[2] A.N. F^{17} 11708, prefect of Nord to Emperor, 14 Oct. 1853 (copy).
[3] Ibid., rector of Var to minister, 12 Sept. 1853.
[4] Fortoul papers, A.N. 246 AP 21, meeting of officials, 8 Oct. 1855.
[5] A.N. F^{17} 11708, minister to rectors of Douai, 8 Aug. 1856, Aix, 30 Sept. 1856.
[6] Ibid., Jaume to Fortoul, 14 May 1856. Cf. L. Bourrilly, 'L'Instruction publique dans la région de Toulon de la Restauration à la Troisième République', *Bulletin de l'Académie du Var*, new series, xviii (1895), pp. 88–9.

thought that that was where his mission lay, while Denniée, following Fichet, aimed at the 'rich industrial bourgeoisie'.[1]

At Lille, the school was saved after a reorganization in 1856–7. Denniée was dismissed, the debts paid off, and a capable local official put in charge. In 1861, the school took on a completely new character. It became the 'École des arts industriels et des mines', taking the sons of the rich business class after they had completed their secondary education and giving them a higher technical training.[2] In this new guise, the school was very successful, and was similar to the 'École centrale lyonnaise' founded by local initiative at Lyons in 1857. The model for both schools was the École centrale, an engineering school founded in 1829 (Dumas was one of those involved) as a civilian counterpart of the Polytechnique; the École centrale was taken over by the state in 1857, and became one of the *grandes écoles*. There was clearly a demand for this higher form of education, and it might have been met by Fortoul in 1853 if local conditions had been studied more carefully. The importance of respecting local needs was perhaps the chief lesson of the failure of the *écoles professionnelles*.

One reason for Fortoul's loss of interest in them was that by 1854, in the context of a general reform of higher education, he was pursuing a new scheme for teaching 'applied science' in the faculties of science, or in towns without faculties in new institutions called 'écoles préparatoires à l'enseignement supérieur des sciences et des lettres'. These were to be founded in co-operation with the municipal councils, and were often based on public lecture courses already organized by them. The new course in applied science was to last two years, and to include mathematics, mechanics, physics, chemistry, and natural history. As with the reform of the lycées, it was felt that scientific education needed to be accompanied by more elevating studies, and the courses were to include French literature, French history, geography, and drawing. A 'certificate of capacity' would be given at the end of the course.[3]

Although organized as part of higher education, this teaching was thought of as a form of *enseignement professionnel*. There was a

[1] A.N. F¹⁷ 11708, Denniée to Rouland, 27 Sept. 1856.
[2] *Enquête sur l'enseignement professionnel*, i, pp. 211 ff. (evidence of Bernot, director).
[3] Decree of 22 Aug. 1854, *arrêté* and instruction of 26 Dec. 1854; cf. *Journal général de l'instruction publique*, xxiv (1855), pp. 246–7.

minimum age of sixteen, and the teaching was supposed to be at the level of the higher forms of the lycées. But discussion among officials in 1855 revealed great confusion about its nature and purpose. Dumas (whose hand can be seen behind this reform, whereas he had nothing to do with the *écoles professionnelles*) seemed to envisage going even below the age of sixteen, and taking pupils from higher primary schools. Cournot thought that it was basically for the sons of the rich. But Fortoul described it as 'the teaching of our age', and looked forward to its extension throughout France. It would meet the needs of the *classes moyennes* or *bourgeoisie intermédiaire*, and allow the abolition of the special courses in the lycées.[1]

Écoles préparatoires were founded in 1855 at Nantes, Rouen, Angers, and Mulhouse. In the faculties, serious efforts were devoted to the teaching of applied science at Grenoble and at Lille, where Pasteur had been made dean of the new faculty.[2] But the original purpose, which was to attract full-time students who would work in the laboratories as well as attend lectures, failed almost entirely. The number of registered pupils in the *écoles préparatoires* was only 62 in 1857, and declined to 43 by 1865.[3] By 1867, only 16 certificates of capacity had been awarded by the faculties and 77 by the schools—56 of them at Mulhouse, the only one which was at all successful.[4] The experiment failed because it met neither the need for intermediate education (because the level was too high) nor the demand for higher technical training (because the courses were too general and there was no practical contact with industry).

The *écoles préparatoires* survived, but as with the faculties their courses became chiefly public lectures attended in the evenings by outsiders. The courses on literature and history actually proved the most popular, though the scientific ones seem often to have attracted a working-class audience. Some figures for the school at Rouen in 1856 show the typical pattern. The average attendance at each course was:[5]

---

[1] Fortoul papers, A.N. 246 AP 20–21, meeting of officials, 3–4 and 8 Oct. 1855.

[2] Cf. L. Pasteur, *Pasteur. Correspondance, 1840–1895* (1940–51), i, pp. 287–92, 299–301, 305–9, 323–7.

[3] *Statistique de l'enseignement supérieur 1865–1868* (1868), p. 6.

[4] Jourdain, *Rapport sur l'organisation et les progrès de l'instruction publique*, p. 204.

[5] A.N. F[17] 4346, report of director of school to *conseil académique* of Caen, Nov. 1856.

mathematics	93
mechanics	99
physics	79
chemistry	231
natural history	98
literature	156
history	331

By 1856, then, various attempts had been made by Fortoul to meet what were thought to be the needs of industry—the scientific sections in the lycées, the *écoles préparatoires*, the *écoles profession-nelles*; and alongside these innovations the special courses in the lycées and colleges continued. This dissipation of effort was one reason for the lack of achievement. Fortoul had no over-all strategy for *enseignement professionnel*, and he was not prepared to back the innovations which he made with money or with vigorous action; the Fichet episode, indeed, casts doubt on his judgement and competence. But behind the political failure lay deeper problems. The history of Fortoul's initiatives suggests that the many experts who thought this an unsuitable field of action for the University were right. Fortoul claimed that it was the duty of the University to extend its teaching to keep abreast of scientific and industrial progress. But in fact it was difficult to attempt innovation with the machinery which existed. The University's administration was better adapted to inspecting and supervising a system which ran by the momentum of tradition and routine than to intro-ducing new concepts of education or imparting a dynamic of change.

Moreover, the University's educational ideal could not easily be reconciled with the kind of vocational specialization which *enseignement professionnel* seemed to demand. The University was a national body which believed in imposing uniform programmes, while the success of *enseignement professionnel* depended on variation to fit in with local needs. With both the *écoles profession-nelles* and the *écoles préparatoires*, Fortoul automatically thought in terms of a uniformly imposed syllabus, and applied to his new creations the administrative pattern of the municipal colleges: the state provided the teaching, but local councils were expected to provide the bulk of the funds. Without the sympathy of local opinion, this would not work. Where efforts were made to gain that sympathy, as at Mulhouse, the schools were successful—in that town, indeed, they were virtually taken over by an employing class notable for its energetic interest in education.

The fifties, then, saw little advance in the field of technical education, and what there was owed more to local initiative than to government action. The Second Empire certainly recognized the connection between industrial progress and education, but it cannot be said that it tackled the problems with any great understanding. This was partly, no doubt, because of their novelty. The world of industry and commerce, where professions were not defined by examinations and qualifications, and where the different grades—proprietors, managers, engineers, foremen, skilled workers—were difficult to distinguish, was an alien world for the University. Advice and experience were indeed available if the government had chosen to use them, but in the fifties men like Fichet were more readily listened to than the competent but republican Pompée.

Most of the experts would have agreed that the most urgent need was for *enseignement professionnel* in the general sense—for an intermediate education which was short, practical, and open to primary school pupils. The failure to provide this was perhaps the greatest weakness of the Second Empire's educational policy. The gap left by the demise of the higher primary schools was not filled, and neither Fortoul's reform of secondary education nor his innovations in the technical field really met the practical needs of the 'intermediate' class. There was too much vague rhetoric and too little realism—even Dumas, who had defined the problems clearly in his 1847 report, could fail to relate his schemes to the ages of the potential pupils. What was needed above all was more information—about who the intermediate classes were and what they wanted, about the desires of employers and workers, and about the local conditions into which the schools had to fit. When the question of *enseignement professionnel* was tackled again in the sixties, it was to be on a firmer basis of extended discussion and investigation.

4. BIFURCATION IN PRACTICE

Fortoul's reform of the lycées was soon found unsatisfactory; practical difficulties were encountered, and the teachers were very hostile to it. Bifurcation was first modified and then abolished by Fortoul's successors. But it does not seem to have been so unpopular with the parents whose needs it was intended to meet. For some years, the scientific sections attracted more pupils than the literary ones, and although the popularity of science later declined over-all it remained strong in areas where local conditions were favourable. These included the most industrialized regions, which suggests that the reformers' idea of offering a form of education attractive to the industrial and commercial bourgeoisie was partly fulfilled. On the other hand, the scientific sections did not replace the 'special courses' of the lycées and colleges, which survived alongside them.

In 1852 and 1853 the administration collected statistics on the division between the two sections in each school, and compared them with the situation before the reform. The following table shows how pupils were divided between the various types of education given:[1]

| | | Lycées | | Colleges |
	1851	1852	1853	1853
Special mathematics	425	361	453	
Higher division:				
Letters	6,339	4,023	3,587	3,515
Science	1,970	4,560	4,743	2,088
Lower division	5,819	6,049	6,352	
Elementary forms	2,366	2,389	2,634	
Special courses	2,557	2,291	2,615	
Total, all pupils	19,476	19,673	20,384	27,905

It will be seen that the success of the scientific sections was immediate, and it was greatest in the lycées, where the sections took over the task of preparation for the government schools. In the colleges (where the reform was in any case only applied in the larger schools) the special courses continued to meet much of the demand for modern education, and even in the lycées the growth of the scientific sections was not really at the expense of these courses.

No general figures of this kind were recorded after 1853, but we do have annual figures for each school collected in 1864.[2] The

[1] A.N. F17 6806, summary table for lycées, F17 6833, situation of colleges in 1853. Cf. F17 6833, figures for individual lycées. The 'science section' figures for 1851 refer to the old 'elementary mathematics' form.

[2] A.N. F17 6843–6849, replies to circular of 16 July 1864, question II. 2.

general pattern which emerges is that the scientific sections retained their popularity until around 1858, when the literary sections began to outnumber them. This tendency was accelerated after 1860–1. The figures for the baccalaureate examination show a similar pattern. More baccalaureates in science than in letters were awarded in 1854 and 1855, but not in any subsequent year. The gap was not, however, a wide one: in 1855, for example, 2,055 were awarded in letters and 2,123 in science, in 1861 2,872 and 2,103.[1]

There were considerable differences between individual schools. In some, the scientific sections remained popular to the end, while in others they never really caught on at all; even in 1853, the literary section was larger in 18 out of 60 lycées.[2] There was a fairly clear regional pattern, science being strongest in the north and east and weakest in the centre and west. It is worth looking at some individual cases in some detail, because these figures provide a chance to illustrate the way in which secondary education varied according to local conditions and the needs of its clientele.

It is important to remember that the primary purpose of the scientific sections was preparation for the examinations of the government schools. There was therefore no necessary connection between the popularity of science and the presence of industry, and the scientific sections were strong in the Paris lycées and in the larger provincial lycées which tended to attract candidates for the government schools from the whole of their region. Especially 'scientific' lycées were those in towns which had a strong military tradition—like Metz and Nancy in Lorraine, where the scientific sections well outnumbered the literary even in 1863–4.[3] The same was true of the naval port of Brest, where from 1852 to 1858 the literary section never had more than 20 pupils and the scientific never fewer than 100. Even in 1864, 10 of the 13 pupils in the Philosophy class were taking the literary baccalaureate only with a view to entering the naval medical services.[4] Preparation for the naval school was concentrated in naval towns—other schools showing a similar pattern were Lorient, Rochefort, and Toulon, where the inspectors in 1857 complained that 'the teaching of

---

[1] *Enquêtes et documents relatifs à l'enseignement supérieur. XXI. État numérique des grades, 1795–1885* (1886), pp. 66–75, 168–77.
[2] A.N. F¹⁷ 6833, figures for individual lycées.
[3] A.N. F¹⁷ 6814, reports of inspectors-general, 1864.
[4] A.N. F¹⁷ 6848, reply of *proviseur* of Brest to circular of 16 July 1864.

letters bears little fruit, and indeed in the higher forms is largely abandoned'.[1]

Another source of local variations was competition with Catholic schools. It will be recalled that to strengthen the University's competitive position after the *loi Falloux* was one of the motives of the 1852 reform. A local example shows how this worked in practice. At Montluçon, a Catholic school was opened in 1853 after a campaign by the Catholic party, and the position of the municipal college was threatened. The reaction of the administration was to strengthen the scientific teaching and to introduce bifurcation at once. The ministry was urged to appoint a young and active science teacher, and the municipal council was persuaded to spend 200 francs on scientific apparatus. A new weapon of competition was thus added to the more conventional devices of mobilizing liberal opinion and government influence.[2]

The result was that in areas where Catholic competition was strong the state schools tended to concentrate on science because they taught it better, while Catholic schools remained 'literary'. In the Breton department of Ille-et-Vilaine, for example, science predominated by 93 to 76 in the public schools (chiefly the lycée of Rennes), but letters by 201 to 92 in the private schools. The lycée, where the scientific section was larger until 1861, was thus untypical of the department as a whole.[3] The same happened in the Vaucluse, where the lycée of Avignon was in direct competition with a Jesuit college. In 1855, the lycée had 53 pupils in the scientific section (which remained the larger until 1862) and 33 in the literary, but the Jesuits had no scientific section and 133 senior classical pupils.[4]

What of towns where these special factors did not apply? The popularity of science would depend on the nature of the school's clientele, and the careers which the pupils aimed at, and these varied considerably. Broadly speaking, science was most popular in towns where commerce and industry were important, and

[1] A.N. F¹⁷ 6775, report of inspectors-general, 19 June 1857.

[2] A.N. F¹⁷ 2480, monthly reports of rector of Allier, Apr., June, July, Sept., Oct., Nov. 1853, Jan., Feb., June 1854.

[3] A.N. F¹⁷ 6813, report of *inspecteur d'académie* of Ille-et-Vilaine to *conseil académique* of Rennes, 10 June 1855.

[4] A.N. F¹⁷ 4344, report of *inspecteur d'académie* of Vaucluse to *conseil académique* of Aix, 1855. Cf. Strasbourg in R. Anderson, 'The Conflict in Education', in T. Zeldin (ed.), *Conflicts in French Society* (1970), p. 80.

weakest where the schools were patronized by the old-established middle class who aimed at the traditional liberal professions for their sons. But this was not always the case; the industrial towns of Rouen, Amiens, and Nîmes, for example, did not have notably 'scientific' lycées. One reason for this was that in towns of this kind *écoles professionnelles* and similar schools may have taken away part of the potential clientele. Another was that the scientific sections did not always compete successfully with the special courses, which the 1853 figures show to have been organized on an extensive scale even in the largest lycées. There were substantial numbers of 'special' pupils, for example, at Marseilles (153), Lyons (124), Caen (142), Nantes (111), Rouen (99), Saint-Étienne (99), and Saint-Omer (96).[1] In some towns, the special courses were clearly being used by the industrial and commercial bourgeoisie as well as the lower middle class. At Le Havre, which had a large municipal college, bifurcation was never organized, as the special courses, created in 1850, successfully met the demands of local commerce. The courses reached a high level, and in 1858 included more than a third of all pupils.[2]

But there were towns where the success of the scientific section was clearly due to the presence of commerce and industry. This could be combined with an interest in the government schools. Science was popular in Nantes, for example, because 'the instincts of the people of Nantes give them a preference for the Government schools or careers in industry'.[3] 'The pupils generally choose science with the idea that if they later fail in the entry examinations for the imperial schools, they will always be able to use the excellent lessons of their science teachers in industry.'[4] The same was said at Nancy in 1864.[5]

In other towns, the government schools were less important, as at Lille or Reims. It was reported from Reims in 1854 that the scientific section was far larger than the literary, but that standards

[1] A.N. F¹⁷ 6833, figures for bifurcation in individual lycées. Cf. R. Anderson, 'Secondary Education in Mid Nineteenth-Century France: some Social Aspects', *Past and Present*, no. 53 (1971), p. 139.
[2] A. Anthiaume, *Le Collège du Havre* (1905), ii, pp. 316–19. Cf. A.N. F¹⁷ 4342, annual report of *conseil académique* of Seine-Inférieure, 1853.
[3] L. P. de Lafforest, *Rapport sur l'instruction dans la Loire-Inférieure* (1855), p. 4.
[4] L. P. de Lafforest, *Rapport sur l'instruction dans la Loire-Inférieure* (1856), p. 4.
[5] A. N. F¹⁷ 9099, reply of *proviseur* of Nancy to circular of 5 Oct. 1864.

were low because 'most of the families mean their children to go
not to the government schools where entry is by competition and
requires serious preparation, but into the wine or cloth trade,
which requires nothing of the kind and yet promises them more
lucrative positions'.[1] The scientific sections did well in most of the
smaller towns of the north and east, and also in small industrial
centres in the south like Albi and Castres. They could also be
popular in rural areas. In the Indre department in 1852, most of
the pupils in the college of Châteauroux and all of those in the
colleges of Issoudun and La Châtre had chosen science. This was
attributed to 'the calm and positive nature' of the local population,
which meant presumably their lack of ambition to enter the liberal
professions.[2] Similarly at Mâcon, 'bifurcation has at first succeeded
only too well, in the sense that no pupils are left in the literary
section'. It was explained that 'the habits of the Mâconnais mean
that no great importance is attached to classical studies', and that
the lycée could not survive without its primary (i.e. special)
classes.[3]

The character and traditions of the local community were also
invoked by officials to explain why in some cases science was less
popular. In 1858, for example, it was reported that the classics
were flourishing at Paris only at the lycée Bonaparte, patronized by
'rich and elegant families', who still retained the old taste for a
literary education.[4] Elsewhere, the dominance of local society by a
traditional legal bourgeoisie was often noted as a factor favouring
the classics. At Aix in 1857, literary pupils outnumbered scientific
ones two to one; 'In a town where the influence of the Magistrature
must tend to the conservation of literary traditions, this state of
affairs is only natural.'[5] At Grenoble, families were strongly
conscious of their *parlementaire* tradition, and thought its survival
depended on the maintenance of literary culture.[6] And at Orléans,
it was said that science was unlikely to be popular with the local
families, who belonged to the nobility and magistrature; 'a marked

---

[1] A.N. F¹⁷ 6813, report of inspectors-general, 1854.

[2] A.N. F¹⁷ 4342, annual report of *conseil académique* of Indre, 1853.

[3] A.N. F¹⁷ 6813, report of inspectors-general, 1854. The figures show that this
was somewhat exaggerated.

[4] A.N. F¹⁷ 1641, report of *inspecteur d'académie* A. Nisard, Apr. 1858.

[5] A.N. F¹⁷ 6775, report of inspectors-general, 19 June 1857.

[6] A.N. F¹⁷ 4244, rector's report on meeting of *conseil académique* of Grenoble,
June 1855. Cf. F¹⁷ 1640, monthly report of rector of Grenoble, Mar. 1857.

pre-eminence will always be given here to Letters, which develop the urbanity of the mind, and its *most aristocratic* faculties, so to speak.' Families from outside the town, however, drawn from less exclusive social strata, would welcome a more practical education.[1]

The impact of Fortoul's reform, then, depended very much on local conditions. Where the interest in science was mainly related to the government schools, the scientific sections merely served an old need in a new way. Where it was at a lower, practical level, they could not replace the special courses—and the reform was not applied at all in most smaller colleges. But where conditions were favourable, the sections did seem to meet some of the needs of industry and commerce, and attract those who wanted an education which was modern as well as solid and complete. The reform must have been one cause of the University's recovery from the blow dealt it by the *loi Falloux*: numbers in the lycées had at first fallen sharply, but began to rise again in 1852 and had passed the pre-1848 figure by 1856. As the following table shows, the recovery of the colleges was slower:[2]

	Lycées		Colleges	
	Schools	Pupils	Schools	Pupils
1847	53	23,207	314	28,385
1850	56	20,453	307	27,488
1855	64	22,746	247	25,235
1860	72	27,372	240	28,531
1865	77	32,630	251	33,038

Since the Catholic schools were also expanding, this was in fact one of the fastest periods of general growth for secondary education in the nineteenth century.[3]

Where it was successful, bifurcation retained its popularity with parents until the end, and some officials were to oppose its abolition by Duruy. But in the intervening years, it had been found wanting by the teachers, and Fortoul's system had been dismantled piece by piece. While Fortoul was minister, criticism within the University was suppressed, although to his irritation the

[1] A.N. F¹⁷ 2482, weekly report from lycée of Orléans enclosed in monthly report of rector of Loiret, May 1852.

[2] *Statistique de l'enseignement secondaire en 1865*, Tables 13, 23.

[3] Cf. Prost, *Histoire de l'enseignement en France*, p. 32; V. Isambert-Jamati, *Crises de la société, crises de l'enseignement* (1970), pp. 376–7.

conseils académiques which had been created in 1854 began to pass
resolutions deploring the drop in standards.[1] Fortoul's death,
however, released the safety-valve, and in 1857 there appeared the
first balanced critique of the reforms, Ernest Bersot's *Lettres
sur l'enseignement*; Bersot was one of the liberal teachers who
had left the University in 1852 rather than take the oath of
allegiance.

Rouland's policy in secondary as in primary education was to
restore the morale of the teachers and regain their confidence. In
1857, and again in 1863, he encouraged the teachers in the Paris
lycées to give their opinions on bifurcation and to suggest what
modifications should be made. In 1857, giving evidence to the
commission of inspectors which Rouland had set up, the teachers
let out the accumulated resentments of five years, and revealed a
fundamental hostility to Fortoul's reform and a desire to be rid of
it. The tone of anger, bitterness, and bewilderment behind the
teachers' comments is striking. The professor of rhetoric at the
lycée Charlemagne was typical of his colleagues: he 'would like to
abolish bifurcation, of which he has a *horror*, as he says, along with
everything connected with it'.[2]

These inquiries centred on the question of the decline of
standards—*abaissement des études*. All agreed that this decline had
occurred. Duruy was quoted as complaining that 'The pupils no
longer have the habit of writing, even in Rhetoric; they no longer
read; they hardly understand the questions which one puts to
them; some cannot spell.'[3] But the teachers' view was a limited
one. By 'standards' they meant essentially the standards of Latin
teaching, and the University's idea of measuring the progress of
education was to compare Latin proses written at different periods
(Duruy was to initiate such an inquiry when minister). Progress in
other aspects of teaching was overlooked—though even in 1857 it
was admitted that there had been some improvement in the
teaching of science. When bifurcation was discussed, and criticized,
by the *conseil académique* of Douai, it was Pasteur who pointed out
that a reform of such significance could not be judged by the
standards of a previous system, or by its effects on one generation
of schoolchildren. He thought that the weakness of the reform was

---

[1] Fortoul papers, A.N. 246 AP 20–21, meeting of officials, 2, 6, 10 Oct. 1855.
[2] A.N. F17 9096. Other papers relating to this inquiry in F17 68781.
[3] A.N. F17 9096, inquiry at lycée Napoléon.

the shortage of good science teachers, and that effort should concentrate on their training;[1] shortly afterwards, Rouland made
Pasteur head of the scientific side of the École Normale.

Rouland's inquiries did reveal some practical problems. One
was that the common subjects were not working, and the weakness
of the scientific pupils when the two sections were taught together
created many difficulties. Another was that the choice of subjects
was imposed too early, and the teachers demanded unanimously
that the point of bifurcation should be one year later. Rouland,
however, moved cautiously, stressing that the principle of bifurcation was not in question. As a man of practical experience, he
recognized the claims of the new scientific age, and as a conservative
he was reluctant to repudiate the actions of a previous minister of
the Emperor. Nevertheless, his policy of 'prudent ameliorations'[2]
gradually destroyed the unity of Fortoul's system.

Rouland's personal remedy for the improvement of bifurcation
was the phasing out of common instruction, though this was not
backed by experts like Cournot.[3] In 1859, the two sections were
separated for Latin and French teaching in the Paris lycées. The
other major structural change was making the baccalaureate in
letters the entry qualification for medicine, which immediately
transferred pupils out of the scientific sections.[4] Rouland also
abolished 'comparative grammar', and restored the old system of
teaching history in strict chronological order.

Other changes were designed to restore the morale of the
University and improve the daily lot of the teachers. The more
vexatious of Fortoul's measures were repealed or fell into disuse.
Under a new director, the École Normale began to revive, and the
old specialized *agrégations* in grammar, science, and history—
though not yet philosophy—reappeared. In 1858, Rouland found
the funds for a salary increase. He seems to have succeeded in this
way in gaining the sympathy of the University and introducing an
easier atmosphere. Surveying the end-of-year prize-giving speeches
made in 1858 and 1859, the semi-official *Journal général de
l'instruction publique* concluded that 'the struggle between science
and letters' was over, and that 'the country has confidence in the

---

[1] A.N. F¹⁷ 4348, minutes of *conseil académique* of Douai, 12 June 1857. Pasteur
was a pupil of Dumas and no doubt familiar with his ideas.

[2] Rouland, *Discours et réquisitoires*, ii, p. 13.

[3] A.N. F¹⁷ 6878¹, observations of Cournot, undated (? 1857).

[4] See above, p. 70.

University, and the University has confidence in the state'.[1] The University could once more feel that its traditions were safe and its national mission respected. By 1861, it was possible for a high official to make disparaging references to bifurcation and to declare that 'for the last few years, we have done little but work to reconstruct the ruins and to restore what it was attempted to destroy'.[2]

In 1863, Rouland again consulted the teachers in the Paris lycées. This time their comments were far more moderate, and while still unfriendly towards bifurcation they were now willing to acknowledge that the decline of standards might have other causes, and that the picture was not all black—many agreed that the general standard might be higher even if the standard of the élite had fallen. Nevertheless, the inquiry made clear the teachers' fundamental conservatism and uncompromising devotion to the classics. The teachers of Rhetoric, for example (in this inquiry the form teachers from each lycée came together), defended all the traditional exercises, and wished to see no change. 'The system followed by the University is good; it is excellent. . . . If the fashion is for easy studies, let us resist the fashion.' They hoped that Rouland would restore

a complete plan of liberal studies, such as our traditions impose on us, with that character of intellectual exclusiveness which should remain the mark of public education. . . . France will not forget the names of those who, struggling against opinion and fashion, work for her true glory and maintain her legitimate influence in the world.[3]

Fortoul and Dumas had thought that France's international position depended on her exports; the University thought that it depended on her guardianship of the classical tradition.

The weight of the teachers' attack was now directed at the baccalaureate rather than at bifurcation. The baccalaureate, it was said, destroyed the leisurely traditions of the University by encouraging boys to cut their studies short; examination-mindedness was a product of the 'spirit of the age' and the materialistic ambitions of parents. This had been a problem ever since the

---

[1] *Journal général de l'instruction publique*, xxviii (1859), p. 683, xxvii (1858), p. 646.

[2] Ibid., xxx (1861), p. 525 (speech of Artaud, vice-rector of Paris).

[3] A.N. F^{17} 9098, report of Rhetoric committee, 15 Mar. 1863.

'certificate of studies' (requiring candidates for the examination to prove attendance at classes) had been abolished in 1849. It had lain behind the concern about declining standards in the 1850s, and behind the desertion of the Philosophy form. In 1855, Fortoul had considered re-establishing the certificate of studies, but this could not be done without infringing on the freedom of private schools.[1] Its restoration was demanded again by the teachers in 1863, along with alternatives like raising the minimum age or splitting the examination into two parts taken in succeeding years— a system which Rouland had introduced for the scientific bacca-laureate in 1859.

These discussions showed that the teachers now realized that the tendencies which they deplored were rooted in the conditions of their society and their age, and that to reverse the work of Fortoul would not itself solve the underlying problems. The heat had now gone out of the bifurcation issue, although the teachers still wanted to see it postponed by one year. The other main demand (not much heard in 1857) was for the restoration of philosophy to its rightful name and its place of honour in the schools; this was the burden of a thoroughgoing attack on Fortoul's reform published by one of the Paris philosophy teachers in 1862.[2] The restoration of philosophy was to be one of the first acts of Rouland's successor Duruy, and when he also put bifurcation back by a year as the teachers demanded it was only as a prelude to the total abolition of Fortoul's system.

---

[1] Fortoul papers, A.N. 246 AP 21, meeting of officials, 6 Oct. 1855.
[2] C. Bénard, *L'Enseignement actuel de la philosophie dans les lycées et les collèges* (1862). Cf. Bénard's evidence in 1857 in A.N. F¹⁷ 9096.

CHAPTER SIX

Church and state

1. THE DEVELOPMENT OF CATHOLIC EDUCATION

Conflict between Church and state was inevitable while both bodies had comprehensive ambitions in the educational field. Nineteenth-century Catholics refused to abandon the idea that education was an essential part of the Church's mission, and that in a Catholic country schools of all kinds should come under its moral supervision if not its control. Under the Third Republic, when state education became anticlerical, Catholics bent their energies to the creation of a complete 'parallel' system of education, running from the infant school to the faculty. In earlier years, when the state admitted the Church's claims to influence, this was less necessary, but the Church still fought a constant battle to extend its influence as widely as possible. In some areas, like girls' secondary education, this influence was satisfactorily over-whelming; in others it was disturbingly limited—notably in higher education, where the state maintained its 'monopoly'. These were the chief areas of conflict at the end of the 1860s, when the state made its first hesitant interventions in the education of middle-class girls, and when it seemed that freethinking tendencies were being given their head in the faculties. But for most of the Second Empire the Catholic educational campaign concentrated on two things: building up a network of 'free' secondary schools for boys, and extending (or later defending) the hold of the teaching orders over primary education.

The teaching orders were the Church's main educational agency, and little could have been achieved without the devotion which led individual Catholics into them. Some of the orders, like the Jesuits and the Christian Brothers, were powerful and autonomous enough to act independently of the hierarchy, although this also meant that they incurred the suspicion of the state. Napoleon I's ecclesiastical legislation put formidable legal weapons in the hands of hostile governments, and the orders had become dependent on privileges (the letter of obedience for nuns, exemption from military service for teaching brothers) which a jealous state could easily withdraw.

The burden of defending the Church's interests politically fell on the bishops. The life of the Church centred around them, especially as the French Church had no national organization, and although chosen by the government of the day they were independent thereafter. Under the Second Empire, the hierarchy was represented in the Senate, and in the departments the bishop was a public figure on a par with the prefect. Within the University's own administration, the bishops or their representatives sat on the various councils from the national Conseil impérial downwards. Within his diocese, the bishop could count on the obedience of the parish priests, whose influence in the villages was reinforced by their right to enter and supervise the school.

Equally important was the support, both moral and financial, of Catholic laymen. The Church was formidable as a political force because its views were backed by the 'notables', especially those who sat on *conseils généraux* of departments and on the municipal councils whose decisions were so important for primary education. The degree and nature of this support varied from one part of France to another, but it is probably true to say that in the 1850s the Church got the support of the 'establishment', of right-thinking men throughout France, by presenting itself as the friend of property and order. For a time the authority of state, Church, and public opinion acted in unison, and in many places even the University's administration was run by clerical officials appointed after 1850.

In some areas, like Catholic Brittany, this situation was to persist. There was a Catholic consensus, with the notables supporting the Church and the University forming an alien force struggling to establish its influence. But in other parts of France, the rift between Church and state after 1860 and the revival of middle-class liberalism brought about a new situation in which the Church could not rely on general support but had to ally with one party in the local political struggle. It found its allies mainly among the rich upper class, and this led the Church into an alliance with political legitimism which was in the long run to appear unwise.

For the time being, however, the upper class were powerful

allies who could provide Catholic education with political protection, money, and customers in the shape of their own children. Nor
was government influence necessarily against them, for prefects
often found it expedient to work with the Catholic party. And
there were always government officials whose sympathies were
obvious, like the magistrate in the Gers in 1853 who was 'an enemy
of the government by instinct; . . . one of the most ardent adversaries of the University, one of those who propagandize most
actively for the clergy'. However, this official 'who sends his
relatives' and friends' children to the seminary, does not dare to
take his own son away from the Lycée'.[1] Many other officials did
patronize Catholic schools with impunity. With such sympathies
working for it, the Church was able to build up powerful provincial
entrenchments, vividly described by Taine in his account of his
travels around France as an examiner for Saint-Cyr. His conclusion
(in the mid-sixties) was that 'the priests are the true masters of the
provinces'.[2]

For an active bishop, like Dupanloup at Orléans or Parisis at
Arras,[3] the promotion of Catholic education was a never-ending
task. A first and very legitimate preoccupation was the recruitment
of priests, often by no means easy where popular faith was
declining. Bishops had seminaries under their direct control, fed
by *petits séminaires* (some departments had two or three) which
differed little from ordinary secondary schools. Most deliberately
widened their recruitment in this period, though it was sometimes
found that the vocation of the prospective priests suffered from
contact with more worldly pupils. The Church remained faithful
to the idea that priests, most of whom came from the peasantry,
should be chosen young and educated in an intensely Catholic
atmosphere; one of the duties of Catholic teachers at all levels was
to pick out and encourage likely candidates.

In 1865 there were 137 *petits séminaires*, and 70 'diocesan
colleges' also run by the bishops; the latter were often former
municipal colleges transferred to the bishops under the *loi Falloux*.
These secondary schools under episcopal control outnumbered

[1] A.N. F¹⁷ 1636, monthly report of rector of Gers, Oct. 1853.

[2] H. Taine, *Journeys through France* (1897), p. 177.

[3] There are useful studies of these two: Guillemant, *Pierre-Louis Parisis*;
C. Marcilhacy, *Le Diocèse d'Orléans sous l'épiscopat de Mgr Dupanloup, 1849–
1878* (1962).

those run by religious orders (43, of which 14 were Jesuit),[1] and the bishops also had much influence over the girls' convent schools. With primary education, the aim was not to promote private Catholic schools, but to persuade municipal councils to entrust their schools to a teaching order rather than a layman. The law gave the councils the right to express this preference (though not, since 1852, to choose the teachers themselves), but it was a right closely limited by the government. It could be exercised only when there was a vacancy, and since teachers tended to stay in the same post for life this was not often. A determined Catholic campaign, however, might force the lay teacher to resign. The priest could make his position difficult by obstruction, by malicious complaints to the authorities, and by stirring up discontent among parents. In the last resort, a rival private school could be opened, and pressure put on parents to transfer their children from the 'atheist' school. Another tactic was for a local employer to offer the teacher another job. But these methods only really worked in areas where the local notables were sympathetic, and it is perhaps significant that in a set of reports of 1864 cases of this kind are reported only from the Catholic west.[2]

The male teaching orders could make more progress when new schools were founded, especially perhaps in the industrial areas where Catholic employers were impressed by an education which was at the same time Christian, cheap, and efficient.[3] Another factor was that when new schools were founded it was often with money given or bequeathed by philanthropists who made it a condition that the school should be run by an order. Between 1850 and 1853, 47 per cent of new public schools for boys were entrusted to orders; in 1863–9, when the government was hostile, the figure was 5 per cent. The corresponding figures for girls were 60 per cent and 33 per cent; here expansion was easier because of the continual creation of separate girls' schools to replace mixed ones.[4]

---

[1] *Statistique de l'enseignement secondaire en 1865*, Table 26.

[2] *État de l'instruction primaire en 1864 d'après les rapports officiels des inspecteurs d'académie* (1866), ii, pp. 641–2, 699–700, 733 (Vendée, Côtes-du-Nord, Finistère).

[3] G. Duveau, *La Vie ouvrière en France sous le Second Empire* (1946), pp. 449–51.

[4] G. Rigault, *Histoire générale de l'Institut des Frères des Écoles Chrétiennes* (1937–53), v, pp. 343–4.

There was a natural momentum to the expansion of Catholic education. The conscientious bishop or priest saw its promotion as part of his pastoral duty, just as the University's officials worked automatically to extend and improve state education. The results of this activity can be indicated statistically. There are full figures for only two years, 1850 and 1863, but they leave no doubt that the fifties saw a massive expansion of the Church's influence over primary education.

Number of schools[1]

	Lay teachers		Run by orders	
	1850	1863	1850	1863
Public schools:				
Boys and mixed	33,201	35,348	1,227	3,038
Girls	4,178	5,998	5,237	8,061
Private schools:				
Boys and mixed	4,563	2,572	399	536
Girls	8,325	7,637	3,449	5,571
Total, all schools	50,267	51,555	10,312	17,206

This table shows the relative unimportance of private schools, except for girls, the disparity between boys' and girls' schools from a religious point of view, and the major expansion of teaching by orders. The last point is also illustrated by figures comparing the status of teachers in 1843 and 1863:

Teachers, public and private schools[2]

	1843	1863
Men:		
lay	44,173	40,817
members of orders	3,128	8,768
Women:		
lay	14,404	21,009
members of orders	13,830	38,205

Finally, the proportion of children taught by the orders, taking both public and private schools into account: in 1863 they taught 22 per cent of all boys, and 54 per cent of girls, against 15 per cent and 45 per cent in 1850.[3]

[1] *Statistique comparée de l'enseignement primaire (1829–1877)*, Tables 6–8.
[2] Ibid., pp. lxxviii–lxxix. [3] Ibid., Table 37.

These were national figures, but the pattern varied considerably between different areas. This was especially so with boys; the popularity of the Christian Brothers and similar orders was localized, and their pupils tended to be concentrated in the towns. If the 1863 figures are broken down by departments, we find that the orders taught over 50 per cent of the boys in only seven departments (two in Brittany and the others in the Rhone valley and Provence); there were nineteen, mostly in the north and east, where they had under 10 per cent. The strength of the female orders also varied locally, but there were only a few departments where they taught fewer than 30 per cent of the girls, and four where they had over 80 per cent.[1]

The Christian Brothers had an influence disproportionate to the numbers they taught because of their strength in the large towns, their modern and efficient methods, and their experiments with technical and near-secondary education. They had a strong sense of their independence and traditions, and ran their schools with little reference to the University's prescriptions. The order was directed from 1838 to 1874 by Frère Philippe, a man of tact and moderation who presided over a great expansion both within France (there were 3,656 brothers teaching in 1848, 8,202 in 1869)[2] and abroad. Unlike the Jesuits and some other orders, the Christian Brothers abstained from political polemic and intrigue, leaving others to fight the political battle on their behalf. They won wide respect for their devotion to the poor and their concentration on (to use the contemporary phrase) their modest and useful functions.

The progress of Catholic secondary education must be measured by its effectiveness in competing with the University. For a few years after 1850, the Catholic sector expanded rapidly as new schools were opened and a previously frustrated demand was met. The University suffered at first. But by the mid-fifties the situation stabilized itself and public and Catholic schools began to expand at a similar rate without much change in their share of the total numbers. In 1865, for example, the lycées and colleges had 46 per cent of the pupils, the Catholic schools 24 per cent, and lay private schools (a declining sector) 30 per cent.[3] The Catholic schools differed among themselves. Those run by the Jesuits, the

---

[1] See maps annexed to Maurain, *La Politique ecclésiastique*.
[2] É. Levasseur, *L'Enseignement primaire dans les pays civilisés* (1897), p. 97.
[3] Anderson, in Zeldin (ed.), *Conflicts in French Society*, p. 59.

Marists, the Assumptionists, and other orders were patronized by the upper class and some of the rich bourgeoisie, as were some of the *petits séminaires*. But most of the latter, the 'diocesan colleges', and the smaller Catholic schools, appealed more to the better-off peasantry and lower middle class; they competed with the municipal colleges rather than the lycées, and were successful because of their low fees, not their social exclusivity.

In the schools favoured by the rich, a consciously élitist form of education was developed, nearer than anything else in France to the English public school. These were boarding-schools, often set in the countryside, which had an intense communal life and put as much emphasis on character training as on academic achievement. They were one of the means by which the legitimist upper class retained its corporate identity and its values, and for that reason became a political target for liberal governments.

The teaching in these schools was generally even more classical than in the lycées. Catholic teachers were ill-equipped to meet the challenge of the industrial age—we have seen how Fortoul sought to exploit this—and in the 1850s 'science' was something of a dirty word for conservatives. 'The exclusive study of material science means materialism; materialism means socialism; socialism put into practice means the total destruction of society.' This was a Catholic headmaster's message at his prize-giving in 1853.[1] A Jesuit writer, however, said that 'we must think actively of the apostolate of the mathematical and physical sciences, by opening special schools where Religion will sanctify the cradle of the scientific generations'.[2] In practice, the Jesuits sought to serve the Catholic élite by adapting their teaching to the modern age, and in particular by giving very successful specialized preparation for the military schools. The long-term result, significant at the time of the Dreyfus Affair, was that Jesuit-trained officers were prominent in the upper ranks of the French army.

It was, however, the Christian Brothers who did most to expand Catholic teaching into new fields by opening *pensionnats*, boarding-schools for the middle class. This expansion into secondary education was strongly disapproved of by the University authorities, but the schools kept within the law by not teaching Latin (thus remaining technically primary). The result was that

[1] J. F. C. Peschoud, *Discours sur l'éducation* (1868), p. 319.
[2] A. Cahour, *Des études classiques et des études professionnelles* (1852), p. 74.

they gave a sort of education for which there was a real demand among the middle and lower bourgeoisie, one which was non-classical but also carried to a high level. The course was based on French, history, mathematics, science, modern languages, commercial subjects, and drawing (a subject in whose teaching the Christian Brothers were pioneers). This programme was first worked out in the *pensionnat* of Béziers in the forties, and by 1850 there were eight of these schools. Seven or eight more were founded in the fifties. In Paris, there was a *pensionnat* at Passy which had 600 pupils in 1855. At Clermont-Ferrand, the scientific teaching in the sixties rivalled the lycée's. In 1861, the Christian Brothers at Marseilles 'want to take the pupils who follow the special courses away from the lycée. . . . Their power at Marseilles intimidates everyone.'[1] At Quimper, the *pensionnat* had a bias towards agriculture, and attracted several hundred pupils.[2]

The *pensionnats* gave a general education at something above the 'higher primary' level. The order also ran some more specialized institutions. In Paris, there was the Maison des Francs-Bourgeois, a commercial school founded in 1843.[3] At Beauvais, the Institut agricole was opened in 1855.[4] In 1862, the Christian Brothers took over the Oeuvre de Saint-Nicolas, an institution with two schools in Paris which combined moral care and technical training for apprentices.[5] These *oeuvres d'apprentis* or *patronages* were a feature of Catholic philanthropy at the time.[6] Finally, the Christian Brothers, like lay teachers, gave evening courses for adults and young workers. These efforts on behalf of the urban working class earned the order a good deal of official commendation, and underlined the Church's claim to be able to provide a complete range of educational institutions suited to the needs of all classes.

The energy and financial sacrifice which went into building up Catholic education were impressive. The contribution to France's intellectual life was perhaps less so. The intellectual level of the

---

[1] A.N. F¹⁷ 2650, quarterly report of rector of Aix, 15 May 1861.
[2] On the *pensionnats* generally: Rigault, *Histoire générale*, v, pp. 387 ff., 512–15, 518, 526.
[3] Ibid., v, pp. 265–6.
[4] J. Bavencove, *Institut agricole de Beauvais (Oise)* (n.d.), p. 32.
[5] A. Prévot, *L'Enseignement technique chez les Frères des Écoles Chrétiennes au XVIIIe et au XIXe siècles* (n.d.), pp. 132–3.
[6] J.-B. Duroselle, *Les Débuts du catholicisme social en France 1822–1870* (1951), pp. 553 ff.

French priesthood remained mediocre, as was shown by its performance in the new religious controversies of the sixties. The lack of any Catholic higher education was felt, and the secondary schools did not become nurseries of independent thought. In the Church of Pius IX, the emphasis was increasingly on authority and obedience, and Catholic thinkers tended either to avoid controversial problems or to take refuge in assertive rhetoric rather than argument. Churchmen were concerned to maintain spiritual values amid the materialism and selfishness of the nineteenth century, but often they did this by turning their backs on the modern world and refusing to try to understand it. In education, this was expressed in the denunciation of science as materialist, and the maintenance of the old idea of a classical-Christian utopia for the consumption of schoolchildren. In politics, the same nostalgia for the ancien régime led the Church to support legitimism. Finally, the Church tied itself to the property-owning classes because this seemed to make its position in state and society secure. The conventional ideas and social prejudices of the bourgeoisie were endorsed from the pulpit, and the Church willingly allowed itself to be used as an instrument of social control. This policy meant great material gains for the Church under the Second Empire, notably in the field of education; but it corrupted its moral authority, and sowed the seeds of a bitter harvest in later years.

2. CATHOLIC IDEAS ON EDUCATION: DUPANLOUP

Catholic education expanded in the 1850s because it had the support of the established classes, and it had their support because they were persuaded that religion was the enemy of socialism and the friend of property and order. These themes were eagerly embraced by Catholic preachers and writers. The ultramontane *abbé* Gouget, for example, in a book on 'education envisaged from the social point of view', argued that only an education which was fundamentally Catholic and given by Catholic teachers could save society. 'All the disasters of 1848 came from contempt for religious authority', and the liberal bourgeoisie were to blame for 'accepting an education that cares nothing for God, as long as it respects the family and property'. Now they should appreciate that 'there is an intimate and necessary connection between Catholic truth and social truth'.[1] Gouget believed that education should be kept within 'sages limites', and that 'too extensive education is a social calamity'. Primary education should be limited to 'the elements of prayer, reading, and writing. . . . It would even be desirable that three-quarters should not be able to read well enough to enjoy it', for that led the urban population to read corrupting literature, and the peasants 'to study the civil code, which causes so much litigation between individuals, and to covet the management of municipal affairs, which leads to so many divisions within communes'.[2] And like other conservatives at the time he tried to prove that there was a connection between education and the growth of crime.[3]

Views like this were a product of the overheated atmosphere of the early fifties. A more moderate and representative picture of Catholic educational ideals is presented by the writings of bishop Dupanloup. Between 1850 and 1866, Dupanloup published two three-volume works on the general problems of education, and he frequently intervened in current controversies—notably at the time of Duruy's experiment with girls' secondary education. He came to be looked on as the leading educational expert of the day, and his experience was wide: he had made his mark in the forties as head of a Parisian *petit séminaire*, he was a leading spokesman of the Church in the discussions preceding the *loi Falloux*, and as bishop of Orléans after 1849 he vigorously developed Catholic education in his diocese. That Dupanloup's works were representative of orthodox opinion may be inferred from the frequency with which he is quoted or paraphrased by others. Although Dupanloup was given to impulsive exaggeration, his views were essentially moderate, and he belonged to the liberal or Gallican party in the Church. He was not, however, a very original or profound thinker.

Dupanloup's first volume appeared in 1850, and included some outbursts of anti-egalitarian rhetoric. But there was nothing exceptional in his view that 'education must accommodate its teachings to the social and providential position of the pupil, to the role which he is called on to fill in society', or in his distinction between different levels of education: popular for the working classes, intermediate for the *classes moyennes*, and 'higher literary

---

[1] Gouget, *Essai sur les conditions de l'éducation, envisagée au point de vue social* (1853), pp. 39, 90.
[2] Ibid., pp. 68–70. [3] Ibid., pp. 78–81.

education, for the upper classes of society'.[1] It was this higher
literary education that Dupanloup knew most about, and three of
his volumes were devoted to it. They formed a manual of practical
advice for Catholic teachers, and a sustained defence of the
classical tradition, against both the materialists and the followers
of the *abbé* Gaume.

Dupanloup's remarks on other branches of education were very
generalized, and his main interest was always in the education of
the upper class. His contacts with the nobility were close throughout his ecclesiastical career, which he had begun by reconciling
Talleyrand on his deathbed to the Church, and consolidated by
becoming the fashionable confessor of the faubourg Saint-
Germain. In Dupanloup's view, one of the functions of Catholic
education was to restore the social leadership of the landed class.
Many of the new schools founded after 1850 were of course
patronized by that class, and Dupanloup's ideas were shared by
other teachers; in 1853, an educational review which circulated
among Catholic teachers devoted an article to the special problems
of education for the nobility.[2] Dupanloup's views on this were tied
up with his fervent patriotism, which was also typical of Catholics
at the time. France could only be great when she was Catholic—
as the seventeenth century, the 'grand siècle', showed—and could
only recover from her recent tribulations by a religious regeneration. The lead in this must be taken by the upper classes. Disaster
had come about because they had turned into a frivolous and
parasitic class, and this was due to 'the weakening of that strong
and ancient education which the great European stocks once
received'.[3]

'Let me say it once more to those heads of great families: if you
can give your numerous sons [for he also urges them to reproduce]
a higher intellectual education, they will be the leaders of their
fellow citizens at all times and places.'[4] At the very least, a sound
education will equip the rich to manage their fortunes and avoid
being cheated by their agents.[5] But it is also needed to restore their
proper political influence. In recent years, and especially since
1848, society has been threatened by the rise of the half-educated

---

[1] F. Dupanloup, *De l'éducation* (1850–61), i, pp. 26–7, and cf. p. 262.
[2] *Revue de l'enseignement chrétien*, ii (1853), pp. 321–41.
[3] *De l'éducation*, ii, p. 602.
[4] Ibid., i, p. 238.   [5] Ibid., i, pp. 239–40.

demagogue. 'In a nation where every village has at least one municipal councillor who aspires to the reputation of an orator and wants to rule over the commune, including the church, the school, and the *château*, it is more than ever essential that a well-brought-up and educated gentleman should be able to express himself suitably on every subject.'[1] Like Gouget, Dupanloup saw that universal suffrage combined with rural education meant a challenge to established social authority.

Dupanloup used this rather naïvely as an argument for teaching traditional rhetoric in the schools. This was of a piece with his old-fashioned view of who had the real power to change society—the men of letters, the historians, the orators, and the philosophers. Dupanloup's definition of the upper class included the professional and intellectual élite as well as the nobility, but industry, commerce, and science had little place in his scheme of things.[2] He had a practical appreciation, however, of the problems faced by upper-class families. There was, for example, the delicate question of what to do with 'those for whom this higher education is evidently not suitable, but who are nonetheless born into a position which seems to demand it'. For some, he recommended modern education without Latin; for others, 'instructive and amusing reading' combined with physical exercise was the thing. In such cases, he suggested, a 'vocation' for the navy might often be discovered.[3]

The motto which appeared on the title-page of Dupanloup's volumes was 'Education is a work of authority and respect'. This is the key to many of his ideas. Respect and unquestioning obedience to authority were the basic principles on which society should rest, and to inculcate this was a central aim of education. The same principle of authority applied to the relations between child and parent, between pupil and master, between worker and employer, and between the lower classes generally and their betters. It was a congenial idea in the 1850s, and Dupanloup had no hesitation in endorsing on behalf of the Church the words of Thiers: 'Catholicism is the greatest and holiest school of respect that the world has ever seen.'[4] In particular, the Church's claim to control popular education was based on the fact that only her teachers could preach patience and industry to the poor, obedience

---

[1] F. Dupanloup, *De la haute éducation intellectuelle* (1855–66), i, p. 360.
[2] Ibid., i, p. 96; *De l'éducation*, i, p. 262.
[3] *De l'éducation*, i, pp. 328–30. [4] Ibid., ii, p. 485.

and respect to their children, and resignation and hope to the young worker. The courage and resignation shown by the Irish people in face of the great famine demonstrated what Catholic education could achieve.[1]

Dupanloup devoted four chapters to the role of Respect in education, and defined the child's duties under the 'law of respect' as also including docility, attention, and gratitude.[2] Catholic teachers were perhaps over-influenced by their experience in educating priests, which they transferred to the education of ordinary children. The aim of the seminaries at this time (as indeed, to a large extent, of the *écoles normales*) was to produce docile and malleable instruments of authority.

They were also influenced by their belief in the inherent sinfulness of children. The three special faults of children (Dupanloup devoted a chapter to each) were pride (*orgueil*), sensuality, and 'frivolity, or curiosity'. Sensuality naturally provided many problems for the educator—Dupanloup believed in maintaining complete sexual ignorance ('innocence') into adulthood. And reprehension of 'frivolity' lay behind Dupanloup's conservative attitude on what to teach; he was suspicious of subjects, like history, which were too easy and enjoyable, and believed in Latin grammar and verse because their aridity was a moral challenge.

But the greatest childhood sin was pride, and to break this pride was the teacher's main task. Like Thomas Arnold, Dupanloup saw the teacher always wrestling with the wickedness of boy nature: 'education . . . is a constant and terrible struggle against all the evil instincts and all the evil forces of depraved human nature, in oneself and in others!'[3] A teacher who thought like this was likely to be torn between his natural kindliness and the stern demands of duty. Dupanloup's ideas were enlightened in some ways—he stressed that discipline should be paternal rather than mechanical, and that education must respect the child's character and individuality—but his practical advice was harsh. The psychological punishments which he preferred to physical ones were aimed at humiliating the child, and his remedy for offences against religion or morality was instant expulsion. For he believed both in original sin and in the full moral responsibility of children.

This mixture of tenderness and oppression seems to have been

[1] Ibid., i, pp. 293-7.   [2] Ibid., ii, p. 483.
[3] Ibid., ii, pp. 367-8.

characteristic of the Catholic boarding-schools of the time. Dupanloup was a strong believer in boarding education. Education should be an all-embracing experience in which the voices of religion and morality alone were heard, and children were cut off from evil influences. For the educator had to struggle against the decadence of the age as well as the evils of human nature. Dupanloup carried this to the point of thinking a child safer in a boarding-school than in his own family. Parents were sadly lax in enforcing the rule of authority and respect, too inclined to indulge the whims of their children and even to undermine the work of the school by emotional scenes at the end of the holidays, or by listening to the child's complaints about the food or the teachers. Moreover, nowhere was a child more exposed to the corruptions of the age—newspapers, novels, balls, theatres, and so on—than in the upper-class home.[1]

Here Dupanloup parted company with the conventional sentiment of the age, which gave the highest place to the family—'the most sacred of human institutions', as the cliché went. When priests tried to interfere with its inner life, and especially to come between father and son, bourgeois anticlericalism began. But in general belief in the family was one of the complex of conservative values which the Church supported and profited from in this period. Its importance was underlined when the Academy of Moral Sciences set the 'role of the family in education' as a prize subject. Reporting on the entries in 1857, Guizot noted with satisfaction that they were full of sound ideas and moral tendencies.[2] The first prize was won by Théodore Barrau, an educational writer who had already published a book on a similar theme in 1852.

Barrau's books are of interest because they obviously represent middle-of-the-road bourgeois opinion, and what is striking is how close his views are to Dupanloup's. Barrau too sees the task of education as combating the materialism of the age, calls on the rich to turn from idleness to intellectual effort, proclaims the law of obedience and respect, wants to make religion the foundation of education, and thinks boarding essential. The main difference is that Barrau is hostile to the excessive influence of the Church, prefers laymen to priests as teachers, and is sympathetic to the

---

[1] Ibid., ii, pp. 251–7, 580 ff.

[2] *Séances et travaux de l'Académie des sciences morales et politiques*, 3rd series, xix (1857), p. 163.

University.[1] But the pretensions of the state were also to be resisted. In Guizot's words, the lesson was that the family should be the main instrument of education, aided 'by two great external forces, the State and the Church, indispensable but not sovereign auxiliaries'.[2] This profound liberal belief in the family was long to delay progress towards compulsory education. But what is significant in this context is that the approach of all parties to education in these years after 1848 was essentially moralistic rather than practical, and this was a mood which greatly favoured the Church in its campaign to recatholicize French education.

3. FROM FORTOUL TO DURUY

France's intervention in 1859 in the Italian war of liberation caused a breach between the government and the Church, and was one reason for the evolution of the authoritarian empire into a 'liberal' one. In the sixties, educational policy became openly anticlerical. But as we have seen, even Fortoul had defended the state's educational interests and asserted its right to control the Church's activities. In 1853, for example, he introduced a new system of inspecting private girls' schools, primary and secondary, which he considered a triumph for the civil power;[3] in fact, concessions had been made to the Church in the course of nego-tiations with Parisis, and the only inspectors allowed to enter convent schools were priests specially appointed for the purpose. This inspection was only carried out twice before falling into disuse. More successful was the attempt to force the Christian Brothers to charge fees: Rouland continued the pressure applied by Fortoul, and the order gave way in 1861.[4]

More significant than these minor changes in legislation was the fact that the University's officials began to oppose the Church's influence actively at local level. If they were confronted by Catholic intrigues against the University, they fought back, and competed with the Catholics for the support of mayors, councillors, magistrates, and notables. This was especially so after the appoint-

---

[1] T.-H. Barrau, *De l'éducation dans la famille et au collège* (1852), pp. 4–8, 73 ff., 163, 166–8; *Du rôle de la famille dans l'éducation* (1857), pp. 127–8, 257 ff., 225 ff., 266–9.

[2] *Séances et travaux de l'Académie des sciences morales et politiques*, 3rd series, xix (1857), p. 174.

[3] Fortoul papers, A.N. 246 AP 20, meeting of officials, 5 Oct. 1855; decree of 31 Dec. 1853.   [4] Rigault, *Histoire générale*, v, pp. 376–9; cf. above, p. 82.

ment of the new rectors in 1854. At the same time, political control of primary education was transferred to the prefects, who soon began working to restrain the expansion of the teaching orders.[1] As Cournot pointed out, few issues aroused more passion in local politics than the appointment of schoolteachers, and lay teachers had obvious electoral value.[2] The Catholic educational campaign was part of a political machine which in the long run could not be allowed to develop unchallenged by a government which based its local influence on a system of managed elections and official candidates. When the machine was put at the service of legitimism, it became a force to be combated openly.

In 1855, Fortoul held a meeting of the new rectors at which they reported progress. 'In the academy of Toulouse', said the rector Laferrière, 'I found an influence which was hostile to us—the influence of the religious orders. I have taken it as my first duty, as representative of the University, to wave the University's flag', notably by strengthening the lycée against the Jesuits.[3] Another rector, Mourier, who was responsible for Brittany, later recalled how after the law of 1854 'the regular clergy opened their campaign, getting on their side all the élites, in the army, the magistrature, and the rich bourgeoisie; the nobility were in the front rank of this crusade'. The lycées and colleges suffered, but under Mourier's guidance 'they found a clientele [in social strata] where they had not before penetrated, without losing the sympathy of the liberal classes, whose spirit they represented; and we obtained from the towns and the departments the credits which we asked for for their schools at every level'.[4]

Mourier's ideas are interesting because he was no radical, but a Gallican Catholic and conservative *universitaire*. They also show the limitations of this official anticlericalism. First, Fortoul's policy (and Rouland's) insisted that if the University was to regain middle-class confidence it was essential (in the words of Mourier's predecessor at Rennes) 'that the teaching of the Lycée should be severely orthodox and its discipline irreproachable'.[5] Outward religious conformity was enforced, and carefully watched over by

[1] Maurain, *La Politique ecclésiastique*, p. 153.

[2] Cournot, *Des institutions d'instruction publique*, p. 494.

[3] Fortoul papers, A.N. 246 AP 20, meeting of officials, 2 Oct. 1855.

[4] Mourier, *Notes et souvenirs*, pp. 98, 113.

[5] A.N. F^{17} 2481, monthly reports on secondary education, Ille-et-Vilaine, Oct. 1853.

E

officials: records were kept of how many pupils took mass at Easter, and Mourier described the figures which he forwarded in 1859 as 'most attractive and edifying'—the abstentions at Rennes had fallen from 24 to 13.[1]

Secondly, the defence of secular education concentrated on the lycées, and was most vigorous where Jesuit competition was found. The rectors cared less about primary education in the fifties. This was because of the traditional feeling that the governing class needed a common education, and that national unity was threatened if schools with contrary ideals produced 'two hostile Frances'.[2] The objection was not to Catholicism itself, but to extremism, for the ideal was that unity should be achieved around a moderate Catholicism shared by the University. In 1855 the question arose whether the college of Charleville should be turned into a lycée; the rector advised against it because the college courses were used by the pupils of the *petit séminaire* (once a common arrangement). If the school became a lycée, this would cease, as the archbishop of Reims thought a lycée would not offer sufficient 'guarantees' (i.e. would be less amenable to his influence). The rector did not want to see 'the rupture of this unity, which seems valuable to me from every point of view—the point of view purely of the University itself, and the social point of view. . . . It is not uncommon in a commune in this department to find a mayor and a notary, a priest and a schoolteacher, who have been brought up together, had the same education, and share the same ideas. One can imagine all the advantages which such a situation presents in everyday life.'[3]

When Rouland replaced Fortoul in 1856, the ministry of education was headed by a man whose legal background made him an instinctive Gallican and defender of the state's authority. The Italian crisis allowed him to act according to his instincts, and in 1860 there was a major shift in government policy. Rouland outlined his principles in a memorandum submitted to the Emperor. The influence of the Church—now seen as an enemy both of modern ideas and of patriotic interests—was to be combated especially by curbing the religious orders. In education, this meant stopping their expansion in the primary sector (this was the real

[1] A.N. F^{17} 6777, rector of Rennes to minister, 4 Apr. 1859.
[2] Mourier, *Notes et souvenirs*, p. 98.
[3] Fortoul papers, A.N. 246 AP 20, meeting of officials, 4 Oct. 1855, report of rector of Douai (Guillemin).

change compared with earlier years) and 'supporting the State's education vigorously, for it is the true national education'. Since 1850, 'the legitimist-Catholic party has been able to perpetuate among the younger generation that division of castes and ideas which the unity of the University's education might have caused to disappear. It has thus been able to ensure the continuance of its social and political doctrines through the children who are educated by the orders.'[1] At the beginning of 1861 a committee of senior ministers laid down the details of the new anticlerical policy, which was already being put into force.[2]

In secondary education, the main decision was to allow no new schools to be opened by 'unauthorized' orders, a legal category which included the Jesuits. The Jesuits were refused permission to open a school at Brest in 1860, and the general ban lasted for the rest of the Empire. At the same time, Rouland strengthened the University by spending money on rebuilding and re-equipment, creating new lycées out of municipal colleges, and persuading town councils to reclaim for the public sector some of the colleges which had been transferred to bishops since 1850.[3] Between 1861 and 1867, the lycées and colleges gained 10,000 pupils, though the Catholic schools held their own with an extra 5,600.[4]

Resisting the expansion of the orders in primary education meant bringing pressure on the municipal councils. The law was now narrowly interpreted to limit the expression of their preferences (this had begun in 1859), and after 1860 prefects were generally successful in preventing councils transferring schools to the orders and overriding their wishes where necessary. The expansion of the orders virtually ceased, though they held on to what they had achieved. The government also used its right to authorize new orders: the decision was taken in 1860 to authorize no new male orders (a policy in fact applied by Rouland since 1856) and few female ones—authorizations of the latter, lavish in the fifties, dwindled to a handful after 1860. Other decisions taken were to act against the *pensionnats* of the Christian Brothers, and to restrict the freedom to make donations and legacies which tied public schools to a religious order.[5] The other side of this policy was

---

[1] Maurain, *La Politique ecclésiastique*, pp. 457–8, and cf. 470.
[2] Ibid., pp. 468 ff.   [3] Ibid., pp. 463, 465, 469–71, 580–1.
[4] Anderson, in Zeldin (ed.), *Conflicts in French Society*, p. 59.
[5] Maurain, op. cit., pp. 215 ff., 438–40, 468–74, 581–92.

Rouland's desire to raise the morale of the lay teachers, which has already been discussed; he pointed out in his memorandum that gaining their loyalty had advantages 'from the point of view of universal suffrage'.[1] For the first time since 1848, the teacher could feel that his superiors would support him in conflicts with the priest or local notables, and could see the administration offering protection of his interests and status as well as demanding obedience.

The new policy towards the Church was undoubtedly congenial to Napoleon III himself. Otherwise he would not have chosen Victor Duruy to succeed Rouland in 1863. Duruy was an 'old soldier of the University militant' (his own words),[2] a man who had followed the classic path from a humble home to the École Normale. As a historian, he had attracted the attention of Napoleon when the latter was writing a 'Life of Caesar', and the Emperor's influence had gained him advancement in the University. When appointed minister, he was an inspector-general. He lacked political experience, but soon proved himself one of the most talented and energetic of the Empire's ministers.

Duruy was a democrat and an anticlerical, though his anti-clericalism had quite different roots from Rouland's. His political and intellectual stance is not very easy to label. Under the Third Republic, he came to be seen as one of the 'precursors' of its policies, and this caused his republicanism and anticlericalism to be exaggerated. He shared many of the basic ideals of republic-anism, but had no special attachment to the republican regime. He declared that 'social evil is my personal enemy, and the greatness of France my religion', and was prepared to support any government which sincerely promoted the interests of France and of progress.[3] He had a strong personal admiration for Napoleon III, and remained loyal to his memory. But he was a democrat, and his ideas fitted in with the democratic Bonapartism which was one of the political tendencies of the sixties—though not, unfortunately for Duruy's own position, the dominant tendency in the Empire's ruling circles.

The creed to which he gave his allegiance was, in the words of

[1] Ibid., p. 457.
[2] Mourier, *Notes et souvenirs*, p. 328.
[3] Duruy, *Notes et souvenirs*, i, pp. 52–3. His position is well described in J. Rohr, *Victor Duruy, ministre de Napoléon III* (1967), pp. 18 ff.

the Catholic historian La Gorce, 'a disciplined, patriotic, educated democracy, strongly coloured by free thought'.[1] His anticlericalism was inspired both by his belief in free thought and by his enthusiasm for progress, science, and the achievements of the modern world: the University, he thought, was the ally of these forces, and the Church had to be fought because it was obscurantist and medieval. In a letter to Napoleon in 1866, he laid down an anticlerical programme in terms very similar to Rouland's memorandum of 1860, and gave high priority to containing the influence of the orders over primary education.[2] The events of his ministry left no doubt of his hostility to clericalism.

At the same time, Duruy's position was not the same as Ferry's twenty years later. He belonged to the generation influenced by Cousin and Michelet, not to the new positivist school, and his personal beliefs were of a vaguely deist kind characteristic of *universitaires*. His University background was also reflected in his belief that teachers should conceal their personal views, and should respect the fact that most parents were Catholic; like his predecessors, he expected the University to conform outwardly to the demands of religion, and did not feel that there was anything false in this.[3] In office, he showed a tolerance and a genuine liberalism which were rare in Church–state relations. He enforced the law, but without harassment and petty persecution. He was prepared to give credit where it was due to Catholic education, and to learn from its achievements. His relations with the Christian Brothers, for example, remained courteous.[4] On the whole, this moderation was not reciprocated by the Church, whose leaders attacked Duruy savagely.

Duruy came to office when the intellectual atmosphere in France was changing rapidly. A new generation of thinkers was reaching maturity, and the restrictions on freedom of expression were being relaxed. In the sixties began a many-sided debate between religion and science, and a hostility to religion which went far deeper than old-fashioned anticlericalism gained more and more supporters— especially after Pius IX's denunciation of liberal and modern ideas in the Syllabus of Errors of 1864. It was inevitable that this

---

[1] La Gorce, *Histoire du Second Empire*, iv, p. 272.
[2] Duruy, *Notes et souvenirs*, i, pp. 330–3.
[3] Ibid., i, pp. 23, 45–6, 67, 325–8.
[4] Rigault, *Histoire générale*, v, pp. 356–7.

movement of ideas should affect the University, and create problems
for ministers who were trying to maintain a façade of orthodoxy.
The most celebrated case was the 'Renan affair'. Ernest Renan
was appointed in 1862 to the chair of Hebrew at the Collège de
France, and in his inaugural lecture he made clear his disbelief
in the divinity of Christ. Rouland suspended him, and after the
publication of his *Vie de Jésus* Duruy felt obliged to deprive him
of his post, though he made his personal sympathies clear.[1] Another
controversial figure was the young philosopher Taine, one of those
who had been forced out of the University by Fortoul's persecu-
tions. In 1863, he became an examiner for Saint-Cyr despite
clerical protests; in 1865 he was nearly dismissed, and it took the
personal intervention of the Emperor to reinstate him, though he
was successful in 1864 at getting a post in the École des Beaux-Arts.[2]
Problems of this kind were to dog Duruy throughout his period of
office, and to provide much ammunition for Catholic critics.

They arose from the basic ambiguity of the government's
position during the 'liberalization' of the Empire. Having lost
support on the right, the Empire tried to build it up on the left.
But it was not fundamentally willing to make the concessions,
either political or religious, which were needed if liberals and
democrats were to be convinced of its good faith. It was not
prepared to make a final break with the Church and abandon the
use of religion as a guarantee of political and social order any more
than it was prepared to defy the prejudices of the middle class and
introduce a real democratization of education. Duruy's position
summed up this dilemma. His closest links in politics were with
liberal parliamentarians and anticlerical journalists, while there
was a gulf of incomprehension between him and his fellow
ministers. In Parliament, he often had the sympathies of the
opposition rather than the majority. He was kept in office by the
Emperor's personal backing, but was eventually dispensed with
when his anticlericalism became too inconvenient politically. While
in office, he had to undergo many humiliations and frustrations
arising from this situation, of which the most striking was the
failure of his attempt to make primary education free and
compulsory.

[1] Maurain, *La Politique ecclésiastique*, pp. 593–4, 679, 682–3.
[2] Ibid., pp. 633, 749.

CHAPTER SEVEN

Democracy and education

1. THE REVIVAL OF DEBATE

The coming of the 'liberal Empire' created an atmosphere in which educational problems could again be freely discussed. Political activity revived, and many books and articles explored the conditions under which France might advance towards greater democracy. Throughout the sixties, the idea that fresh legislation was now needed to make primary education universal gained in strength, partly through the campaigning of liberals and democrats who worked to win public and official opinion over to this cause. What political forces were involved in this campaign, and what were the limits of debate? The first point to make is that one should not read back into this period the aims of the eighteen-eighties, and suppose that all who wanted the extension of education rallied to the cause of free, compulsory, and secular education. Of the four men who did most in the campaigns of the sixties—Jules Simon, Victor Duruy, Charles Robert, and Jean Macé—only Macé fully shared the ideals of the founders of the Third Republic.

The demand that education should be secularized, whether by removing religion from the syllabus or by relying exclusively on lay teachers, was relatively muted in this decade. It was still thought a radical idea and associated with republicanism; 'respectable' theorists did not suggest that moral education could be dispensed with, and the concept of a 'lay morality' independent of religion was not yet widely accepted. By contrast, the idea of making education free by the abolition of fees was in no way radical. It was what the Church had always believed in, and it appealed to many of the University's administrators precisely because it might undermine clerical competition. It already existed in most large towns, and the only real objection to making it universal was that it would cost the taxpayer money. In fact Duruy was able to bring about an extension of free education in the law on primary education which he introduced in 1867.

It might be thought that the principle of compulsory education would be easily accepted in a country where the tradition of state action was strong. Indeed, the case for it had been argued by Eugène Rendu, an official in Fortoul's ministry, at the height of the authoritarian Empire,[1] and there was the example of several other countries to appeal to. Yet middle-class opinion remained obstinately hostile to compulsion, and there was no real chance of its being approved by the parliaments of the Second Empire. One reason was that it might affect the Church schools and 'liberty of teaching', but the main one was the strength ot the liberal doctrine of non-intervention, which is a striking feature of the sixties. Suspicion of the state, a natural enough phenomenon after France's recent political experience, was an element common to the liberal orthodoxy of middle-class writers and the Proudhonian ideas characteristic of radical and working-class writers at the time. Much of the debate about education centred on the principles of liberalism, and on how they might be reconciled with making education free and compulsory. The champions of universal education had to contend not so much with the old obscurantism which was content to leave the masses in ignorance, as with the progressive orthodoxy of the age, which saw compulsion as an interference in the rights of the family and free education as a threat to the initiative and self-respect of the individual.

Jules Simon's *L'École* (1865), the most influential plea for wider education published in this period, concentrated on the case for compulsion. Simon was a former *universitaire* and a moderate republican prominent in the politics of the Second Republic; as the Third Republic's first minister of education, he was later to demonstrate his lack of sympathy with extreme anticlericalism. In the sixties, he led the educational campaign in Parliament (where other men of 1848 like Carnot also reappeared after the 1863 election), and became known nationally through his writings and speeches. The issues which Simon took up included the salaries of teachers, the inferiority of girls' schools, the need for public libraries, and the question of factory children. The problem of *enseignement professionnel* was also revived as one aspect of popular education, especially as economic justifications for its extension were now coming to the fore. The old argument that modern industry needed brain rather than brawn, and that education made

[1] E. Rendu, *De l'enseignement obligatoire* (1853).

the human capital of industry more productive,[1] was given new point by the free-trade treaty of 1860 and the London International Exhibition of 1862, which made men more aware of the vulnerability of French industry. The more idealistic spoke of France's need to hold her place in the peaceful struggle between nations which had now replaced war. Later in the decade, the military and industrial rivalry of Prussia created special alarm, and well before 1870 the weaknesses of France's education had been identified—by Duruy among others—as a danger to her position as a great power.

The importance of the economic argument is shown by the part which industrial interests took in the campaign for universal education. The enlightenment of the industrialists of Mulhouse and their contributions to technical education have already been noted. In the sixties the whole Alsace region, where primary education was already at a high level of development, and where the presence of industry coincided with the influence of Protestantism and the direct example of Germany, was the seat of a movement of opinion which spread from its local base to have national influence—something of a kind uncommon in France.

But the economic arguments for better education were not confined to those with a direct interest. Even Dupanloup, proclaiming his support for popular education at an international Catholic congress, stressed the theme of international competition.[2] The old idea of 'moralizing' the workers now faded away, or appeared in a new form inspired by democratic idealism rather than fear. Another argument which was gaining in popularity was that universal suffrage required universal education as its corollary; Napoleon III, however, did not seem to accept the logic of this, for education was still neither free nor compulsory in 1870. All the efforts of the reformers, and of Duruy himself, had failed to shift the government from an essentially timid and parsimonious attitude to popular education.

Of the various groups involved in the educational debate, the liberal economists deserve pride of place because of the pervasive influence of their theories. The *Journal des Économistes* frequently published articles on education, but their subjects show that it was

[1] e.g. H. Baudrillart, in *Journal des Économistes*, 2nd series, xxiv (1859), pp. 321–2.
[2] F. Dupanloup, *Discours prononcé au Congrès de Malines* (1864), pp. 25–6.

middle-class education which really interested this segment of opinion. The economists campaigned for the introduction of economic teaching in the lycées and faculties, and (like Bastiat earlier) attacked the classics and demanded modern secondary education. In 1859, a Swiss disciple of Bastiat, Charles Clavel, published a comprehensive denunciation of the French classical tradition; one of his arguments was that literary education was 'essentially aristocratic' and was kept up by the bourgeoisie as a mark of class exclusiveness.[1] When it came to primary education, the economists were on the side of expansion but were inhibited by their principles from calling on the state. Doctrinaires like Clavel maintained that 'the sole duty of governments towards education is complete abstention'.[2] In 1861, the Société d'économie politique staged a discussion of the question: the pure liberal position was held by many, but more realistic members argued that state action had to be accepted because of the historical situation in France, especially the need to counter the Church's influence.[3] In the event, some liberals persuaded themselves that education might be compulsory but not free,[4] others the reverse; few approached the question with enthusiasm.

Classic liberalism seems to have been incapable of making the imaginative leap to a concept of state action which went beyond the *loi Guizot*. The same is true of the pure political liberalism of the Orleanist school, whose leading younger representative, Prévost-Paradol, took remarkably little interest in popular education.[5] It needed an injection of the republican tradition to create the necessary idealism and energy, and it was the 'men of 1848', and their allies in industrial circles, who exerted the most effective pressure for improvement. Anticlericalism, restored to respectability by the change in government policy, was also an element in the alliance. The anticlerical newspaper *L'Opinion nationale*, founded in 1859, had close connections with the

[1] C. Clavel, *Lettres sur l'enseignement des collèges en France* (1859), pp. 183–5.
[2] C. Clavel, *Oeuvres diverses—éducation, morale, politique, littérature* (1871), i, p. 236.
[3] *Journal des Économistes*, 2nd series, xxix (1861), pp. 465–75. Cf. *De l'enseignement obligatoire. Discussion entre M. G. de Molinari . . . et M. Frédéric Passy* (1859).
[4] e.g. H. Rozy, *L'Instruction primaire obligatoire mais non gratuite* (1870) (Rozy was one of the first economics professors in the University).
[5] P. Guiral, *Prévost-Paradol (1829–1870). Pensée et action d'un libéral sous le Second Empire* (1955), pp. 551–6.

industrial milieux of Alsace, and had a writer, Charles Sauvestre, who specialized in scandalous anecdotes about nuns and Christian Brothers (and whose wife was active in the field of technical education for girls). Sauvestre and his paper enjoyed close relations with Duruy when the latter was in office, as indeed did Jules Simon, who was a personal friend of Duruy and shared many of his ideas.

Men of this kind could make their voices heard in Parliament, in the newspapers read by the liberal middle class, and even in the corridors of power. There were, of course, other writers and propagandists with more radical ideas, but their action was necessarily less effective, though they are often of interest in the light of future events. The positivists, for example, can hardly be neglected in view of their influence on Jules Ferry and the other founding fathers of the Third Republic; it was in April 1870 that Ferry made a later famous speech on equality in education.[1] Positivism took on a new coherence with the foundation of the review *La Philosophie positive* by Littré in 1867, but it cannot be said that the school's contribution to the debate on education was very large or striking. Like the economists, the positivists were hostile at this time to state action, and did not join in the call for free and compulsory education.[2]

The late sixties also saw the revival of working-class political activity, and the discussion of educational ideas was stimulated by the foundation of the First International. This subject has been dealt with comprehensively by Georges Duveau,[3] but one may pick out for special comment a group of writers who had been associated with the working-class newspaper *L'Atelier* in the forties, and who now founded the 'Bibliothèque utile', a series of cheap books for working-class readers. One of them, *De l'instruction en France* (1861), by Victor Guichard and Henri Leneveux, put the case for universal education. Another was Anthime Corbon's *De l'enseignement professionnel* (1859); as we shall see, other members of this group were to take a leading part in discussions of *enseignement professionnel* in the sixties.[4]

The 'Bibliothèque utile' group were on the left wing of

---

[1] For this whole subject, see L. Legrand, *L'Influence du positivisme dans l'oeuvre scolaire de Jules Ferry* (1961).
[2] Ibid., pp. 51, 58. [3] Duveau, *La Pensée ouvrière*.
[4] See below, pp. 195–6. Cf. Duveau, *La Vie ouvrière*, p. 4 57.

republicanism, and attacked the élitism of the lycées, wishing to establish true social equality through a common primary education for all classes. Leneveux thought that this would lead to the disappearance of class divisions, which were simply a relic of the past.[1] But perhaps the most radical ideas of the period were those of Paul Robin, a left-wing positivist, who started from the theory that every individual's faculties should be developed to the maximum, and came near to the principle of secondary education for all.[2]

Those who criticized the lycées often described the men they produced as a 'mandarinate' or 'caste' cut off from the people by their esoteric education—this was said by the liberal economists as well as the left.[3] An attack on the University itself followed naturally from this theme, and from the left it appeared as a stronghold of reaction rather than a refuge of liberalism. It was, after all, founded by the despotic Napoleon, was an instrument of state authority, and enforced religious orthodoxy. One severe critic was Clarisse Gauthier-Coignet, a feminist, Protestant, and libertarian who wrote one of the few radical books on education to appear in the fifties. She wanted to see an autonomous University, run by the teachers themselves, with political power decentralized to the communes.[4] Arsène Meunier too denounced the University as the 'worm-eaten debris of the imperial edifice'.[5]

Suspicion of state action and of the University, then, was one of the difficulties with which Duruy had to contend, and part of the context of his work as a reformer. He was aided by a current of opinion favouring the extension of popular education, which was flowing strongly even before he took office. But it would be wrong to assume that his attempt to move towards free and compulsory education had the support of all men of good will: there were objections of principle which still seemed convincing to responsible opinion. In the sixties Frenchmen awoke to the need to complete their system of popular education, but were still debating how this should be achieved.

[1] Guichard and Leneveux, *De l'instruction en France*, pp. 119–21.
[2] P. Robin, *De l'enseignement intégral* (1869), *passim*.
[3] e.g. Courcelle-Seneuil in *Journal des Économistes*, 2nd series, xlv (1864), pp. 176–7.
[4] C. Gauthier-Coignet, *De l'enseignement public, au point de vue de l'Université, de la commune et de l'État* (1856), pp. 93 ff., 317–28.
[5] Meunier, *Lutte du principe clérical*, p. 507.

2. THE CAMPAIGN FOR UNIVERSAL EDUCATION

The cautious improvements in primary education made by Rouland already indicate some stirrings of public opinion, and his teachers' essay competition was to provide material for reformers: one of its judges, Charles Robert, published two selections of extracts from the essays to illustrate the backwardness of rural education.[1] Robert, who was then an official of the Conseil d'État, was chosen by Duruy to be secretary-general of his ministry, and became in effect his chief adviser on primary education policy. Robert had a strong general interest in social problems, and like Duruy himself he had faith in the benevolence of the Emperor and the ability of his regime to satisfy the legitimate demands of the working class.

It is interesting to note that Robert was a native of Mulhouse, and a spokesman for the industrial interests of Alsace. In 1861 he published a book on compulsory education to support a petition which the Société industrielle of Mulhouse had submitted to the Senate. Robert justified compulsion by referring to the effects of the Anglo-French treaty, to the need for a better-educated working force, and to the fact that 'primary instruction and religious education, by moralizing the worker, give regularity to his labour, prevent debauchery and distress, and save the employer more money on the relief funds than the school and the teacher could cost him'.[2] The Mulhouse petition was accompanied by others from Strasbourg and Montbéliard, and the Conseil général of the Haut-Rhin had passed resolutions calling for compulsory education in 1858, 1859, and 1860; but in his account of these events Robert admitted that this awakening of public conscience was still confined to the east. The Senate rejected the petition without discussion, and Rouland made his opposition clear.[3] Even the arrival of Duruy did not make an immediate difference, for secondary education at first absorbed his attention.

An important turning-point was the publication of the govern-

[1] C. Robert, *De l'ignorance des populations ouvrières et rurales de la France et des causes qui tendent à la perpétuer* (1863) and *Plaintes et voeux présentés par les instituteurs publics en 1861 sur la situation des maisons d'école, du mobilier et du matériel classiques* (1864).
[2] C. Robert, *De la nécessité de rendre l'instruction primaire obligatoire en France et des moyens pratiques à employer dans ce but* (1861), p. 8.
[3] C. Robert, *L'Instruction obligatoire* (1871), pp. 15–24.

ment's report on the 'state of the Empire' to the new Parliament elected in 1863. This included a section on education which, while stressing the progress made in recent years, admitted that there were still 1,018 communes without schools of any kind, and estimated that 600,000 children were escaping schooling altogether. This figure was naturally seized on by the advocates of compulsion —some of them asserting that the true figure should be around 800,000—and it was repeated again and again in Simon's writings, along with other significant statistics like the proportion of illiterate conscripts (27·4 per cent in 1862) and the remarkable discrepancies in literacy between different parts of France, which were the subject of a study presented to the Institute in 1864 by General Morin.[1] Morin's figures also impressed Duruy, who had maps made showing the departments in various shades of grey.

In Parliament, the opposition put down an amendment to the address demanding the complete abolition of fees. The speakers on this included Havin (director of the anticlerical newspaper *Le Siècle*) and Simon, who developed another favourite theme: the contrast between the government's prodigal spending on the army and on prestige projects like the new Opéra and its meanness towards education. In *L'École* Simon asserted, again using Morin's calculations, that 29·5 per cent of the budget went on military expenditure, only 1·1 per cent on education.[2] The opposition also campaigned in 1864 for the improvement of girls' education, Carnot speaking on this in Parliament and Simon publishing an article in the *Revue des Deux Mondes* which underlined the wretched position of lay schoolmistresses and the high rate of female illiteracy revealed by the marriage registers—44 per cent generally, but 48 per cent if rural areas only were counted. Simon blamed this backwardness partly on the mediocrity of the teaching orders, and demanded the abolition of the 'letter of obedience'; the anticlerical side of the campaign was clear from the start.[3]

Duruy could therefore expect some support for legislation to extend the scope of primary education. But it was, of course, support from the small parliamentary opposition, and here lay the dilemma which confronted him throughout his period in office. It

[1] See Simon, *L'École*, pp. 209–26, and below, p. 159.
[2] *L'Instruction populaire en France. Débats parlementaires* (n.d.), pp. 137–8; Simon, *L'École*, p. 109.
[3] *Revue des Deux Mondes*, 2nd period, lii (1864), pp. 948–68.

was not these men that he had to persuade, but his colleagues in the government, the officials of the Conseil d'État, and the conservative majority in Parliament. Their priorities were the preservation of the regime, the maintenance of public order, sound public finance, and (increasingly, as the Empire came under stronger attack from the left) conciliation of the Church. The more progressive Duruy's measures, the more suspicious they became. His only asset was Napoleon's willingness to keep him in office, though not to support him on every occasion.

Duruy tried to base all his policies on a sound foundation of statistics and other information gathered at home and abroad. In 1863, he set on foot the collection of data for a complete statistical picture of primary education—by the time he left office, the same had been done for higher and secondary education. In 1864, he sent all the *inspecteurs d'académie* a long questionnaire to establish the state of primary education in the provinces and to elicit their views on how it might be improved. Reports were also compiled on Germany and other countries, especially those where compulsory education was the practice.[1] According to Robert, Duruy thought compulsion the first priority, but soon saw that it could not be applied fairly without the abolition of fees.[2] By the end of 1864, he was ready to act, and began to sound out his colleagues; at this stage he had three projects, combining compulsion, free education, and local option in different ways in order to cope with various levels of opposition.[3]

In the event, he underestimated this opposition and badly over-reached himself. In February 1865, in his speech opening Parliament, Napoleon declared that 'in the country of universal suffrage, every citizen should be able to read and write', and promised a bill to extend primary education. Duruy believed that he had won the Emperor over, especially as a report which he had prepared justifying the free and compulsory principles came back from Napoleon with his approval minuted. This report was a document of remarkable breadth of views, and dealt scathingly with the conventional conservative arguments. Duruy saw compulsory education as the complement of universal suffrage, and argued that by introducing it the government would be furthering social progress and responding to the desire of the masses. He laid down

---

[1] By Baudouin and Monnier: see Bibliography, section II E.
[2] Robert, *L'Instruction obligatoire*, pp. 45–6.   [3] Ibid., pp. 49–53.

the principle that 'popular instruction is a great public service', to be paid for by the community as a whole. 'A great movement is carrying humanity towards the domination of the material world through science, and the conquest of well-being through wealth,' he concluded; France must regain her position at the head of this movement by fortifying 'the intelligence and morality of her laborious classes. Society forms an immense pyramid: the wider, higher, and more solid the base, the stronger and more secure are the intermediate levels, and the higher too will the peak climb into the light.'[1]

In March, Duruy published this report in the official *Moniteur*, which implied that it reflected government policy. But later the same day a disavowal was published; it was explained that the report expressed only Duruy's personal views, and that the bill being considered by the government was of more modest scope. A month later, when the question was debated in Parliament, the government spokesman again repudiated Duruy's views. This was a humiliation for Duruy; he offered his resignation to Napoleon, but it was refused, and he stayed in office having learnt like Fortoul that a minister of education was free to make ambitious plans but usually lacked the political weight to push them through.[2]

The bill which Duruy had ready for Parliament did not go quite as far as he wished: the principle of free and compulsory education would have been made adoptive, each local council deciding for itself whether to apply it. But the bill was radical in another way, as it would have modified the *loi Falloux* by allowing individuals to open private schools without having a teaching qualification.[3] This extension of 'liberty of teaching' was characteristic of Duruy: he wanted a strong state system free of clerical interference, but minimal state control of the private sector; the Church should have the same rights as private individuals, but no special privileges. In the more modest bill which eventually became the law of 10 April 1867, these controversial proposals were dropped. The law made significant changes in two areas. First, it was made easier for councils to abolish fees altogether if they chose, by altering the system of financing schools and making a special fund available

---

[1] *L'Administration de l'instruction publique de 1863 à 1869. Ministère de S.E. M. Duruy* (n.d.), pp. 186–7, 211–12.

[2] Cf. Gontard, *Les Écoles primaires de la France bourgeoise*, pp. 170 ff.

[3] Robert, *L'Instruction obligatoire*, pp. 147–54.

for encouraging the change; Duruy had already abolished in 1866 the quota on free places imposed in 1853.[1] Second, the law of 1867 lowered the population level at which communes had to provide a separate girls' school from 800 to 500 (this change had been planned by Rouland in 1862), and there were various improvements in the condition of women teachers; for the first time, they had a minimum salary fixed by law, though it was lower than that for men. This led to significant improvements in girls' education, and two-thirds of the new schools set up as a result of the law were taught by lay schoolmistresses.[2]

The provision of the law which aroused most passion was an incidental one concerning the *engagement décennal*. This was the promise to teach for ten years which teachers in public schools made in return for exemption from military service. By convention, the exemption had extended to all members of teaching orders, whether they were teaching in public or private schools. Duruy now tried to limit this privilege to public teachers. He had logic on his side, and patriotic feeling at a time when the Prussian threat was leading the government to consider changing the system of military service; but his action was inevitably seen as a provocation by the Church, whose representatives in Parliament had already marked Duruy down as an enemy and were working for his downfall. He did not improve matters by an angry outburst denouncing the fact that heads of religious orders could create exemptions 'with three yards of black or grey cloth'.[3] He won his point in the 1867 law, but in practice the Christian Brothers continued to enjoy their traditional immunity.[4] It is perhaps surprising that Duruy did not try to abolish the letter of obedience —Simon introduced an amendment to the bill directed at this 'privilege of ignorance'.[5]

Duruy's law, though less than he wanted, was the first real step forward since 1850, and was not his only contribution to primary education. Although he lacked personal experience in this field, and did not give it the same detailed attention as he did his reforms in secondary education, he did try to broaden its base and raise its

---

[1] Decree of 28 Mar. 1866.

[2] Maurain, *La Politique ecclésiastique*, pp. 774–8. Duruy's first bill also obliged every town larger than 2,000 inhabitants to maintain a *salle d'asile*, but this did not appear in the law.

[3] Gontard, op. cit., p. 180.   [4] Rigault, *Histoire générale*, v, pp. 380–6.

[5] *L'Instruction populaire en France. Débats parlementaires*, p. 231.

level. He recommended that the more informal and child-centred methods of the *salles d'asile* should be extended to the primary schools.[1] He made history and geography compulsory subjects, and introduced gymnastics.[2] He laid down a programme of agricultural education, and provided training in the subject in the *écoles normales*.[3] This seems to have had little permanent effect, but Duruy attached great importance to it as a means of making rural schools more attractive to parents. He also had plans for central schools of agronomy and horticulture.

In an attempt to encourage children to stay on at school, Duruy urged rectors to set up a leaving examination (*certificat d'études primaires*) so that those who stayed till the end would have something to show for it. He also suggested *écoles de persévérance* for older pupils, which would have been a revival of the higher primary schools (as Simon was demanding).[4] Other policies of Duruy broke new ground: he encouraged the provision of hot meals in *salles d'asile*,[5] and in the 1867 law introduced *caisses d'écoles*. These were funds to be financed by voluntary contributions as well as public money, and were intended to encourage school attendance by giving prizes and financial help to poor families.

Like most ministers of education, Duruy saw that the key to real improvement was the teachers, and he succeeded in getting them on his side and making them feel that their services were valued. One example of this was his use of the Exhibition in Paris in 1867. The Exhibition had a section on education, for which Charles Robert was mainly responsible, and Duruy, who lost no chance of reaching public opinion, used it to the utmost to demonstrate the achievements of his ministry. In addition, a special visit was arranged by a group of 700 teachers from all over France, who were given a series of lectures on educational subjects by Duruy's experts, and received by the Emperor himself. This symbolized the 'definitive rehabilitation of the lay teachers, the end of the long disgrace that had followed the *loi Falloux*';[6] the teachers' gratitude was reflected in the enthusiasm with which they undertook the voluntary work of running adult courses, a success of Duruy's

[1] Circular to prefects, 12 May 1867.
[2] Law of 10 Apr. 1867; decree of 3 Feb. 1869.
[3] *Arrêté* of 30 Dec. 1867.   [4] Circulars of 20 Aug. 1866, 30 Oct. 1867.
[5] Circular to prefects, 14 June 1869.   [6] Gontard, op. cit., p. 187.

ministry which will be dealt with in the next section. Duruy also gave thought to the future, reorganizing the *écoles normales* and liberalizing their regime, and urging more departments to set up *écoles normales* for girls—there were still only eleven in 1863.[1]

Duruy's departure in 1869 was not quite the end of the Second Empire's interest in primary education: his successor Bourbeau introduced a bill making all public education free, but this soon ran into difficulties both in government circles and in Parliament, and Bourbeau gave way to the conservative Segris. By 1870, however, partly as a result of the interest and controversy provoked by Duruy's policies, public consciousness of educational problems and public support for extending primary education were far stronger than at the beginning of the decade. New forces, too, had appeared on the scene, of which the most significant was Jean Macé's Ligue de l'Enseignement.

Jean Macé was a republican who, after the failure of the hopes of 1848, had retired to teach in a girls' boarding-school at Beblenheim in Alsace. He first became known in the sixties as an author of children's books, and was then active in Alsace in the movement to encourage 'popular libraries'. In 1866, in the columns of *L'Opinion nationale*, he launched the idea (borrowed from Belgium) of a league uniting all men of good will who supported the cause of popular education; it would be an 'educational Landwehr' standing behind the regular army of teachers.[2] The idea obviously touched a responsive chord: local 'circles' of the League were formed more or less spontaneously, and by the end of 1867 there were nearly 5,000 members. The propaganda of the League liked to dwell on the fact that the first three members were a policeman, a railway guard, and a stone-cutter, but the majority of members were middle class. In Rouen, for example, the League was composed mainly of professional men, merchants, and manufacturers, and even included liberal Bonapartist officials and the local deputy.[3] More commonly, the League was taken up by local groups of republican politicians and journalists, as it offered possibilities of political action as well as representing a cause at the centre of republican idealism. There were close connections in many places

[1] Decree of 2 July 1866; circular to prefects, 6 July 1869.
[2] J. Macé, *La Ligue de l'Enseignement à Beblenheim 1862–1870* (1890) (the principal source for what follows), p. 211.
[3] M. Boivin, 'Les Origines de la Ligue de l'Enseignement en Seine-Inférieure 1866–1871', *Revue d'histoire économique et sociale*, xlvi (1968), pp. 207–8, 214.

with Masonic lodges, and the League soon became the target of clerical attacks. Even Duruy was suspicious of it at first.[1]

Quasi-political organizations were still looked on with great suspicion, and to ensure the survival of the League Macé directed it cautiously. In principle, it simply co-ordinated the action of the local circles without having policies of its own, and the League itself did not campaign for universal education. Macé encouraged the circles to second the efforts of the lay public schools, not to found schools of their own; at Le Havre, for example, the circle tried to persuade reluctant parents to use the schools, made gifts of clothing and stationery to the poor, and gave prizes for regular attendance.[2] Other circles did the same, but the main practical effort in most towns was the organization of evening courses for adults. Several local circles also organized political campaigns. The Le Havre group initiated a campaign for free and compulsory education in 1870, and was supported by those in Mulhouse, Colmar, Sainte-Marie-aux-Mines, and Rouen.[3] Also in 1870, a 'propaganda committee' based on the Strasbourg circle of the League organized a petition for universal education which attracted 300,000 signatures from all parts of France; this petition, the culmination of the primary education campaign under the Empire, was in support of a bill introduced in Parliament by Simon.

Once more, the impulse came from eastern France, and the success of the League was in fact limited to certain areas. In 1870, there were 59 circles and 17,856 members; but 5,846 of the members were in the east. There were 5,543 in the south, including two large circles in Marseilles, and 2,718 in the west, where the League was strong in the industrial Seine-Inférieure. There was also an influential circle at Paris. But virtually no impact had been made on the rural west and centre, or on the industrial areas of the north, where Catholic influence was strong and public opinion lethargic on educational matters.[4]

The activities of the League and its circles show new forces breaking the surface of political life. In many major towns, there was a democratic opposition within sight of taking municipal

---

[1] Gerbod, *La Condition universitaire*, p. 505.
[2] Boivin, in *Revue d'histoire économique et sociale*, xlvi (1968), pp. 223–4.
[3] Robert, *L'Instruction obligatoire*, pp. 86–8.
[4] Macé, op. cit., pp. 476–81.

power; these groups would undoubtedly exploit municipal autonomy to alter educational policy, and since the imposition of compulsory education was not within their power they would seek above all to take the schools out of the hands of the teaching orders. If the Empire had survived, there would probably have been much friction over this question, and in some towns the shift to the left was already apparent. At Saint-Étienne, for example, the municipal council adopted a policy of balance between lay and 'congregational' schools in 1865. Previously all the schools except one had been run by orders; now all new schools were lay, fees were abolished, and a hard line was taken towards the orders—the council insisted, for example, on all assistant teachers having the *brevet* as well as the head.[1] At Lille, all the schools of the Christian Brothers were laicized in 1868.[2] At Bordeaux, a lay school opened in 1864 was deliberately non-denominational, and this seems to have been the case in several towns.[3] It was illegal for schools, whether public or private, to exclude religious teaching altogether, but some local groups nevertheless opened private secular schools. We hear of this at Épinal (where the local circle of the League took the initiative), Marseilles, and Saint-Étienne.[4] At Lyons, where the municipality was solidly conservative, a militantly anticlerical 'Société d'instruction libre et laïque' created three such schools in 1870. The government of the Second Empire failed to act against them, but they were the cause of a major political conflict in the seventies.[5]

The men involved in these enterprises were those who were to seize power in their towns when the Empire collapsed. It is obvious from their actions then, and from the history of the Paris Commune, that both radical republicans and the urban working class thought the secularization of education an essential and urgent democratic

---

[1] M. Devun, 'La Politique scolaire de la ville de Saint-Étienne du Premier Empire à la Troisième République', *Actes du 89e Congrès National des Sociétés Savantes. Lyon, 1964. Section d'histoire moderne et contemporaine*, ii (1965), pp. 580–5.

[2] B. Ménager, *La Laïcisation des écoles communales dans le département du Nord (1879–1899)* (1971), pp. 98–9.

[3] L. Desgraves and G. Dupeux, *Bordeaux au XIXe siècle* (1969), pp. 459–60.

[4] P. Zind, *L'Enseignement religieux dans l'instruction primaire publique en France de 1850 à 1873* (1971), p. 228.

[5] Gontard, *Les Écoles primaires de la France bourgeoise*, p. 199, and 'Une Bataille scolaire au XIXe siècle: l'affaire des écoles primaires laïques de Lyon (1869–1873)', *Cahiers d'histoire*, iii (1958), pp. 271–3.

task. The last years of the Empire saw a revival of traditional anticlericalism, and a polarization of political and religious attitudes which was to continue in the seventies and determine the treatment of educational questions. Even the history of Duruy's ministry had suggested that anticlericalism was inseparable from the complex of ideals which led men to work for the extension of popular education. It is possible that the Empire, which knew how to keep the Church under firm control, might have been able to initiate educational progress without unleashing religious conflict at the same time. But any chance of this was lost when the regime failed to rise to the challenge offered by Duruy in 1865.

3. LITERACY AND POPULAR CULTURE

The 1860s, the period when the significance of universal suffrage became clear and when the railways were opening up the country-side and bringing greater national uniformity, also saw the arrival of mass literacy as a social fact and a problem. Those who thought about education sought answers to some of the practical problems which it posed, and were also led to reflect on the relations between education, class, and culture. Mass literacy was still, of course, very imperfect. The majority of children did now attend school, but often irregularly and only for a few years. 'Half at least of the children on the register belong to the school only on paper,' said Louis Hachette; and nine-tenths of those who learnt to read did not use their skill and soon forgot it.[1] As a bookseller and publisher, Hachette had a special interest in the question, but he was not alone in urging that literacy must be consolidated by providing suitable reading matter and organizing evening courses so that adults and adolescents would not lose touch with education altogether.

The encouragement of these 'adult courses' was one of the achievements of Duruy's ministry. The idea of evening courses was not in itself new. Technical education for workers had long been given in this form, by municipalities and philanthropic societies, and Paris had two of the latter—the Association poly-technique founded in 1830, and the Association philotechnique which split off from it in 1848. These associations had many distinguished supporters, and both Rouland and Duruy presided at their annual prize-givings. But Duruy tried also to encourage

[1] L. Hachette, *L'Instruction populaire et le suffrage universel* (1861), pp. 13–14.

courses which would take adult education into the rural communes, and would normally be conducted by the *instituteurs* after their day's work. He relied essentially on voluntary effort by the teachers; little money was available for paying fees, but Duruy did his best by awarding prizes and medals and by less tangible marks of official favour for those who distinguished themselves in this way. The teachers seem to have responded to Duruy's appeals with genuine enthusiasm, although this could not have sustained the movement for more than a few years. The campaign for adult courses got going in 1865, and although the statistics published by Duruy are rather untrustworthy it is clear that there was a remarkable expansion. In 1863, there were 4,986 courses for men and 182 for women, with 115,673 and 9,974 pupils respectively. By 1869 there were 28,172 courses for men and 5,466 for women, and the figures for pupils were 678,753 (it had been higher in 1868) and 114,383.[1] These figures included privately run courses—the activity of the Ligue de l'Enseignement in this field has already been mentioned—and the religious orders also played their part.

Some of these courses were vocational, others on subjects of general interest; but a large number seem to have been directed at those who had recently left school, and concentrated on the elements of literacy. It was claimed that of 595,506 students attending in 1866, 249,199 were completely or virtually illiterate at the start, but only 17,940 remained partly illiterate at the end; in 1867, 357,406 of the 829,555 attending were illiterate.[2] Duruy believed that the improvement in the literacy of conscripts—between 1850 and 1860 it rose from 64·6 per cent to 70·1 per cent, but by 1868 was already 80 per cent—could be attributed to this campaign directed at adolescents;[3] the adult courses were perhaps doing the same work here as Sunday schools in Britain.

Once basic literacy was achieved, what use would peasant and working-class readers make of it? This was a question which preoccupied most of those who thought about education. The old idea that it was better for the poor not to read at all was disappearing, but both liberals and conservatives still saw popular

[1] *Statistique comparée de l'enseignement primaire (1829–1877)*, pp. cxl–cxli; Rohr, *Victor Duruy*, pp. 149–56.

[2] L. Maggiolo, *Souvenir des conférences pédagogiques de la Sorbonne. Septembre 1867. Des cours d'adultes—Des bibliothèques scolaires—Du régime disciplinaire et des concours* (1868), p. 51.

[3] Duruy, *Notes et souvenirs*, i, pp. 229–34.

taste as something that could be moulded and directed from above rather than left to the readers themselves or to commercial interests. The commercial interests were of course active, though the book trade was hampered by legal restrictions which made it difficult to sell books outside the large towns; the removal of these controls was one aim of campaigners like Simon and Hachette, and one of the first acts of the republicans in 1870. Traditionally, the countryside relied for the supply of books on itinerant chapmen (*colporteurs*), but their numbers were now declining, and they were not to survive the Second Empire for long. They suffered from government control, from the coming of the railways, which opened new channels for the distribution of books and periodicals, and from the growing sophistication of public taste.[1] The staple fare of the chapmen had been of a kind established for centuries, almanacs and the volumes of stories and folk wisdom known as the *Bibliothèque bleue*. These were now giving way to cheap novels of a sentimental or melodramatic kind. Moreover, the same kind of reading matter could now be provided by cheap newspapers, using the railways to establish a national circulation; the *Petit journal*, founded in 1863, was the first and most successful of these popular newspapers based on stories and anecdotes.[2]

These novels and newspapers were what conservatives called 'bad' books. The most energetic efforts to replace them with good ones were those inspired by religion. In an article published in 1863, Simon listed the numerous charitable societies engaged in distributing tracts and running periodicals; the Société de Saint-Vincent-de-Paul, for example, published 125,000 copies monthly of its *Petites lectures illustrées*, and Protestants were also very active in this work.[3] On the liberal and democratic side, however, the effort went into encouraging the growth of lending libraries rather than sponsoring publications. There was no tradition in France of municipal lending libraries, and an attempt to found a 'Société des Bibliothèques communales' in 1850 had failed. In 1861–2, however, there was a wave of activity. In 1861, the Bibliothèque des Amis de l'Instruction was founded in Paris; this was a working-class initiative inspired by the well-developed reading habits of the

---

[1] See J.-J. Darmon, *Le Colportage de librairie en France sous le Second Empire* (1972).

[2] Ibid., pp. 192 ff.

[3] *Revue des Deux Mondes*, 2nd period, xlvii (1863), pp. 363–4.

Paris artisans.[1] In 1862, perhaps responding to the demands of the teachers in his essay competition, Rouland issued a regulation requiring every school to have a *bibliothèque scolaire* looked after by the teacher; some books would be sent from Paris, others might be acquired locally, and all except school textbooks would be available for lending to parents. Circulars of Rouland in 1859 and 1860 had already paved the way for this regulation, which remained the basis of public library provision for the rest of the century. In 1865, there were 4,833 school libraries with 180,854 books; in 1869, 14,395 libraries and 1,239,165 books.[2]

All books in these libraries had to be officially approved, and it is not surprising that liberals saw them as 'an instrument of government rather than of civilization'.[3] The year 1862 also saw the foundation of the Société Franklin, a private body supported by philanthropists of all political parties, but with a strong liberal tendency; Robert and Simon were its moving spirits. The aim of the society was to encourage and co-ordinate the efforts of local libraries, and to help them by compiling lists of suitable books. By 1870, there were 817 libraries affiliated to the society, of which 341 were run by municipal councils, 111 by societies founded for the purpose, and 46 by circles of the Ligue de l'Enseignement. As might be expected, the library movement was especially strong in eastern France.[4] This was partly the work of Jean Macé, whose main public activity before founding the League was the organiza- tion of the Société des bibliothèques communales du Haut-Rhin. Started in 1863, the society tried to stimulate local initiative through propaganda and publicity, and was the model on which Macé based the League itself.[5]

The library movement had its opponents, for it was seen as a threat to the influence of the Church, and could be denounced as a social menace if books by dangerous authors appeared on the shelves. In 1867, the Senate debated a conservative petition against a library at Saint-Étienne which offered its readers books by Voltaire,

[1] Duveau, *La Vie ouvrière*, p. 456.
[2] Circulars of 25 July 1859, 31 May 1860 and *arrêté* of 1 June 1862; J. Hassenforder, *Développement comparé des bibliothèques publiques en France, en Grande-Bretagne et aux États-Unis dans la seconde moitié du XIXe siècle (1850–1914)* (1967), p. 55.
[3] Simon in *Revue des Deux Mondes*, 2nd period, xlvii (1863), p. 369.
[4] Hassenforder, op. cit., pp. 53–4.
[5] Macé, *La Ligue de l'Enseignement*, pp. 74 ff.

Rousseau, Proudhon, Michelet, Renan, and Balzac, among others. The Senate at this time saw several clerical attacks on the new intellectual tendencies of the sixties, and on this occasion as on others free thought found a vigorous champion in the writer Sainte-Beuve.[1]

The Société Franklin tried to recommend books which were known to have popular appeal rather than to promote a special type of book written for workers, for experience showed that books too obviously designed to force moral lessons on their readers were rejected. But they hoped that in due course a 'popular literature' would emerge. By this they meant not the old *Bibliothèque bleue* (though one may detect some nostalgia for the passing of the old popular and oral culture: critics like Charles Nisard and Champfleury were beginning their systematic study, and Fortoul had sponsored a collection of French popular songs), but books written for the working class by sympathetic intellectuals who could capture the right tone. It was generally assumed that in the long run universal education would mean universal access to high culture, but that in the meantime something simpler was needed. Simon, however, believed that the newly literate could at once appreciate the French classics, that 'nothing is too good for the people', and that Corneille and Racine could be genuinely popular.[2]

The liberals were anxious not to appear condescending, but their own didactic aims were often barely concealed. The economists, in particular, believed that if only workers could grasp the principles of political economy they would cease to agitate for social change, and they tried to promote knowledge of economics through pamphlets and adult courses. Duruy supported this cause, and like many French observers he was impressed by the calm of the Lancashire workers during the cotton crisis of the sixties, and attributed it to their superior education. Another form of didacticism was the ideology of 'self-help'. Simon, Robert, and Michelet thought that biographies of men like Arkwright and the Stephensons, who had risen from humble origins to be great benefactors of humanity, were an ideal form of popular literature—the very name

[1] R. Bellet, 'Une Bataille culturelle, provinciale et nationale, à propos des bons auteurs pour bibliothèques populaires (janvier–juin 1867)', *Revue des sciences humaines*, xxxiv (1969), pp. 453–73.

[2] J. Simon, *Les Bibliothèques populaires* (1865), p. 5; cf. *L'École*, pp. 416–17.

of the Société Franklin reflected this approach. Quite a few biographies of this kind were published, and, as a review of Mignet's life of Franklin said in 1849, 'no form of popular teaching could be more intelligible and profitable, for it is of a kind to awaken truly sound reflections on the dignity of man and the power of labour, and finds daily application among the vicissitudes of a life of toil'.[1] Details given by Macé of the books bought for libraries in Alsace suggest that biographies were genuinely popular with working-class readers, along with novels and stories, travel books, history (especially of the Revolution and Napoleon), popularizations of science, and works dealing with the practical aspects of industry and agriculture. Collections like the *Bibliothèque utile*, and illustrated periodicals like the *Magasin pittoresque*, also met this last demand.[2]

Thus not all workers read cheap novels, and perhaps there was no harm in it if they did. Conservatives like de l'Étang, who wanted to replace *colportage* by a system of distributing 'good' books through the village teachers, did indeed condemn novels for discontenting people with their lot by transporting them into a world of fantasy[3] (the idea that escapist literature might rather reconcile them to their lot did not occur to him); but those with more direct experience of the working class were more tolerant. Leneveux pointed out that reading novels at least kept literacy alive, and that instructive information could be got over in novel form.[4] Émile Levasseur believed that novel-reading was simply an initial stage in the flowering of intellectual interest; the publishers of cheap books had begun with novels, but now that they had created a public with the taste for reading they were moving on to more serious works.[5] Levasseur also made the justified comment that in reading mediocre novels the working class was only following the example of the bourgeoisie. The friends of the working class were rather too inclined to set it heroic standards,

---

[1] H. Desprez in *Revue des Deux Mondes*, new period, i (1849), p. 782. Smiles's *Self-Help* was translated in 1865, and was in a fourth edition by 1869; his life of the Stephensons was translated in 1868.

[2] Macé, *La Ligue de l'Enseignement*, pp. 120 ff.; Duveau, *La Pensée ouvrière*, pp. 299–302.

[3] E. A. de l'Étang, *Des livres utiles et du colportage comme moyen d'avancement moral et intellectuel des classes rurales et ouvrières* (1866), pp. 16–17.

[4] Guichard and Leneveux, *De l'instruction en France*, pp. 110–11.

[5] É. Levasseur, *Histoire des classes ouvrières en France depuis 1789 jusqu'à nos jours* (1867), ii, pp. 490–1, 550.

expecting the worker who returned from twelve hours' labour at once to depart for an evening course or to take up an improving book.

Thus some of the problems created by mass literacy were being considered. Could the barely literate masses be expected to participate in the traditional high culture of the nation? Would they have to be content with a bastardized version of middle-class culture, or could a distinctively popular culture emerge? Was popular taste to be abandoned to commercial exploitation, or might it be guided on to a more healthy path by those with the interests of the masses at heart? Another sort of question was how the relations between the classes would change when education was no longer the monopoly of an élite. If the cultural gap between the classes was closed, what would happen to the social leadership of the middle class? As we have seen, many republicans thought that the classes would fuse together if everyone passed through a common education, and they attacked the classics for maintaining an artificial cultural barrier and creating a 'mandarinate'.

The conservative view, of course, was that maintaining a cultural gap was one of the functions of secondary education, since (as the *lycéens* of Rouen were told at their prize-giving in 1866) 'in a country where the political edifice rests on universal suffrage, . . . power is reserved to those whom a strong classical education has raised above their fellow-men.'[1] In another prize-giving speech, Désiré Nisard urged the pupils to work harder to keep ahead of advancing democracy, so that they would 'remain the first among equals through the accepted privilege of a more elevated education. . . . The dialogue between those who emerge from the primary schools and from our lycées would be embarrassing if the former did not feel the ascendancy of the latter.'[2] The idea that in a democratic society those with secondary education formed a legitimate élite, an 'aristocracy of intelligence', was also expressed by Duruy, and became a commonplace of the Third Republic.

The liberal Clavel, however, argued that the cult of the classics endangered the leadership of the élite because of the 'spirit of caste' which it created. Those who had a classical education were

[1] Marquis de Belbeuf, *Discours prononcé le 7 août 1866 à la distribution solennelle des prix au lycée impérial de Rouen* (1866), pp. 3–4.

[2] D. Nisard, *Discours académiques et universitaires (1852–1868)* (1884), pp. 279–80.

no longer able to communicate with the masses or understand their needs, and so were powerless to influence them. The lack of a popular literature by which the minds of the people might be reached was due to 'the system of public education which has raised a barrier between the cultured classes and the remainder of the nation'. Only when there was 'community of culture' would the 'intellectual aristocracy' be truly accepted and influential.[1] Clavel also noted how even those of modest social origins were alienated from their background by classical education,[2] a theme developed by the democratic theorist Vacherot. Parents, he said, make great efforts to send their sons to the lycée, 'but no sooner have the sons tasted these fruits reserved for the aristocracy than for the most part they disavow their parents, and they are noted for their hard and scornful attitude in the ranks to which they have been raised by the weary arms of their heroic families. What a triumph for democracy!'[3]

Clavel saw the problem from a middle-class point of view, and used his argument to justify modernizing secondary education. For more radical thought based on the same perceptions we must turn to the writings of Michelet. Michelet was one of those who had risen from the people, but he had not forgotten it. His mystic belief in the people and their qualities was the inspiration of his historical work, and the subject of his democratic tract *Le Peuple* (1846). In this he deplored the divorce between the people and the educated classes, and consequently between 'instinct' and 'reflection'. Education as then organized killed 'instinct', and created a vulgar and rootless middle class. The problem was to bring instinct and reflection together again, and only the school attended by rich and poor alike could do this. 'What is the first part of politics?' asked Michelet; 'Education. The second? Education. And the third? Education.'[4] And in a famous series of lectures on the eve of the 1848 Revolution he urged his students to go down to the people—'a crusade of men going to meet other men'—and learn from their wisdom.[5]

Michelet had hoped that his own works could bind the classes

---

[1] Clavel, *Lettres sur l'enseignement des collèges*, pp. 212–15, and *Oeuvres diverses*, ii, pp. 113–16.
[2] *Oeuvres diverses*, ii, pp. 121–3, 135.
[3] É. Vacherot, *La Démocratie* (1860), p. 98.
[4] J. Michelet, *Le Peuple* (ed. L. Refort, 1946), pp. 131, 151 ff., 264–6, 269.
[5] J. Michelet, *L'Étudiant* (1899), pp. 26, 29 ff., 195–6.

together by giving them a common national legend, but he was forced to recognize that though his heart lay with the people he could no longer communicate with them. For 'the completely abstract culture which we are given dried me up long ago. . . . That is why . . . I have never attained the ideal of grandiose simplicity which I had before my mind.'[1] When I die, he said, 'Comment viendront les livres populaires?' will be found written on my heart.[2] For Michelet, the problems of 'popular literature' and of cultural alienation through education were bound together by deeply felt personal experience, and his feelings must have been those of many young men who felt the urge to put their science and learning at the service of democracy, or who exchanged the peasant's smock for the black coat of the *instituteur*. Michelet's treatise on education, *Nos fils*, appeared just before the end of the Empire, and shows how some of the best minds of the age were preoccupied by the still relevant problems of the consequences of mass literacy and of an educational system which promoted social mobility.

---

[1] *Le Peuple*, p. 119. [2] J. Michelet, *Nos fils* (1870), p. 363.

CHAPTER EIGHT

Primary education in the 1860s

Two impressionistic sources help us to gain a picture of what primary schools were like in the sixties: the essays submitted by teachers for Rouland's competition, and the reports, later printed, which the *inspecteurs d'académie* sent in response to Duruy's questionnaire in 1864. These can be compared with the reports commissioned by Guizot when he introduced his law, and they leave no doubt of the immense progress which had been made. Although the teachers still complained about the material conditions in which they had to work—we hear of schools in stables and unsuitable rooms, of mud floors, of children having to bring their own firewood for the stove, of schools without desks to write on—these conditions were now the exception, not the rule, and examples nearly always come from poor and backward departments like the Corrèze, where 'seven-eighths of the classrooms are badly laid out, dark, low, often unhealthy, and so small that they are the despair of masters who aim at a methodic organization of their teaching'.[1]

Standards for new school buildings had now been laid down. From 1858, the plans of new schools had to be approved by the ministry before a subsidy would be paid; ventilation had to be provided, and a space standard of four cubic metres per child was prescribed. This measure, based on similar regulations for *salles d'asile* in 1855, marked a new extension of central government action.[2] The efforts of the communes to build schools were already provoking new complaints from the teachers—that they failed to anticipate future demand, or that they built 'little châteaux' with impressive façades but cramped interiors. And one complaint frequently echoed was, 'What a contrast between the presbytery and the school! The presbytery is built in bourgeois style, but the school lodging is designed for a proletarian.'[3]

[1] *État de l'instruction primaire en 1864*, i, p. 508; cf. Robert, *Plaintes et voeux*, p. 12.

[2] *Arrêté* of 14 July and circular of 30 July 1858; decree of 21 Mar. 1855.

[3] Robert, *Plaintes et voeux*, pp. 24–6, 29.

For there is plenty of evidence, even in the published inspectors' reports, for tension between teachers and *curés*, particularly where the teacher was expected to assist in church services; several inspectors demanded that this practice should now be ended. The teachers' restiveness was growing, and so was their consciousness of themselves as a force in the nation—it was in the sixties that the term *instituteur* finally replaced *maître d'école*.[1] But we should not necessarily think of them as republicans—little of the spirit of 1848 was left by the sixties[2]—or militant secularists. The teachers were trained in *écoles normales* where the tone was strongly religious and authoritarian, and their superiors continually impressed on them the duty of subordination and the need to set an example of conduct and piety.[3] The teacher might well be conscious of his dignity and his role as the bearer of enlightenment, but the feeling that he was an agent of the state, and a member of a disciplined and hierarchical service, must have been equally strong. From 1863, the government even laid down what furniture was to be supplied to the new teacher (walnut in the living room, deal in the kitchen),[4] and in return for this solicitude he was expected, by Duruy no less than by other ministers, to use his moral influence in the government's interest at election times.[5]

Where teaching methods and the organization of schools are concerned, the best information for this period is on Paris, where the schools came under the influence of Octave Gréard, one of the University's dominating figures under the Third Republic. Gréard, one of the brilliant generation of students who had been at the École Normale during the Second Republic, had been a teacher in the lycées until in 1864 Duruy appointed him *inspecteur d'académie* in Paris. Duruy had a gift for choosing talented subordinates; in 1865 Gréard was put in charge of the education service in the Seine department, a post which he retained until 1879. The schools in

[1] Prost, *Histoire de l'enseignement en France*, p. 147.

[2] Cf. V. Wright, 'L'Enseignement primaire dans les Basses-Pyrénées de 1848 à 1870', *Bulletin de la Société des Sciences, Lettres et Arts de Pau*, 4th series, iv (1969), pp. 172–3; Lévêque, in *Annales de Bourgogne*, xxxvii (1965).

[3] e.g. E. Rendu, *Manuel de l'enseignement primaire* (5th edn., 1858), pp. 74–5, 85, 230–3. Cf. J.-P. David, *L'Établissement de l'enseignement primaire au XIXe siècle dans le département de Maine-et-Loire 1816–1879* (1967), pp. 287–322, 396–9.

[4] Circular of 26 Sept. 1863.

[5] A.N. F¹⁷ 2682, circular to rectors, 9 June 1864; and other correspondence in that file.

Paris came under the authority of the prefect Haussmann, with whom Gréard was able to establish good working relations.[1]

Haussmann's rebuilding of Paris itself represented a challenge to the school administration. The boundaries of the city had been extended in 1860, and as the new suburbs rapidly filled up with families displaced by development new schools were an urgent need. A large school-building programme (including new higher primary schools modelled on the École Turgot as well as elementary schools) was one of Gréard's achievements; the city's annual school budget, 1,170,000 francs in 1859, had already risen to over 5,000,000 by 1866 and was 30,000,000 by 1874.[2] But Gréard was also interested in the quality of the education given, and especially in making the more efficient simultaneous method universal. The simultaneous method was of course used by the religious orders, and in Paris the administration ran both lay and 'congregational' schools in each quarter so that parents would have a choice;[3] but in the lay schools, it was the mutual method, in a modified form, which was still relied on to cope with overcrowded schools. This was the case in most large towns, and few administrators before Gréard had shown much interest in changing things (though the 'individual' method was finally forbidden under Rouland).[4]

Until 1853, the lay schools in Paris had consisted of one class, taught through monitors. In that year, schools with over 150 children were divided into two classes, with the higher one limited to 60–80 pupils. The arrangement of teaching at this time was very simple: there were three hourly classes in the morning (religious instruction, reading, writing) and three in the afternoon (arithmetic, writing, reading); the higher class varied slightly with history, drawing, and singing being taught on some days of the week.[5] In 1857, one school was organized experimentally on the Christian Brothers' pattern, with classes no bigger than one teacher could handle. This was a success, and the system was gradually adopted in other schools. But when Gréard took over, the lay schools still lagged badly behind. In 1867, only two out of 106 schools run by

---

[1] F. Buisson, *Nouveau dictionnaire de pédagogie et d'instruction primaire* (1911), art. Gréard.

[2] Levasseur, *Histoire des classes ouvrières*, ii, p. 463; Du Camp, *Paris: ses organes, ses fonctions et sa vie*, v, pp. 92–5.

[3] *État de l'instruction primaire en 1864*, ii, p. 208 (Seine).

[4] Circular of 15 June 1863. For the different methods, see above, p. 33.

[5] Rendu, *Manuel de l'enseignement primaire*, pp. 262–7.

F

the orders were divided into fewer than three classes, whereas in the lay sector, of 60 boys' schools 8 had one class, 29 two, and 33 three or more; of 54 girls' schools, 10 had one class, 33 two, and only 11 three or more. Large classes, therefore, still existed, and the 'mixed method' was used: the more advanced classes were taught by the teacher as a unity, but in the larger elementary classes the teacher took only part at a time while monitors drilled the rest in mechanical routines. The full monitorial system, which involved teaching the monitors in a special class, had now been dropped, and the monitors were simply children older or more forward than the rest of the class.[1] This mixed method was in fact the prevailing method throughout France.

The conditions in which this teaching took place are illustrated in a book on recent school architecture in Paris published in 1862. In the suburbs, there was room to expand; the school at Petit-Montrouge was arranged in classic small-town fashion, with separate boys' and girls' schools on either side of a square and the *mairie* in between. Each school had two classrooms holding 150 children; the schools were run by religious orders, and included their living accommodation. An example of an urban school run by an order was that of the Soeurs de Saint-Vincent-de-Paul in the rue Parmentier. This included on the same site the sisters' lodgings, a *salle d'asile*, a girls' elementary school, and a centre for the order's charitable activities. The girls' school had three classrooms, with room for 100, 70, and 60 children. By contrast, the lay boys' school in the rue Saint-Hippolyte had a single classroom for 280 boys, though a second classroom for 170 had been created by converting the covered playground; this school had originally been designed for 200 pupils. The most elaborate of the schools illustrated was in the rue de Vaugirard. It had four storeys, occupied (going upwards) by a *salle d'asile*, a girls' school, a boys' school, and a set of rooms for evening courses. A complicated system of separate entrances, staircases, and playgrounds ensured that the pupils of the three schools did not meet. But each school had only one classroom, holding 200 pupils.

In the classrooms, provision for the monitorial groups was made by marking semicircles in the floor around the window piers. The

[1] O. Gréard, *L'Enseignement primaire à Paris et dans le département de la Seine de 1867 à 1877* (1878), pp. 59–61; O. Gréard, *Éducation et instruction. Enseignement primaire*, pp. 62–4.

only other feature of note was the arrangement of the *salles d'asile*: as seems always to have been the case in France, these were equipped with a gallery (*gradin*), a wooden ramp occupying the end of the room with tiered steps on which the children sat. The *gradins* illustrated could hold up to 220 pupils. In England, the gallery was also used for older children, but in France the system of desks in rows had always been standard.[1]

Clearly, the teachers were often working in badly overcrowded conditions, and many of the existing schools were difficult to adapt to the simultaneous method. Despite this last difficulty, Gréard's first priority was always smaller classes. In 1867–8 he introduced a new 'pedagogic organization' based on elementary, middle, and higher divisions (as officially recommended ever since the days of Guizot), with subdivision into separate classes where required. The class size originally aimed at was 120 in the elementary division, 80 in the middle, 60 in the higher (later this fell to 80, 70, and 40); in the average school, the two lower divisions had two classes and the higher only one, giving a total of five separate classes. The divisions still contained children of varying ages staying for more than one year, but Gréard tried to rationalize teaching by insisting that entry and promotion should take place only at the beginning of the year. Formerly, he complained, the programme was constantly disrupted by new arrivals: 'thus it might happen, for example, that a class which in grammar had arrived at the pronoun in December had hardly reached the verb in March; and the teacher was lucky if he was not forced by the weakness of the newcomers to go right back to the adjective.'[2] Another important principle in Gréard's plan was that each division should give as far as possible an education complete in itself, so that even those who did not stay the course received some benefit; thus history and geography were taught in all divisions, and drawing (considered an important subject in Paris, and given much attention) in the upper two.[3]

Other initiatives of Gréard in the sixties included the promotion of the *certificat d'études primaires* for school leavers, and attempts to fill a surprising gap—the absence in the department of an

[1] T. Vacquer, *Bâtiments scolaires récemment construits en France et propres à servir de types pour les édifices de ce genre* (n.d.).

[2] O. Gréard, *Éducation et instruction. Enseignement primaire*, p. 67 n. 1.

[3] Ibid., pp. 69 ff., and *L'Enseignement primaire à Paris*, pp. 61–8.

école normale, even for men. Evening courses to prepare girls for
the *brevet* were organized at the Hôtel de Ville, and in 1866 Gréard
introduced a system of salaried pupil-teachers on English lines.[1]

Despite these advances, conditions even in the capital were
clearly far from ideal, and over the country as a whole ignorance
was still widespread. As we have seen, the government estimated
that some 600,000 children were not attending school in 1863. This
was certainly an improvement over some earlier estimates: in 1848,
675,501 boys and 996,945 girls, 28 per cent and 41 per cent
respectively of those eligible;[2] in 1857, 400,000 boys and 450,000
girls.[3] But when Duruy compiled his statistics, he found that the
children at school fell short of the estimated 4 million in the age-
group (7–13) by 884,887. The problem in making this calculation
was that it did not allow for the many children who attended for
less than six years; Duruy estimated the number of children who
escaped education *wholly* at 200,000. Those who stayed for only a
short time might learn little, and Duruy established that only
60 per cent of the children who left school in 1863 had mastered
the three Rs.[4]

The 1866 census revealed that among the total population
39 per cent were illiterate, 10 per cent able to read only, and 50 per
cent able to read and write.[5] Continuous series of literacy statistics,
however, suggest that in the sixties about one in five men, and one
in three women, were escaping effective education. Illiteracy
among conscripts, for example, tested at the age of twenty and thus
reflecting the state of education eight to ten years before, evolved
as follows:[6]

(Averages)	1851–55	38%
	1856–60	34
	1861–65	30
	1866–68	24
	1872–75	20
	1876–80	17

---

[1] *Éducation et instruction. Enseignement primaire*, pp. 272–3.

[2] F. Ponteil, *Histoire de l'enseignement en France. Les grandes étapes, 1789–1964*
(1966), p. 210.

[3] E. Rendu, in A. Hill (ed.), *Essays upon Educational Subjects* (1857), pp. 93–4.

[4] *L'Administration de l'instruction publique de 1863 à 1869*, pp. 152–6.

[5] *Statistique comparée de l'enseignement primaire (1829–1877)*, pp. clvi–clx.

[6] Based on figures in Cipolla, *Literacy and Development in the West*, Appendices II–III. (The figures for conscripts include as illiterate those who could
read but not write.)

For men, these figures correspond closely with those taken from the marriage registers, which were first collected in France in 1854; the average age of marriage was nearer thirty than twenty.

Newly married people unable to sign their names

	Men	Women
1854	31%	46%
1855	32	48
1856–60	31	46
1861–65	28	42
1866–70	25	38
1872–75	22	33
1876–80	17	28

The disparity between men and women, which was narrowing only gradually, explains why Simon, Duruy, and others thought the improvement of girls' schools such an urgent task.

In a country where education is not compulsory, the reasons for failure to attend school are of considerable interest to the historian. In the case of France, there were very marked regional differences, which make any generalization difficult. This is shown by the accompanying map, which illustrates the differences in the literacy of conscripts in 1862. In the whole north-eastern corner of France, rural as well as industrial, and in the Paris region, illiteracy was below 10 per cent; but in Brittany and considerable areas of central France it was over 40 per cent, while in three departments (Finistère, Haute-Vienne, Allier) it was over 60 per cent. As time passed, these differences were evening themselves out, and south-eastern France in particular had progressed considerably since the thirties.[1]

No single factor, religious, political, or economic, provides a key to these disparities. A high level of general prosperity no doubt favoured education, but in some circumstances poverty had the same effect: in the Basses-Alpes, for example, parents knew that their children would have to seek work in towns or in other parts of France, and 'it is in the poorest areas that education is sought after with the most eagerness'.[2] This perhaps explains the generally high literacy of the Alpine region.

[1] Cf. Prost, *Histoire de l'enseignement en France*, pp. 104–7.
[2] *État de l'instruction primaire en 1864*, i, p. 43. This and other factors had worked in the same way under the ancien régime: see Gontard, *L'Enseignement primaire en France de la Révolution à la loi Guizot*, pp. 17 ff.

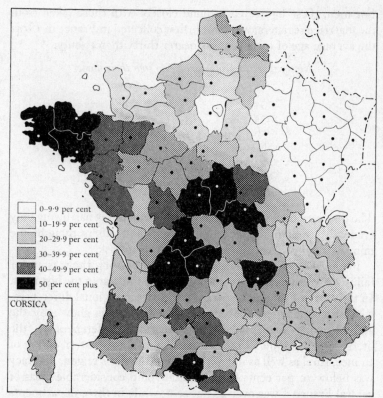

Source: J. Simon, *L'École*, p. 219 n.

There were also variations within departments, especially
between town and countryside. Nationally, the literacy of married
couples was higher in urban communes than rural ones: in 1869,
80 per cent against 72 per cent for men, 65 per cent against 60 per
cent for women.[1] And Émile Levasseur declared that 'if ignorance
still defends itself against the assaults of civilization, it is less in the
manufacturing towns than in the depth of the countryside'.[2]
Literacy was certainly higher in most industrial towns than in the
most backward rural areas; but within individual departments
school attendance might well be worse in the towns. This was, on
the whole, the view of Duruy's inspectors in 1864, concerned as

[1] *Statistique comparée de l'enseignement primaire (1829–1877)*, p. clxvi.
[2] Levasseur, *Histoire des classes ouvrières*, ii, p. 458.

they were with the effects on attendance of factory labour.[1] Recent
scholarly studies suggest that generalization is risky. In Seine-et-
Marne, for example, relatively unaffected by modern industry, the
towns seem to have been more advanced, while in the Calvados it
was the reverse; in the Gard, attendance was low in the mountainous areas, but high in Protestant ones and in the mining towns,
where the Christian Brothers were encouraged by the companies.[2]
Everywhere the obstacles to full attendance combined in different
ways. They may be analysed under five heads: the absence or
inadequate provision of schools, inability to pay the fees, the need
for children to work on the land, the impact of industrial labour,
and the indifference of parents or local notables.

Virtually every commune now had a school, though in the
smaller ones some parents may have preferred to keep their
daughters at home rather than send them to a mixed school. But
the school might still be difficult for many children to reach, and
bad roads were often given as a reason for non-attendance. This
also has some bearing on the regional disparities: in the east, the
north, and much of the south, where settlement was in compact
villages, school attendance was easy. But there were problems
where the population was scattered in small hamlets or isolated
farms, as in mountainous areas and the *bocage* country of the west.
In the law of 1867, Duruy tried to remedy this by encouraging
'hamlet schools', small auxiliary schools under assistant teachers.
This idea was borrowed from the Alpine regions, where the
schools followed the villagers in their summer migration.[3]

In theory, school fees should not have been an obstacle to
attendance since the children of poor families were admitted free.
Duruy's officials in 1864, perhaps biased because of their opposition
to free education, generally reported that neither fees nor the lack
of books or clothing were a cause of non-attendance. But it is

---

[1] e.g. *État de l'instruction primaire en 1864*, i, pp. 123 (Doubs), 319 (Manche),
676, 687 (Aisne), 707 (Ardennes).

[2] A. Chatelain, 'Le Niveau d'éducation des classes laborieuses en Seine-et-
Marne en 1848', *Bulletin de la Société d'études historiques, géographiques et
scientifiques de la région parisienne*, no. 80 (1953), p. 2; J. Gourhand, 'Aperçus
sur la situation de l'enseignement primaire dans le Calvados sous le Second
Empire', *Bulletin de la Société des Antiquaires de Normandie*, lvii (1963–4),
pp. 461–4; R. Huard, *La Bataille pour l'école primaire dans le Gard (1866–1872)*
(n.d.), p. 12.

[3] Law of 10 Apr. 1867, circular to prefects, 12 May 1867. Cf. J. Lovie, *La
Savoie dans la vie française de 1860 à 1875* (1963), pp. 332–3, 452.

difficult to believe that neither the quota imposed between 1853 and 1866 nor the stigma of charity had a deterrent effect. We also learn that exemptions were manipulated by local councils to suit their own prejudices. At Mulhouse, for example, fees were only remitted for the first years of education, so that poor children had to leave at eight or nine when they could begin work in the factories.[1] At Marseilles and at Brest the authorities had abolished all fees in their schools, but admitted to them only children who qualified for free education on grounds of poverty, forcing those who could afford fees to use private schools. This policy, which may well have been more widespread, was deplored by Duruy's officials.[2] Another practice condemned by them, and later forbidden by Duruy, was the provision of separate classes for free and paying pupils; this seems to have been common in girls' schools run by nuns, but not otherwise.[3]

The proportion of pupils admitted free varied little (in public schools, 39 per cent in 1850, 38 per cent in 1863, 41 per cent in 1866).[4] One aim of the law of 1867 was to encourage more communes to abolish fees altogether, and 3,000 did so between 1867 and 1869.[5] This was a modest result: even though the state's direct subsidy to primary education rose from some 2,700,000 francs in 1865 to 6,500,000 in 1869, far more would have been needed to make a real difference, for the bulk of the cost of primary education was still met from the fees paid.[6] In any case, we find that Duruy's officials in 1864 were generally opposed to the extension of free education, on the grounds that attendance was more regular when parents paid for what they were getting. There was an implication in many of their remarks that free education had been tried and found wanting, and indeed the movement was not all one way: in 1846 the very progressive Nancy municipal council had introduced fee-paying for the first time in order to produce more money for expansion.[7]

Even if fees were not a major obstacle, financial constraints

[1] Oberlé, *L'Enseignement à Mulhouse*, pp. 70–1.

[2] *État de l'instruction primaire en 1864*, i, pp. 1–2, ii, pp. 719–20.

[3] Rohr, *Victor Duruy*, p. 164.

[4] *Statistique comparée de l'enseignement primaire (1829–1877)*, p. cxxxiii.

[5] Gontard, *Les Écoles primaires de la France bourgeoise*, p. 183.

[6] *Statistique comparée de l'enseignement primaire (1829–1877)*, Table 67 and p. clxxvii.

[7] P. Clémendot, 'L'Enseignement primaire à Nancy de l'ancien régime à 1850', *Annales de l'Est*, 5th series, xxi (1969), pp. 52–3.

operated when parents could not afford to do without their children's labour. In the countryside, it was the universal and seemingly ineradicable custom for the schools to empty in the summer when the children were needed to work in the fields, and many were taken away from school permanently after a few years. This was inevitable in a rural economy based on the family holding, and there are some signs that it was becoming more necessary than ever in this period. The sixties saw the first great wave of migration from the countryside to the towns, and the first to go were the day-labourers and farm servants on whom small proprietors as well as large had depended; hence 'the scarcity and dearness of labour, which causes children of school age to be called on to work'.[1] This rural proletariat which was now beginning to disappear, incidentally, had probably formed the hard core of rural illiteracy along with those on the margin of society like woodcutters and itinerant workers of various kinds.

Traditional patterns of temporary migration also affected school attendance. In the Limousin, in particular, the adult men worked during the summer in the building trade in Paris and other towns, and children's labour on the farms was all the more essential. In the Creuse, it was also reported that children from the age of ten were now joining this migration, and whole families were going away and not coming back.[2] In Savoy, it was the children who were sent away as chimney-sweeps while the adults stayed at home.[3]

These customs are a reminder that regular school attendance was something alien to the traditional rhythms of country life. The idea of childhood and education as a phase of life preceding entry into the world of work did not correspond with the experience of peasant or indeed artisan families, where the home was the workplace and the child was familiar with the family's labour from his earliest days. Both boys and girls were expected to take their share as soon as they were able, and even the youngest children could watch over animals or scare birds. It was often said that unless children were broken in to rural labour at an early age they would never 'contract the habit of whole days spent in the open air through cold, heat, and rain'.[4] Thus the concept of full-time

---

[1] *État de l'instruction primaire en 1864*, i, p. 472 (Allier); cf. i, p. 513 (Corrèze), ii, pp. 68-9 (Lozère).
[2] Ibid., i, pp. 545-6; cf. p. 513 (Corrèze).
[3] Ibid., i, p. 420 (Savoie).   [4] Ibid., ii, p. 491 (Vienne).

schooling with a 'leaving age' was an urban one, which had to be imposed on a reluctant peasantry. The 1864 reports leave little doubt that rural opinion was at that time hostile to compulsory education, and with few exceptions the inspectors thought it impracticable and undesirable. Those in the west expressed this view most strongly, while among the few to support compulsion were those for the Ardennes and the Vosges, in the north-east, who saw it as the only way of ending the abuses of child labour.[1]

The *inspecteurs d'académie* were thus opposed to both free and compulsory education, and their experience and knowledge of local conditions must carry weight as evidence for what was acceptable to opinion at this time—especially when they knew that a different answer would have pleased Duruy. It is probable, though, that free education would have been much more acceptable in the countryside than compulsion.[2]

In rural areas, the need to work led to irregular attendance, but not necessarily to early leaving. Children could return to school in the winter, and might carry on in this way until the age of fourteen,[3] although there were some forms of 'seasonal' employment which occupied children for long periods—picking olives in the south, market-gardening in the Paris suburbs, sugar-beet refining in the Île-de-France, sardine canning in Brittany.[4] In industry, however, employment was continuous, and once the child had left school to work he was unlikely to return. France's only factory law, passed in 1841, should have made part-time schooling compulsory for factory children aged between eight and twelve. In fact it was widely ignored, mainly because of the lack of inspectors, and even where enforced it only applied to larger factories and was satisfied when the child was given one hour's education a day, on top of eight hours' labour. Reformers like Simon, whose book on the question, *L'Ouvrier de huit ans*, came out in 1867, wanted to see the English 'half-time' system adopted instead.

The inspectors were asked in 1864 to comment on the application of the law of 1841, and what they say supports the conclusions of

---

[1] *État de l'instruction primaire en 1864*, ii, pp. 508 (Charente), 627–8 (Vendée); i, p. 695 (Ardennes), ii, p. 174 (Vosges).

[2] Cf. Chatelain in *Bulletin de la Société d'études historiques, géographiques et scientifiques de la région parisienne*, no. 80 (1953), p. 8; Huard, *La Bataille pour l'école primaire dans le Gard*, p. 26.

[3] *État de l'instruction primaire en 1864*, i, p. 707 (Ardennes).

[4] Ibid., i, p. 83 (Var), ii, pp. 210 (Seine), 426 (Seine-et-Marne), 720 (Finistère).

Duveau's detailed study of this question.[1] The situation varied greatly between different places and industries, and the problem was local rather than national. In some areas, there was little industry to attract child labour, in others child labour was not customary or necessary. The worst conditions were in textiles, where children often formed part of a team with adult workers, and in certain mining areas. The iron industry and engineering, on the other hand, employed few children, and in some cases— including the glassworks and mines of Carmaux, for example—we hear of employers deliberately refusing to admit children of school age.[2] The parents who were generally most anxious to set their children to work were those who worked in factories and mines themselves, or in other poorly-paid and unskilled jobs. Artisans and those who worked in small factories and workshops were much more conscious of the value of education, though we hear of exploitation of their children's labour by weavers and other domestic workers, especially in Alsace.[3]

Some employers set up factory schools (*écoles de fabrique*) which provided education at midday or in the evening, others simply gave time off without trying to enforce school attendance, and others made special arrangements with the public schools. At Nantes, for example, there were no factory schools, but two hours were given for attending school. In the Vosges, factory children either attended the local schools for three hours, or had shorter classes in the factory, which was less satisfactory. In Charente, some employers sent half their children to school in the morning, the other half in the afternoon. In some areas, it seems that the authorities were trying to fill the gap: in Seine-Inférieure, a major industrial area, there were no factory schools, but thirty teachers were subsidized by the department and by certain communes, and taught 1,861 factory children; the inspector thought that little more could be done for the time being to remedy 'a state of affairs which is based on social necessities'.[4] Occasionally employers provided full-scale schools for all their employees' children, but this seems

[1] Duveau, *La Vie ouvrière*, pp. 434 ff.

[2] *État de l'instruction primaire en 1864*, ii, p. 966 (Tarn); cf. i, p. 908 (Saône-et-Loire, metallurgy and mining), ii, p. 674 (Ille-et-Vilaine).

[3] Duveau, op. cit., p. 439; Rendu in Hill (ed.), *Essays upon Educational Subjects*, pp. 94–8.

[4] *État de l'instruction primaire en 1864*, ii, pp. 744 (Loire-Inférieure), 177 (Vosges), 509 (Charente), i, p. 390 (Seine-Inférieure).

to have been usual only where the industry involved created new settlements. Examples are the mining villages of the north, where the companies set up private Catholic schools, and railway towns like Morcenx, in the south-west, where in 1864 the Midi railway company founded schools which were admired by Charles Robert.[1]

The industrial area with the worst educational conditions seems to have been the north. The Nord and Pas-de-Calais departments came well down in the literacy lists, and this was undoubtedly due to the impact of industry: an inquiry in 1872 revealed that in the Nord 60–70 per cent of agricultural workers and 60 per cent of workers in small-scale industry were literate, but only 33 per cent of workers in large-scale industry, a figure which Duveau suggests would be typical for this sort of worker everywhere.[2] This was an area of rapid industrial growth during the Second Empire, and the existing schools were unable to cope—at Roubaix, there was a school with 2,485 children, and the situation was made worse here by an influx of Flemish-speaking workers from Belgium.[3] A recent study shows, however, that the sixties saw a rapid improvement, with school attendance in 1869–70 almost as high as it was to be when education became compulsory.[4] In 1864, the inspector had claimed that the law of 1841 was being enforced and that children working in factories and mines were taught for one hour a day.[5] In other northern departments, however, like the Aisne and Somme, the law was ignored. In the Pas-de-Calais, attempts were made to enforce the law, but there was much evasion, and the inspector called for it to be strengthened and extended to mining, for parents took their children away from school at the age of ten to send them down the pit; though some mining companies, it was said, did more to provide schools than the factory-owners.[6] Child labour in the mines was also reported, incidentally, at Saint-Étienne, and both there and at Lyons the law of 1841 was a dead letter.[7]

---

[1] Ménager, *La Laïcisation des écoles communales dans le département du Nord*, p. 19; C. Robert, *Notice sur l'enseignement donné à Morcenx par la Compagnie des chemins de fer du Midi* (1873).

[2] Duveau, op. cit., p. 438.

[3] *État de l'instruction primaire en 1864*, i, p. 654 (Nord); É. Anthoine, *L'Instruction primaire dans le département du Nord, 1868–1877* (1878), pp. 13–14.

[4] M. Leblond, 'La Scolarisation dans le département du Nord au XIXe siècle', *Revue du Nord*, lii (1970), pp. 388–90.

[5] *État de l'instruction primaire en 1864*, i, p. 660.

[6] Ibid., i, pp. 723–4.   [7] Ibid., i, pp. 883–5 (Loire), 835 (Rhône).

Was the advanced east any better? According to one Catholic critic, the employers of Alsace, who made such an impression in Paris with their demands for compulsory education, themselves maintained second-rate factory schools and turned the towns into islands of ignorance in a sea of literacy.[1] The 1864 reports tend to confirm this: factory schools were common in the Haut-Rhin, but 'irregularly attended, to say the least, and in every case they have only poor results to show'. The classes were held in the evening from 8 to 9.30, when both teachers and children were too tired for much to be achieved.[2] But in the less industrialized Bas-Rhin, the *inspecteur d'académie* declared that industry was not a cause of non-attendance, and that all the factories had schools.[3] There were several other departments in eastern France—Meurthe, Meuse, Moselle, Marne—where it was said that the law of 1841 was enforced and that effective factory schools existed. The inspector at Nancy singled out for praise the schools of the glassworks at Baccarat, and observed that 'in this enlightened region, most of the large industries make a point of honour of the education which they give their workers'.[4] Nevertheless, it seems safe to say that the north-east was educationally advanced in spite of the presence of industry rather than because of it. Where industry existed, the employment opportunities which it offered parents were a danger to prolonged school attendance and even to the maintenance of standards already achieved; and the part-time instruction pre-scribed by the 1841 law was no substitute for true compulsory education.

The final obstacle to the progress of education was the 'indifference' or apathy of parents and local opinion. It was the one most frequently appealed to by Duruy's officials, and they saw it at the root of all the others. If attitudes could be changed, the economic obstacles to attendance would seem less important, and demand would provide a dynamic for expansion independent of politicians and propagandists. They were changing slowly, but there is no shortage of comment in the 1864 reports and in the teachers' essays on the problems created by 'indifference towards primary education, old prejudices, old habits of ignorance, and

[1] J.-I. Simonis, *Lettres à M. Jules Simon sur l'instruction primaire* (1869), pp. 42 ff., 59.
[2] *État de l'instruction primaire en 1864*, ii, pp. 844-5.
[3] Ibid., ii, p. 858.   [4] Ibid., ii, pp. 99-100.

selfish calculations'. We also hear, though usually from the more backward areas, of 'the indifference and sometimes the secret opposition of the local authorities and of a few highly placed persons in certain communes', and sometimes of 'the quite wide-spread opinion, even among people of the upper classes, that it is bad for the inhabitants of the countryside to be able to read'.[1]

It was in the sixties that modern influences began decisively to penetrate the countryside. Thabault has described how in his village in the west new horizons opened up as contacts with the towns and the outside world increased and the value of literacy came to be appreciated, first by the village artisans and shop-keepers, rather later by the farmers.[2] Perhaps the latter were still deterred by what Rouland admitted to be the 'over-vague and over-theoretical character of the teaching'[3]—hence the attempts by Duruy and other reformers to include more that was practically relevant to agriculture.

Duruy's officials expected progress to be made through an ever-widening appreciation of the value of education rather than through government intervention to make it compulsory. They put their faith in the patient improvement of standards, and in working to gain the confidence of parents and dissipate the remaining prejudices. Their allies were 'time, the influence of example, and the counsels of the clergy, who are generally favourable to education'; or 'time, the progress of civilization, and the upward march of ideas'.[4] Their attitudes were optimistic, and they thought that within a generation education would become universal without the need for compulsion; it was an optimism firmly rooted in the accepted ideas of the sixties.

We may end by looking at some of the other problems which preoccupied the administration at this time. One was that an important function of the school was still imposing the use of a single national language. The problem was a lesser one in areas where *patois* was spoken: it was easy for children to speak *patois*

---

[1] *État de l'instruction primaire en 1864*, i, p. 217 (Dordogne), ii, pp. 547 (Indre), 963 (Tarn). Cf. Robert, *De l'ignorance des populations ouvrières*, pp. 2–11.

[2] R. Thabault, *Mon village. Ses hommes, ses routes, son école* (8th edn., 1945), pp. 128–43.

[3] Circular of 20 Aug. 1857.

[4] *État de l'instruction primaire en 1864*, i, pp. 361 (Sarthe), 794 (Ardèche).

at home and official French at school,[1] though we still hear of
children laughed at for speaking 'French' out of school; another
hint that to many peasants the school was an alien, urban institution dispensing a culture remote from everyday life. But *patois* was
now near its end, thanks to mass education and other influences:
'the railways which are now being built will be the best teachers of
French and will complete the work.'[2]

The problem of non-French languages—Basque, Breton,
Flemish, and German—was more intractable. In Alsace and
Lorraine, the use of German was admitted in the schools, but in
general the spirit of the University was very hostile to the survival
of non-French languages, and the action it took was uncompromising. To deal with the Flemish problem, for example, 'the
surest remedy, which has already been used with success, is to
appoint a purely French teacher in the recalcitrant communes'.[3]
This spirit was fully shared by Duruy, who made the promotion
of French a major task of his administration. It was all the more
to his taste because it was a source of conflict with the Church,
which insisted on teaching the catechism in the language which the
child spoke at home. This conflict existed in all the peripheral
areas, but seems to have been worst in Lorraine; a dispute at
Malling (Moselle) attracted national attention in 1868. The rector
for this area, Maggiolo, claimed that victory was in sight when it
was snatched away in 1870. The proportion of children speaking
French had risen, but what was happening was the creation of a
bilingual community rather than the elimination of German.[4]

Another problem that caused Duruy much anxiety was migration
from the countryside. This was seen by contemporaries not as a
necessary part of industrialization, but as a social evil and a
threat to stability. Education itself was blamed by conservatives
for destroying the peasant's contentment with his lot and giving
him a taste for the material way of life and the doubtful pleasures
of the towns; among the peasants themselves, the fear that the

[1] So too in Provençal-speaking areas: ibid., i, pp. 45–6 (Basses-Alpes), 85 (Var),
100 (Vaucluse).

[2] *État de l'instruction primaire en 1864*, i, p. 533 (Haute-Loire).

[3] Ibid., i, p. 663 (Nord). Cf. É. Coornaert, 'Flamand et français dans l'enseignement en Flandre française des annexions au XIXe siècle', *Revue du Nord*, liii
(1971), p. 220.

[4] L. Maggiolo, *Les Écoles en Lorraine ... avant et après 1789. Troisième partie.
1802–1890* (1891), pp. 68–9. Cf. Zind, *L'Enseignement religieux dans l'instruction
primaire*, pp. 247–66.

young men would leave for the towns was one reason for prejudice against education. Duruy was therefore anxious to show that education was not the real cause of migration, and his officials provided him with some ammunition, arguing that 'the lure of the towns attracts the ignorant more than men with some education'[1]— it was the illiterate labourers above all who were leaving. A rather different argument was that 'there are few village schools which give an advanced enough education to allow the children of peasants to obtain jobs in the towns'.[2] In fact, it was difficult to deny that education and emigration were connected, but they were part of a wider tendency of the age outside the control of governments. Duruy could and did argue that the best way to stop migration was to improve rural education, and in particular to end the contrast between free schools in the towns and fee-paying ones in the villages.

'To enlighten men's minds, to show them the results of order and sober thrift, to give them a taste for the charms of a simple life and the laborious habits of the countryside, to teach them to find in them the tranquillity and calm necessary to true happiness; that should be the principal purpose of primary education, at least from the moral point of view.'[3] One of the points which comes out of the 1864 reports is the moralizing function attributed to education. Duruy himself tried to relate the progress of education directly to the decline of crime, and stressed that 'the best way to have empty prisons is to keep the schools full'.[4] Rather more subtly, the inspectors thought that the long-term effect of education was a civilizing one: the coarseness (*grossièreté*), harshness, and uncouth habits of peasant life were giving way to 'des moeurs plus douces, plus polies'.[5] They rejoiced in the decline of superstition, drunkenness, fights, and prejudices (in Alsace, it was noted that anti-Semitic outbursts had ceased),[6] and in the growth of civilized habits and recreations, family life, and the habit of saving. 'The managements of the big industries are well aware what a powerful aid the school is to them for moralizing and disciplining their

[1] *État de l'instruction primaire en 1864*, i, pp. 181–2 (Haute-Saône); cf. ii, p. 522 (Charente).

[2] Ibid., i, p. 18 (Bouches-du-Rhône); cf. ii, p. 561 (Indre).

[3] Ibid., ii, p. 1002 (Tarn-et-Garonne).

[4] *L'Administration de l'instruction publique de 1863 à 1869*, pp. 105, 157–60.

[5] *État de l'instruction primaire en 1864*, i, p. 805 (Ardèche).

[6] Ibid., ii, p. 853 (Haut-Rhin).

workers,' it was reported from the Gard;[1] but the inspectors saw this new spirit of order and discipline spreading in the countryside too. Indeed, the arrival of industry might mean moral disaster. As soon as a factory is set up, complained the rector of Douai, 'the habits of the people are transformed rapidly. Attendance at the school falls, the church is little by little abandoned, the taste for the tavern (*cabaret*) develops, and corruption makes rapid head-way.'[2] The *cabaret* was already seen as the worker's greatest enemy, and both schools and evening courses tried to combat its influence.

This alarm at the morally degrading effects of industrial expansion helps explain the new interest in education manifested in the sixties. Linked with it is another argument found in official circles: the school must be developed because it is today the *only* effective moral influence. In 1853, Eugène Rendu had argued that the traditional moral agencies, the Church and the family, were in decline; 'the Christian tradition, and therefore the social tradition, is broken.' The school was where 'a last stand against corruption of mind and heart' must be made.[3] It was probably Rendu's voice speaking in a circular of Fortoul which deplored the fact that so many children were untouched by 'the moral ideas which con-stitute the traditional life of a civilized people'.[4] Similar views were expressed by the rector Dunoyer,[5] and by Cournot, who argued that strong state education was essential 'for the continued protection of society by the strength of its civil institutions, when the powerful impulse of the religious spirit has become relaxed or broken'.[6] As Pierre Zind points out, the idea of a lay morality is present here. But it is a conservative version, which looks back to the era of Guizot rather than forward to the Third Republic. Indeed, with its concern for morality and its vision of a peasant people living in dignity, sobriety, and ordered calm, the University of the sixties might still be said to be living in the moral climate of the law of 1833.

[1] Ibid., ii, pp. 62–3.
[2] Quoted in Zind, op. cit., p. 172.
[3] Rendu, *De l'enseignement obligatoire*, pp. 8–9.
[4] Circular to prefects, 31 Oct. 1854.
[5] Zind, op. cit., pp. 216–19.
[6] Cournot, *Des institutions d'instruction publique*, p. 29.

CHAPTER NINE

Duruy and classical education

I. THE END OF BIFURCATION

Secondary education was more familiar than primary to Duruy, and he gave it closer personal attention. As a former teacher, he enjoyed making detailed changes in the system and inspecting schools himself. At the same time, he was more open to new ideas than most *universitaires*: he wanted to equip the University's pupils for the contemporary world by strengthening modern subjects in the lycées, and was willing to scrap some of the traditional exercises to make room for a more balanced education. He was responsive to current criticisms of the University, and sought to modify the rigid discipline of the lycées and the heavy burden of work which they imposed. He was also willing to borrow ideas from Britain and Germany if necessary, and was better informed about the facts of education, in France and abroad, than any minister before him. His views on the social function of secondary education, however, were orthodox; if anything, the tendency of his policy was to make classical education more élitist, as his plans for modern and scientific education centred on the rejuvenation of the 'special' courses.

Duruy's first change in secondary education was a symbolic one designed to prove to the University that the memory of Fortoul was to be erased. Logic was renamed Philosophy, and a new programme restored the subject to its place of honour in the syllabus.[1] The next step was the abolition of bifurcation itself, but here Duruy moved more cautiously. As we have seen, Rouland's changes had taken much of the heat out of this issue. In 1863, Duruy did what Rouland had long contemplated by postponing bifurcation for a year, so that the separate sections began after the third instead of the fourth form.[2] Before going further, he decided to collect the opinions of headmasters and officials, and carried out an elaborate inquiry in 1864.

[1] Decree of 29 June 1863, *arrêté* of 14 July 1863.
[2] Decree of 2 Sept. 1863.

Duruy rightly concluded that the weight of opinion in the University favoured abolition, but there were some dissident voices. Provincial headmasters were more in touch with what parents and employers wanted than were the Paris teachers whom Rouland had consulted, and feared they would see their pupils depart if they could no longer offer them an effective scientific education. Their concern about Catholic competition was obvious: at Douai, 'the system is in accordance with the views of the families and the needs of the area. . . . It is principally our adversaries whom . . . the total suppression of bifurcation would profit'; at Besançon, 'the scientific trend is at present very pronounced, and we are having successes which make our recruitment secure, and allow us to fight against the establishments of the Marists and Jesuits and the Catholic college'. It was in the north and east, where the sciences had been most popular, that bifurcation was most strongly defended: 'The abolition of the system of bifurcation would be a disastrous measure for the lycées of the East, and particularly for the lycée of Nancy.' Among the other schools whose heads expressed similar fears were Albi, Amiens, Avignon, Bourges, Brest, Cahors, Épinal, Grenoble, Lille, Nantes, Perpignan, Rennes, Rouen, Saint-Omer, Sens, Strasbourg, Toulouse, and Tours. However, most of them would be satisfied if Duruy's new arrangements made the same provision as before for preparation for the government schools, and this was to be the case.[1]

Duruy's inquiries also showed that the numbers in the scientific sections were falling, especially of course since the 1863 modification. In November 1863, 40 out of 70 provincial lycées had under 30 pupils in their scientific section, while only 14 had over 50.[2] Duruy could claim that the system was 'collapsing of its own accord',[3] and in 1864 he abolished it.[4] The new structure of classes introduced in 1865 returned to the pre-1852 system. There was now again a single series of forms leading up to Philosophy, with special mathematical forms for candidates for the government schools. These forms included non-scientific teaching, like Fortoul's scientific sections, so that the system was not radically

---

[1] A.N. F¹⁷ 9099, replies of *proviseurs* and principals to circular of 5 Oct. 1864, and cf. replies of rectors.

[2] Ibid., note for minister summarizing results of circular of 5 Oct. 1864 for meeting of inspectors-general.

[3] Report to Emperor accompanying decree of 4 Dec. 1864.

[4] Decree of 4 Dec. 1864, *arrêté* of 24 Mar. 1865.

different from bifurcation as amended in 1863; the main differences were that there was no common instruction, and that pupils could transfer to the specialized forms when they chose, with no fixed point of bifurcation. Matthew Arnold, who wrote a useful description of secondary education under Duruy for the Taunton Commission, observed that 'the abolition . . . turns out, when one looks closely at it, to be more apparent than real'.[1]

All the same, Duruy's basic approach was different from Fortoul's. He expounded it in a speech in 1864. The ideal was that there should be no specialization, but a single balanced course ending in a unified baccalaureate. However, the inexorable demands of the government schools made this impossible: the lycées alone provided 500 candidates annually for the Polytechnique, over 300 for Saint-Cyr. The pattern of classical education had to be modified to take account of this. But in future the needs of industry and commerce would be better met by the new special education, which complemented the abolition of Fortoul's system and took over part of its role. Theoretical science would be taught in the higher forms of the lycées, but 'we will place the *applications* in the special college'.[2] Duruy was really taking a step backwards by reasserting the traditional distinction between the liberal professions and the rest, between pure and applied knowledge. The new special education, which was based on the existing special courses, would inevitably be inferior in status to the classics. The 1852 reform, whatever its failings, had at least grappled with the problem of whether secondary education should change fundamentally in an industrial age. Duruy preferred to meet the needs of the new age outside the framework of classical education, which could thus continue on the old lines free of urgent pressures to modernize. Even the *Revue de l'instruction publique*, which generally welcomed Duruy's restoration of the University's traditions, criticized his speech for dodging the real problems.[3]

The actual teaching of science covered the same ground as before, except that for non-specialists the natural sciences were concentrated at the end of the course rather than forming a

[1] M. Arnold, *Schools and Universities on the Continent* (ed. R. H. Super, 1964), p. 83.

[2] *Bulletin administratif du ministère de l'instruction publique*, new series, ii (1864), pp. 71–5.

[3] *Revue de l'instruction publique*, xxiv (1864), p. 289.

sequence as in the 1852 plan.[1] This tended to reduce the status of science as a part of general education, and seems to have been felt as a setback by the science teachers.[2] But in fact scientific education had made permanent gains, and bifurcation had not been a fruitless experiment.

In the first place, Duruy did not return to the pre-1852 system for the baccalaureate. The separate scientific examination remained, enjoying equal status with the classical one, and still necessary for entry to the government schools.[3] In the sixties, around 1,700 scientific baccalaureates were taken each year—fewer than in the fifties, and about half the figure for the classical examination.[4] But as long as the examination existed, it gave scientific education prestige and fixed standards, and prevented a return to the narrow mathematical approach of the early nineteenth century.

Bifurcation had also stimulated the training of science teachers—two were needed to set up a science section, and before 1852 many schools had had only one. The number of scientific *agrégés* in the lycées grew by 52 per cent between 1850 and 1865, the literary *agrégés* by 41 per cent,[5] while Gerbod calculates that by 1865 science and modern languages accounted for 603 of 1,306 teachers in the lycées, a quarter in the colleges.[6] The scientific equipment of the lycées was also improved: under Duruy, questionnaires investigated this subject, and in 1867 a model list of apparatus was issued.[7]

Thus the presence of science could no longer be ignored, and perhaps the effects of bifurcation on attitudes were the most significant. Having once won equality with the classics, the sciences could never return to the pre-1852 position of being squeezed into spare corners of the syllabus and regarded as semi-optional. Science had established its claim to be a part of the general education of the

[1] In 1863, they were all put in the Philosophy form, but in 1865 natural history was transferred to the Second form: *arrêté* of 12 Sept. 1863, circular of 22 Sept. 1863, *arrêtés* of 3 Dec. 1863, 24 and 25 Mar. 1865.

[2] Gerbod, *La Condition universitaire*, p. 490.

[3] Except that from 1867 Saint-Cyr accepted either baccalaureate.

[4] *État numérique des grades, 1795–1885*, pp. 66–75, 168–77.

[5] A.N. F17 6839, unpublished statistical report for 1850, Table 3; *Statistique de l'enseignement secondaire en 1865*, Table 5.

[6] Gerbod, *La Condition universitaire*, p. 426.

[7] Circulars of 28 Sept. 1863, 16 July 1864, 1 June 1867; list in *Bulletin administratif*, new series, vi (1866), pp. 643–64.

whole élite, and the opinion of parents, employers, and local communities had moved decisively in its favour. Although Duruy abandoned bifurcation, he did not intend to devalue science itself; he believed in it as the instrument of material progress and an expression of the spirit of free inquiry. His ultimate aim was a rejuvenated curriculum into which science would be integrated, and with which the University would measure up to the needs of the nineteenth century and triumph over its enemies.

2. THE CHANGING CONTENT OF CLASSICAL EDUCATION

In 1865, Duruy issued a complete set of new programmes for the lycées, but much of it simply reproduced what had gone before. This was partly true even of philosophy, whose 'restoration' did not involve a fundamental change in what was taught. Fortoul had abolished the traditional categories of Psychology, Logic, Ethics, and Theodicy; under Duruy they reappeared, but the actual subjects arranged under these headings underwent only minor modifications, and new ones introduced in 1852, like scientific method and the use of language, remained. Duruy's programme was no more or less 'clerical' than Fortoul's. If anything, the ethical part gained at the expense of logic, and there was more emphasis than in 1852 on the soul and its immortality, on free will, on God and the proofs of his existence.[1] Like Cousin, Duruy claimed that the University's philosophy taught only what men of all creeds could accept, and he was careful to conciliate the Catholics: 'The priest at the altar and the professor at his desk have the same task. . . . They are following parallel lines, but moving towards a common goal.'[2] In this period, the philosophy of the lycées was spared the kind of Catholic attack which it had suffered in the forties.

Duruy was anxious to assert the 'spiritualism' of the University's teaching against allegations of materialism, and his changes were considered to mark a reinstatement of Cousin's doctrines. This was by no means welcome to many of the younger generation, influenced by the devastating attack on Cousin and his philosophy launched in 1857 by Taine.[3] But Taine had to admit that eclec-

[1] *Arrêté* of 14 July 1863, and cf. programme of 30 Aug. 1852.

[2] Speech to Conseil impérial, 20 July 1863, in *Bulletin administratif de l'instruction publique*, xiv (1863), p. 145.

[3] *Les Philosophes français du XIXe siècle* (later retitled *Les Philosophes classiques du XIXe siècle en France*).

ticism, hollow and sterile though it might be, retained its dominance in the schools, for it was a teachable system, tried by experience, and there was no alternative ready to replace it. Cousin died in 1867, but he had many younger disciples—men like Paul Janet and Elme Caro—who sought to modernize and expand the doctrine, and who continued to dominate the University's strongholds in the Paris lycées, the faculties, and the École Normale.[1] The more prominent critics like Taine and Renouvier were outside the University.

The philosopher most favoured by Duruy was Félix Ravaisson; when Duruy restored the *agrégation* in philosophy, Ravaisson became chairman of the *jury*. This post gave its holder much power over new appointments, power used by Ravaisson in a tolerant and open-minded way. A report on the state of philosophy in France, commissioned by Duruy for the Paris Exhibition of 1867, served as Ravaisson's philosophical manifesto. In it, he said that the *agrégation* had revealed a 'spiritualist realism or positivism' as the new philosophy of the younger generation.[2]

Spiritualism in one form or another continued to be the distinguishing mark of the University, but there was much variation of belief. Many philosophy teachers were still sincere Catholics, others disciples of Comte and Littré. There were also some neo-Kantians; this strain in French philosophy, attractive because of its synthesis of the moral and critical approach, of individualism and altruism, was to become the dominant one in the University under the Third Republic.[3] The administration seems to have taken little interest in the philosophical allegiance of teachers, provided that they kept to the syllabus and avoided offending local conservative opinion. The University's experience since 1848 encouraged an attitude of extreme prudence and conformism, compounding the dogmatism which was already inherent in eclecticism. Much of the teaching in this period must have been uninspiring, like that of Nourrisson at the lycée Napoléon: 'Not a single departure from the opinions which he was ordered to hold, not a doubt on the most delicate problems.'[4]

[1] P. Janet, 'Une Nouvelle Phase de la philosophie spiritualiste', *Revue des Deux Mondes*, 2nd period, cviii (1873), pp. 363–70.

[2] F. Ravaisson, *La Philosophie en France au XIXe siècle* (1868), p. 258.

[3] Cf. Gerbod, *La Condition universitaire*, pp. 490–8.

[4] G. Renard, 'Au lycée Napoléon de 1864 à 1867', *La Révolution de 1848*, xxvii (1930), p. 161.

Some teachers did indeed see the purpose of philosophical education as the formation of the 'philosophical spirit', the encouragement of independent and critical thought.[1] More common, however, was the view that it should give the pupil firm beliefs to guide him in a confused world. The professor at the lycée of Marseilles, welcoming Duruy's new policy, saw the answer to the moral and intellectual decadence of the age in 'the return to our University philosophy . . . created by a happy alliance of the tradition of the ancients and the thought of the seventeenth century, impregnated with the purest spirit of Plato and of Descartes'.[2] So too one of Duruy's rectors: 'The greatest minds of antiquity and of modern times have given to all the great questions which arise in the world firm answers. . . . The Professors, familiar with these doctrines, will expound them with that authority which permits of no doubt.'[3]

Duruy may not have wished to change the direction of philosophical teaching, but he was determined that it would no longer be neglected. The baccalaureate was altered so that a philosophy essay was compulsory, and the Philosophy form was made more attractive and important by placing there the new subject of contemporary history. This was the most original of Duruy's innovations. In 1862, Duruy had been appointed to teach history at the École Polytechnique, and had said then that he would like to introduce contemporary history in every lycée as a 'course in patriotism and social education'.[4] The existing course ran in chronological order, ending in 1815, and contemporary history therefore formed a natural conclusion for a syllabus which began with the Old Testament. It now ran, one unfriendly critic said, 'from Adam to Napoleon III, and from the expulsion from Paradise to the evacuation of Mexico';[5] the Mexican expedition was indeed included—being up to date had its dangers.

Duruy's programme for contemporary history—from the middle of the eighteenth century to 1863—remains impressive. It

[1] J. Tissot, *Du développement de l'esprit philosophique comme objet de l'éducation* (1864), pp. 4 ff.

[2] E. Maillet, *Académie d'Aix. Lycée de Marseille. Distribution solennelle des prix, le 9 août 1866. Discours* (1866), p. 15.

[3] Desclozeaux, *Discours prononcé à la distribution des prix du lycée impérial d'Avignon du 12 août 1863* (n.d.), p. 9.

[4] Duruy, *Notes et souvenirs*, i, p. 125.

[5] V. de Laprade, *Le Baccalauréat et les études classiques* (1869), p. 57.

sought to look at society as a whole, and to include economic and intellectual movements as well as political history. The great theme was Progress, material and moral, and the aim was to make the pupils 'men of their age, and to put them in a better state to serve their country according to the necessities of the present time'.[1] This idea of history as the 'history of modern civilization'[2] and the key to understanding the contemporary world was very different from the history traditionally taught in French schools, with its emphasis on heroic actions and great men, for which ancient examples served as well as modern ones. There could be no poetry and no moral lessons, complained Laprade, in the history of tariffs.[3] Duruy disagreed. His new programme included 'notions of political economy'; he claimed that the days of battle-history were past, and that history must include economics 'if it wants to remain what it ought to be: the treasury of human experience and the mistress of life'.[4] This development naturally pleased the *Journal des Économistes*.

Contemporary history was inevitably controversial. How could it be taught without bringing politics into the classroom? Duruy claimed that the objective study of history helped to heal wounds rather than reopen them, and that national reconciliation was the government's aim.[5] But the syllabus itself was by no means impartial—and the first version of it was so biased that he had to make major alterations in the face of press and parliamentary criticism, and of pressure from the Conseil impérial, which he had neglected to consult in the first place.[6]

The provisional syllabus offended both left and right by being both liberal and strongly Bonapartist (an aspect played down by Duruy's later admirers). It was liberal in its hostile tone towards legitimism and the Restoration, in its praise of the rise of tolerance, and in its account of Napoleon III's intervention in Italy (the burning issue of the day). The left were offended by the emphasis on the democratic basis of the Second Empire, and the celebration of its triumph over the 'socialism' of 1848. The first version contained a long catalogue and eulogy of the social, political, and

---

[1] Circular of 24 Mar. 1865.
[2] Duruy, op. cit., i, p. 280.
[3] Laprade, op. cit., pp. 86–9.
[4] Instruction of 24 Sept. 1863.
[5] Ibid.
[6] Programmes of 24 Sept. 1863 (provisional), 15 Dec. 1863 (revised); A.N. F^{17} 6806, papers relating to Conseil impérial, and F^{17} 12957, minutes of Conseil impérial, 16, 24, 25, 26 Nov. 1863.

economic achievements of the regime. It is hardly surprising that Duruy was attacked by the liberals in Parliament as well as the Catholics, and criticized by both Michelet and Dupanloup.[1] The political implications of the programme were well appreciated by Duruy's officials; one rector welcomed it as 'a sure means of attaching the new generations firmly to the Imperial dynasty, by inspiring love for our liberal institutions and safeguarding them from the suggestions of those who turn history to partisan use'.[2] No political incidents were reported when the new syllabus came into operation.

Political motives—a mixture of internationalism and patriotism—were also involved in Duruy's encouragement of modern languages. On the one hand, there was the liberal vision of European unity, with the nations drawing closer together and competing peacefully to make their contributions to prosperity and progress; on the other, there was the threat of Prussia. After 1870, the deficiencies of the lycées, including their weakness in modern languages, were to be blamed as an element in France's defeat. But the mood of self-criticism began with Sadowa in 1866. Duruy was acutely conscious of German rivalry, commercial, intellectual, and military, and in 1867 he noted 'Nobody in the army speaks German, and the Emperor reproaches me with it.'[3]

Duruy radically altered the teaching of modern languages in the lycées. Since 1852, English and German had been taught compulsorily, in a three-year course beginning in the third form. From 1863, languages were begun in the sixth form (about the age of 12), were compulsory for three years, then became optional in the higher forms. Smaller schools were allowed to teach only one language, and Duruy encouraged the introduction of Spanish and Italian in southern France.[4] Since languages were to be started young, he wanted teachers to use 'maternal' or 'natural' instead of formal methods, with emphasis on the spoken language and rapid reading knowledge and as little grammar as possible. This pushed further ideas already found in Fortoul's 1854 instructions. The negative side of Duruy's ideas was that he saw language as a

[1] Parliamentary debates printed in *Journal général de l'instruction publique*, xxxiii (1864), pp. 11–15, 330–6; Michelet, *Nos fils*, p. 272; Dupanloup, *De la haute éducation intellectuelle*, ii, pp. 91 ff.

[2] A.N. F¹⁷ 2650, report of rector of Grenoble, 2 Oct. 1863.

[3] Duruy–Glachant papers, A.N. 114 AP 1, Duruy to Glachant, 13 Sept. 1867.

[4] Instruction of 29 Sept. 1863, *arrêté* of 4 Dec. 1863, instruction of 6 Oct. 1865.

professional tool needed by some, but did not think foreign literatures could have the same educative value as the classics; he had argued on these grounds that languages should be optional when he was an inspector.[1]

New methods of teaching could not be introduced overnight. Duruy relied in the long term on improving the quality of the teachers, most of whom were still of foreign origin and inferior ability.[2] Duruy revived the *agrégation* in modern languages, and he planned to train teachers at the *école normale* which he created for special education.[3] At this time, modern language teachers had begun to write pamphlets calling for improvements and explaining new methods, and they welcomed Duruy's reforms.[4]

Duruy was able to make the changes he wanted in science, philosophy, history, and modern languages; but for the classics he had plans which did not get beyond the experimental stage. This was because he had the controversial idea of cutting out or making optional some of the traditional exercises, in order to make room for modern subjects, and also to shift the emphasis away from style and composition towards reading the classical authors for their own sake. There were senior administrators in the University who shared these ideas, like the rectors Cournot and Théry,[5] but they were likely to be opposed by the ordinary teachers, whose attachment to tradition had been revealed by Rouland's inquiries about bifurcation. Duruy decided to test opinion before acting, and included a number of questions on classical teaching in a questionnaire of 1864. Among his suggestions were: the rapid reading (*lecture cursive*) of classical authors (reactions were divided); making Latin verse optional (almost unanimous opposition); and starting Greek at a later stage (the majority were against). [6]It was clear that the University was unsympathetic, and the fact that some of Duruy's ideas were borrowed from abroad did not help—'it smells too much of Germanism, and is thus condemned in advance

[1] A.N. F^{17} 7563, report of Duruy and Roustan on Avignon, 17 June 1862.

[2] Cf. P. Lévy, *La Langue allemande en France, pénétration et diffusion des origines à nos jours. II. De 1830 à nos jours* (1952), pp. 48 ff.

[3] See below, p. 219.

[4] See Bibliography, section X F(iv): books by B. Lévy, H. Schmidt, H. Montucci.

[5] Cournot, *Des institutions d'instruction publique*, pp. 66–72; A. Théry, *Projet d'une réforme dans l'enseignement des langues anciennes* (1872), pp. 8 ff.

[6] A.N. F^{17} 6843–9, replies to circular of 16 July 1864, questions II.7, II.14, III.17.

in France' was one inspector's comment on *lecture cursive*.[1] When Duruy reissued the programmes in 1865, he abolished Greek prose composition (*thème grec*) but avoided other major changes.

Duruy's next move came in 1868, when he included a number of suggestions for reform in the statistical report which he published on secondary education. This was an attempt to appeal to public opinion over the heads of the University: 'Since the *universitaires* do not want to carry it out themselves, the reform will be imposed on them. For that I am awaiting the publication of the secondary Statistics, which will give the coup de grâce.'[2] Duruy's new reform programme included optional Latin verse, options in the baccalaureate, classes lasting an hour and a half instead of two, teaching certain subjects by 'sets' according to ability instead of by forms, and (in some versions) making Greek optional in the senior forms.

None of this was introduced definitively, but parts were tried out experimentally, and Duruy continued to test the University's reactions. In April 1868, meetings were held in every school and the opinions of teachers invited;[3] in 1868 and 1869, *conseils académiques* were consulted;[4] Versailles served as a pilot lycée for some reforms, and there were other experiments in the provinces on which reports were collected. Some of Duruy's ideas were applied in the new special education. None of this activity proved welcome to the University. The innovation most widely tried was the shorter classes, and even this met with a surprising amount of opposition from teachers. It was also unpopular with the parents of day-boys, who had their sons sent home for longer periods. 'Some of them are talking of sending them to the Marists, who . . . will keep them all day. . . . There are many parents who measure the merit of schools by the number of hours for which their children are taken off their hands.' This reaction was widely reported, and at Reims a group of rich parents tried to get up a petition, claiming that the University had a legal obligation to give their sons four hours of classical education a day. Officials often feared that innovations would be exploited by the Catholic schools, who would claim that the University's education was being weakened.[5]

---

[1] A.N. F^{17} 6847, replies to circular of 16 July 1864, Paris, *inspecteur d'académie* A. Nisard.

[2] A.N. F^{17} 7533, Duruy's note on letter, Mourier to Duruy, 16 Apr. 1867.

[3] A.N. F^{17} 6853, replies to circular of 22 Apr. 1868.

[4] A.N. F^{17} 4363–4, minutes of *conseils académiques*, 1868–9.

[5] A.N. F^{17} 6872^2, reports from academies, undated, Nancy; Mourier to

The officials were always acutely conscious of Catholic competition, and in this case it was used as an argument for conservatism.

Many in the University thought, probably rightly, that eventually Greek would suffer most from Duruy's plans. In 1867 the 'Association for the encouragement of Greek studies' was formed, including the University's leading Hellenists, and it began a campaign in defence of the subject. A pamphlet was published, a deputation called on Duruy, and the support of the conservative press was secured.[1] This was significant as the first appearance of an organized pressure-group defending classical studies, and it may have had some effect in deterring Duruy from action. But in any case Duruy ceased to be minister in 1869, and had no chance to introduce any of his proposals permanently.

Duruy's plans for reforming the classics did much to create disillusion with his administration in the University, despite his liberalism. This is clear from confidential reports written by his son-in-law, Charles Glachant, one of Duruy's personal team at the ministry. After inquiries in the east, 'one of the most enlightened regions in France', he reported that four-fifths of the teachers wanted no change. After the experience of Fortoul, the University was tired of experiments, and longed to return to settled ways; only formal legislation, backed by public opinion, would force the University to change.[2] In another report, Glachant pointed out that it was useless to introduce measures of which the University disapproved, because the non-cooperation of teachers and officials made them a dead letter, and that there was no evidence that parents were dissatisfied with the status quo.[3] All this suggests that Duruy had reached the limits of effective action. When he was dismissed, the *Revue de l'instruction publique* praised his attempt to shake the University out of its centuries-old routine, but admitted that the University had been unresponsive. 'So much the worse for the University! It is he who was right!'[4]

---

minister, 9 June 1869 (on Reims); and cf. other reports from academies, Oct.–Nov. 1868 and undated, especially Rennes.

[1] É. Egger, *La Tradition et les réformes dans l'enseignement universitaire* (1883), pp. 280–9. Cf. *Annuaire de l'Association pour l'encouragement des études grecques*, iii (1869), pp. xl, xlv; *Journal général de l'instruction publique*, xxxviii (1868), p. 322.

[2] A.N. F^{17} 6879, Glachant to Duruy, 12 July 1868; cf. F^{17} 6872^2, reports of Glachant on experiments at Versailles, 16 Mar. and 6 June 1869.

[3] A.N. F^{17} 9096, Glachant to Duruy, 16 July 1868.

[4] *Revue de l'instruction publique*, xxix (1869), p. 258.

As in other fields, Duruy's percipience about the underlying problems made him a 'precursor' of changes later imposed by the pressure of time. His experience also showed that there would be a formidable rearguard action. The classics remained at the heart of the University's educational ideal, even though other subjects had now ceased to be mere appendages and were claiming their independent rights. As long as the defenders of the classics clung to every practice sanctified by tradition, it was impossible to achieve Duruy's ideal of a streamlined classical teaching taking its place in an integrated syllabus. The alternatives were as they had been before 1852: either some form of bifurcation had to be allowed, or the introduction of new subjects meant an ever-increasing burden of work for the unfortunate pupils.

3. HUMANIZING SCHOOL LIFE

In 1868, a book with the title *L'Éducation homicide* was published by the Catholic poet Victor de Laprade. It was an extreme but not untypical example of a mounting wave of criticism of the physical and moral effects of education in the lycées. Criticism centred on three main points: the excessive burden of work laid on pupils, and the lack of physical exercise; the effect of competition and examinations; and the way in which the French system of discipline repressed the individuality of the pupil. This criticism came from liberals and Catholics rather than from the left, and had no special connection with progressive pedagogic theories.

Laprade's book was directed especially against overwork and the inhumanity of the University's system. Its unfortunate victims worked for eleven hours a day, immobile at their desks, their natural needs for movement and exercise frustrated. The mental strain caused by overloading of the syllabus was not balanced by any concern for physical education, and ruined constitutions were the result. Like other writers on the subject, Laprade feared that this would lead to a physical degeneration of the race, and in particular of the upper classes. Complaints about overloading were not new, and it had been the subject of inquiries by Carnot in 1848 and Rouland in 1863. Laprade himself had sounded the alarm in 1851,[1] and the question had been raised from time to time by

---

[1] V. de Laprade, *De l'enseignement des langues anciennes considéré comme base des études classiques* (1852), pp. 6–9 (speech of 1851).

medical writers;[1] but discussion in press and parliament in the sixties suggests that it was attracting increasing public interest.

Laprade described the lycée as a 'frightful mixture of the cloister, the barracks, and the prison'.[2] Another possible comparison was with the factory, and Duruy observed that the schoolchild worked longer hours than a Paris worker.[3] There could be little doubt that it was desirable to reduce the burden, but it was not easy to see how. Laprade's solution was radical but retrograde: he thought liberal education could rely almost exclusively on Latin and Greek, and proposed a ruthless pruning of unnecessary subjects like history, science, and modern languages.[4] This was hardly to Duruy's taste. The most he could do was to rearrange the order of work, with shorter classes, more short breaks, and more time for private study and reading. An experimental timetable on these lines was introduced at the lycée of Mont-de-Marsan, which Duruy was using as a model school for special education, but there were still ten and a quarter hours of work a day.[5]

Physical conditions in the schools were another danger to health. Only 16 of the 77 lycées in 1865 were in buildings constructed for the purpose (most were in monastic buildings, old Jesuit colleges, or other buildings confiscated by the state during the Revolution and not required for barracks or prisons),[6] and nearly all were on cramped sites in town centres. Rebuilding was necessarily slow. But in 1864 Duruy set up 'hygiene commissions' in each academy to improve the existing premises. They were to look into cleanliness, ventilation, and sanitary arrangements, as well as food, clothing, gymnastics, and recreation.[7] Gymnastics and food had received attention from Fortoul in 1853, when an inquiry had revealed that thin soup and boiled beef (up to five times a week) were the staple fare of *lycéens*.[8] But systematic attention to health questions was something new—the ministry of education still had no medical department. Duruy's personal interest in the question is shown by his plan to teach hygiene in the lycées—'a few notions of physical

[1] e.g. A. C. Clavel, *Traité d'éducation physique et morale* (1855), i, *passim*; J. B. Fonssagrives, *L'Éducation physique des garçons* (1870), pp. 104 ff.

[2] Laprade, *L'Éducation homicide*, p. 103.

[3] *L'Administration de l'instruction publique de 1863 à 1869*, p. 578.

[4] Laprade, *Le Baccalauréat et les études classiques*, pp. 45 ff.

[5] *Bulletin administratif*, new series, vii (1867), pp. 311–13.

[6] *Statistique de l'enseignement secondaire en 1865*, pp. xxxiii–xxxiv.

[7] *Arrêté* of 15 Feb. 1864, circulars of 20 Feb., 10 May 1864.

[8] *Arrêté* of 1 Sept. 1853, and accompanying report.

hygiene combine very well with the moral hygiene provided by the teaching of philosophy'[1]—and by minor measures like the sending of delicate pupils to lycées in the south during the winter.[2]

Duruy said that 'the aspect of the lycées should be simple and gay', and he favoured low buildings, sunny courtyards, trees, and gardens.[3] He also encouraged the idea of separate buildings for the younger pupils, sometimes situated in the suburbs, where a less rigorous regime could be applied. In Paris, Louis-le-Grand had had its *petit lycée* at Vanves since 1853 (Duruy turned this into an independent Lycée du Prince Impérial), and the example had been followed elsewhere. In giving attention to these matters, both Fortoul and Duruy were thinking of competition with the Catholic schools, which had a reputation for their attention to health and comfort and their interest in recreation. At the Christian Brothers' *pensionnat* at Marseilles, visited and admired by Duruy in 1866, there was a swimming bath as well as a gymnasium—something possessed by no school in the University.[4]

In 1864, Duruy floated the idea of introducing cricket and other organized games on the English model.[5] But French schools had no playing fields; gymnastics was the only practicable form of exercise and the one thought most in accord with French (and classical) tradition. However, an inquiry in 1869 revealed that only 42 lycées (of 82) had covered gymnasia, and only 22 colleges; 15 lycées, and most colleges, did not even have any apparatus. A new programme for gymnastics was drawn up by experts and adopted by Duruy.[6] There was one significant difference between his and Fortoul's. In 1854, the inclusion of military drill had been rejected, the foreign minister having told Fortoul that this was not in line with the ideas of the Emperor, then presenting himself as the apostle of peace.[7] In 1869, however, fear of Prussia, and debates about a new system of military service, had created a different mood, and military exercises were included in the new gymnastics syllabus. Duruy himself was always an admirer of the army.

Duruy's views on health questions were remarkably enlightened,

[1] Duruy, *Notes et souvenirs*, i, p. 283.   [2] Circular of 1 Dec. 1866.
[3] Circular of 10 May 1864.   [4] Rigault, *Histoire générale*, v, p. 392.
[5] R. D. Anderson, 'French Views of the English Public Schools: Some Nineteenth-Century Episodes', *History of Education*, ii (1973), p. 167.
[6] Decree of 3 Feb. 1869.
[7] Fortoul papers, A.N. 246 AP 19, memorandum of Drouyn de Lhuys, 18 Feb. 1854.

and he did as much as was practicable to meet contemporary criticisms. He had less sympathy, however, with those who criticized the competitive atmosphere of the schools and blamed the baccalaureate and the examinations of the government schools for fostering it. In condemning over-ambitious parents who demanded too much of their children, and complaining that education was now pursued for career ends instead of its own sake, Laprade was only echoing a perennial complaint of teachers.[1] But the concern about overwork naturally directed fresh attention to examinations. Cournot would have liked to abolish the baccalaureate altogether, replacing it by internal examinations[2] (the German *Abitur* was an example cited by reformers). Others wanted to relieve the competitive pressure by raising the age limits of the government schools, but this was never found practicable.

Attacking examinations raised a political question, because it involved the principle of merit, and because the baccalaureate was a means for the state to control indirectly what was taught in private schools. The abolition of state degrees, or a share in administering them, was the next item on the Catholic programme for extending liberty of education. Duruy had no intention of surrendering the state's control. Nor could he afford to relax the intensive preparation given in the lycées for the government schools, for this was a field where Catholics were competing with the University with increasing success. In any case, Duruy shared the belief of all French teachers in 'emulation'; the life of the classroom revolved around marks, class orders, and individual competition. The supreme expression of this spirit was the *concours général*, an annual competition between the Paris lycées, the victors in which received their prizes from the minister himself in a great ceremony at the Sorbonne. Far from abolishing it, as many reformers advocated, Duruy extended the principle by creating a parallel contest for the provinces. Changes which he made in the baccalaureate, however, did tend to make mechanical cramming more difficult.

Many of those who criticized the disciplinary system of the lycées were liberals who related it to the French tendency to look to the state for employment and for social and economic initiatives. They blamed the University for repressing the individuality of its pupils, and so sapping the energy and enterprise of the French bourgeoisie;

[1] Laprade, *L'Éducation homicide*, pp. 51 ff.
[2] Cournot, *Des institutions d'instruction publique*, pp. 175 ff., 371–5.

G

both France's lack of economic dynamism, and her willingness to submit to dictatorial rule, might be traced to this factor. The obvious contrast was with England, where it was thought that the schools implanted the qualities of individual initiative and self-government. Duruy commissioned a full-scale report on secondary education in Britain, and he took many ideas from it.[1] One was that prefects might replace *maîtres d'études*, for it was the boarding system which was the cause of some of the most criticized features of the French schools. The more radical reformers, like Renan, would have liked the state to withdraw altogether from the provision of boarding.[2] But Duruy was not free to take this course. Boarding provided the lycées and colleges with the bulk of their income—the boarders subsidized the day-boys—and it remained popular with parents. Helped by the growth of the railways, the proportion of boarders in the lycées rose from 41 per cent in 1850 to 56 per cent in 1865, the actual numbers more than doubling.[3] But Duruy thought it might be possible to move away from the huge impersonal *internat* and create more of a family atmosphere. Why should boys not board with the teachers, as in England, or with families in the town, as in Germany? The latter custom had been traditional in Brittany, and Duruy encouraged its revival at Napoléonville (Pontivy), a school where he was experimenting with special education, and also tried it at Mont-de-Marsan.[4]

Duruy thus proved that the administration was not unresponsive to public opinion, and sought to change aspects of education which were rarely discussed or questioned in the University. The advent of a liberal minister had brought a breath of pedagogic fresh air. No doubt the fever of activity at the ministry meant little to the average schoolboy, but his life was slowly improving, as schools were rebuilt, as modern ideas on heating, lighting, and sanitation worked their way through the system, and as middle-class expectations about comfort rose with the expanding prosperity of the Second Empire.

---

[1] Anderson, in *History of Education*, ii (1973), pp. 159–72. The report was by J. Demogeot and H. Montucci; Duruy also had a report on Germany by J. F. Minssen. See Bibliography, section II E.

[2] *Oeuvres complètes de Ernest Renan* (ed. H. Psichari, n.d.), i, pp. 534–40. Cf. J. Simon, *La Réforme de l'enseignement secondaire* (1874), pp. 184 ff.; Cournot, *Des institutions d'instruction publique*, pp. 142–3.

[3] *Statistique de l'enseignement secondaire en 1865*, pp. lxxxvi–xci.

[4] Ibid., p. 414; *L'Administration de l'instruction publique de 1863 à 1869*, pp. 491–5.

4. SECONDARY EDUCATION FOR GIRLS

The idea of doing something about girls' secondary education seems to have occurred to Duruy in 1867, when the question was raised by Carnot and Simon in the debates on the primary education bill. Duruy took no new legal powers, but decided to rely on voluntary effort, as with the evening courses for adults. In a circular of October 1867, he instructed rectors to encourage the municipal authorities to organize courses for girls. The teaching would be provided by the professors of the lycées and colleges, the courses would be based on modern subjects, and fees would be charged since they were aimed at 'well-off or rich families'.[1]

Duruy spoke in the circular of 'founding' this form of education, since it did not exist in France. This was, of course, untrue, as secondary education was given both in convent schools and in private boarding-schools. There were also day 'courses' similar to those proposed by Duruy. In Paris, for example, there was an institution founded in 1856 for the Protestant bourgeoisie, and a number of courses attended mainly by girls who wished to train as teachers.[2] It was true, however, that standards in these schools varied widely, partly because of the absence of external inspection (the system of inspecting convent schools introduced by Fortoul was last used in 1858), and, more significantly, because there was no examination for girls to aim at.

In particular, girls could not take the baccalaureate, because girls' schools were not allowed to teach Latin.[3] The University, supported in this by public opinion, was firmly convinced of the unsuitability of Latin for girls: when the commissioners whom Duruy sent to Britain found girls learning Latin alongside boys in the Scottish burgh schools, the Latin shocked them more than the mixture of sexes.[4] In the absence of any other qualification, many middle-class girls took the higher level of the primary teachers' *brevet*, even if they did not intend to teach. But in 1862 the baccalaureate was first taken by a woman. Rouland had at first refused permission, but had

[1] Circular of 30 Oct. 1867.

[2] *Séance d'ouverture des cours gradués pour les jeunes demoiselles protestantes. Discours prononcés à cette occasion* (1856); Gréard, *Éducation et instruction. Enseignement secondaire*, i, pp. 117–22.

[3] See regulation for girls' secondary schools in Seine department, 7 Mar. 1837.

[4] J. Demogeot and H. Montucci, *De l'enseignement secondaire en Angleterre et en Écosse* (1868), p. 474.

been unable to discover any legal justification for this. The pioneer was not a schoolgirl, but Julie-Victoire Daubié, a teacher and writer on girls' education.[1] Only 49 girls were to take the baccalaureate in the years down to 1882.[2]

Another sign of the times was the appearance of a handful of women in the medical faculties. In 1868–9, there were four—but three of them were foreigners; by 1882, the Paris faculty had given nineteen doctorates to women, but only five of them were French.[3] This was a cause in which Duruy had taken an interest, and in 1870, when out of office but with the backing of the Empress Eugénie, he was planning a private institution for the medical education of women at Paris.[4]

There were thus some signs that the time had come in the sixties for the state to help raise standards. But Duruy's rather innocuous proposals unleashed a Catholic attack of great ferocity, led by Dupanloup. In the words of his biographer, 'the courageous bishop dropped all his other work to combat this peril', seeing Duruy's moves as part of 'a vast conspiracy of free thought against Christian womanhood'.[5] Dupanloup published several pamphlets attacking Duruy, the burden of which was that public courses given by laymen to girls were an affront to morality. Even the most moderate bishops felt obliged to support Dupanloup, though embarrassed by the violence of his language. How is this reaction to be explained? The idea of a free-thought conspiracy was certainly not confined to Dupanloup, and many Catholics welcomed an opportunity to discredit the anticlerical minister. But the underlying reason was that Duruy was proposing to shift the frontier between the recognized spheres of influence of Church and state; this was a field of education where the Church's dominance had previously been unchallenged, and could not be allowed to slip away without a fight.

In one of Dupanloup's pamphlets, some fifty pages were devoted to exalting the unique qualities of 'Christian and French womanhood'. His idea that 'there are only . . . two sanctuaries for these fragile and pure vessels, Religion and the Family'[6] was widely shared by middle-class opinion. It was generally accepted, of course, that

---

[1] J. B. Piobetta, *Le Baccalauréat* (1937), p. 111 n.
[2] Gréard, op. cit., i, p. 153. [3] Ibid., i, p. 153.
[4] Duruy, *Notes et souvenirs*, ii, pp. 196–216.
[5] F. Lagrange, *Vie de Mgr Dupanloup* (1883–4), iii, pp. 98, 101.
[6] Dupanloup, *Discours prononcé au Congrès de Malines*, p. 31.

the role of a woman was to be a wife and mother, and Duruy himself defined the aim of his courses as to prepare her 'to carry with another the weight of the duties and responsibilities of life, without departing from the role which nature assigns to her'.[1] But beyond this there was the concept of female modesty or 'delicacy', which were felt to be in danger if laymen taught girls, if male inspectors visited girls' boarding-schools, or if girls had to appear before male examining boards. It was usual for girls attending day courses to be accompanied by their mothers, and Duruy expected this to be the case in the courses he created. When trying to conciliate the bishops in the Conseil impérial, he stressed that he was against the idea of lycées for girls, though he also attacked the bishops' supposed abhorrence of male teachers as dishonest: nearly 3,000 outsiders already taught in convent schools and *pensionnats*, about 400 of whom were members of the University doing part-time teaching.[2]

Nevertheless, the bourgeois preference for Catholic girls' education was strong enough to make Duruy's experiment a relative failure, despite the support of the Empress, the willing co-operation of the University, and the enthusiasm of many municipalities. Duruy had originally expected the courses to appear wherever there was a lycée or college, but only about forty were organized in 1867–8 and fifty in 1868–9 (when they were especially successful in the progressive East). Their success varied with the influence of the Church, which demonstrated on this issue the moral and social pressures which it could bring to bear; and it was precisely this influence which it stood to lose if Duruy's experiment weakened its hold over the wives and daughters of the bourgeoisie. 'Girls of marriageable age who would not be deterred by the refusal of absolution do not want to be pointed at in the streets,' reported Glachant. 'Against these tactics, the University and the government are powerless.'[3] In some towns where religious influence was strong, the courses could not be started; in others, they were attended mainly by Protestants and the daughters of *universitaires*. Often too the prefects were hostile, especially as the 1869 elections approached; the government was anxious to conciliate the Catholic opposition, and Duruy's campaign was an embarrassment to it.[4]

[1] Circular of 30 Oct. 1867.
[2] A.N. F^{17} 12958, minutes of Conseil impérial, 9 Dec. 1867. These minutes show the embarrassment of the moderate bishops, like Darboy of Paris.
[3] A.N. F^{17} 9096, Glachant to Duruy, 16 July 1868.
[4] Maurain, *La Politique ecclésiastique*, pp. 838–55, 872–3; F. Mayeur, 'Les

The courses survived Duruy's dismissal, and where they were established they carried on until gradually replaced by girls' lycées after 1880.[1] The latter were acceptable to opinion because they were staffed by women; Duruy's use of male teachers was unsatisfactory, but the only course open to him. The lycées were also to give a complete education, whereas most of the girls in Duruy's courses were over sixteen, and only adding to an education received elsewhere.[2] The original plan was for graded courses covering three or four years, but numbers were seldom large enough to allow this. Duruy's syllabus was based on his special secondary education, which excluded Latin; it could become, he claimed, 'the classical education of girls from fourteen to seventeen or eighteen years'.[3] It was something to accept that an education without Latin could be classical; Duruy was also accepting the idea that girls' education had to be different, but that was to survive for many years—the syllabuses were not assimilated until the 1920s, and co-education was not accepted in France until much later. Duruy was a genuine pioneer in challenging deeply rooted attitudes. But for the time being, the bourgeoisie were content to maintain the 'anachronism' in their family life denounced by the left—'The wife belongs to the seventeenth century, the husband to the end of the eighteenth.'[4]

Évêques français et Victor Duruy: les cours secondaires de jeunes filles', *Revue d'histoire de l'Église de France*, lvii (1971), pp. 292–9.

[1] Gréard, op. cit., i, pp. 150–2.
[2] *L'Administration de l'instruction publique de 1863 à 1869*, p. 672.
[3] Circular of 30 Oct. 1867.
[4] Simon, in *Revue des Deux Mondes*, 2nd period, lii (1864), p. 960.

CHAPTER TEN

Education and industry

I. THE DEBATE ON ENSEIGNEMENT PROFESSIONNEL

It was inevitable that the new public interest in education in the sixties would revive the question of *enseignement professionnel*, a term which still caused much confusion. It might mean specialized training for particular occupations—though this began to be called technical education from about 1865—or a general education with a practical bias which made it especially suitable for careers in commerce and industry. How far this practical bias should go, and whether it made manual work (*travail manuel*) a necessity in the school, were matters of dispute.

The economic expansion of the fifties meant that the prosperity of industry was now a question of national concern. The relative stagnation of the sixties, and such events as the free-trade treaty of 1860 and the cotton crisis caused by the American civil war, forced industrialists to take stock of their position and to give attention to the intellectual as well as the material factors of production. Men were conscious of the technological changes in industry, especially in textiles; mechanization and the introduction of new processes seemed to create a need not only for a more educated working force but for an intermediate class of men familiar with the basic principles of science and technology, or with the knowledge of geography and languages needed to sell French products on the world market. These were, to use a favourite image, the N.C.O.s of the industrial army, and to improve their education seemed one of the most urgent needs. The decline of apprenticeship continued too to make the training of skilled workers a problem, while even the officers of the industrial army needed to keep up with the times: 'Many heads of industry', it was said in 1864, 'send their sons to the École centrale to give them a scientific education of which they feel the lack themselves.'[1]

---

[1] *Mémoires et compte-rendu des travaux de la Société des Ingénieurs civils*, 1864, p. 440.

The Great Exhibition of 1851 had stimulated interest in *enseigne-ment professionnel*, and the London Exhibition of 1862 had the same result. It was the first international exhibition to have a special section for educational methods and equipment, and as before French representatives were especially interested in art education. They were impressed by the efforts made in this field in Britain since 1851; both Charles Robert, reporting on art teaching, and Prosper Mérimée, on the decorative arts, thought that French industry was still ahead, but that other nations were catching up fast, and French manufacturers must look to their laurels.[1] The partisans of *enseignement professionnel* emphasized the point: 'England, intelli-gent and egoistic, industrious and jealous, dreams of an artistic Aboukir and a commercial Trafalgar over our French industries.'[2]

The most important result of the 1862 Exhibition was the report on industrial education prepared by General Morin, head of the Conservatoire des arts et métiers, and his deputy Henri Tresca. Their report was turned into a plea for the organization of industrial education in France on a large scale, co-ordinating the existing schools and filling in the gaps in order to form a complete system with three levels. The aim throughout would be to bring scientific knowledge to bear on industrial practice; at the lower levels, teaching would be based on *dessin géométrique* (the application of mathematics to industrial design and draughtsmanship) and 'general technology', defined as 'a succession of studies on tools, raw materials, products, processes, in a word on the whole material side of workshop practice'.[3] Morin and Tresca took firm positions on a number of questions which were to prove controversial over the next few years. First, they thought that industrial education must include manual work. Second, they saw it as a means of developing the potential of the individual worker and improving his social position, not just of benefiting industry in general. In our post-revolutionary society, they said, it is illegitimate to try to tie men to the class in which they are born, and they rejected the idea that *déclassement* was something to be feared. They claimed the

---

[1] *Exposition universelle de Londres de 1862. Rapports des membres de la section française du jury international sur l'ensemble de l'Exposition* (1862), vi, pp. 151–2, 247–8, 262.

[2] C. Bertrand, *Étude sur l'enseignement professionnel* (2nd edn., 1864), pp. 18–19.

[3] *Exposition universelle de Londres de 1862. Rapports*, vi, p. 213.

support of Guizot for the view that 'once you have begun to educate the masses, you have to educate them more and more', and they produced a new argument for *déclassement*: since the middle class tend to abandon industry for the liberal professions, the health of industry demands that the sons of workers should be encouraged to move up to fill the gaps.[1]

Finally, Morin and Tresca thought that the time had come for the state to take over from private initiative and to spend money on creating a network of public schools. 'The State can never spend too much to create . . . an intelligent population, possessing sound notions of technology at every level.'[2] There was no better way of securing the future of French industrial prosperity. However, it was vital that the University should not be the agency of state action, for the methods and approach of the lycées would be quite alien to industrial education, where instruction should be given, often on a part-time basis, by practical men closely in touch with local needs. The co-ordinating role should be played by the ministry of commerce.

The minister of commerce was Eugène Rouher, who was anxious to promote the efficiency and productivity of French industry in the aftermath of the free-trade treaty, and who was a powerful political figure. In 1863, as a direct result of Morin and Tresca's report, Rouher set up a commission to examine the whole question of *enseignement professionnel*. It included Morin, Tresca, Mérimée, Chevalier, Le Play, and Perdonnet, director of the École centrale. There were some industrialists—Schneider of Le Creusot, Arlès Dufour of Lyons, Jean Dollfus of Mulhouse—but they were outnumbered by educational experts and civil servants.[3] This commission set to work collecting evidence and hearing witnesses, and was to report in 1865. In the meanwhile, discussion of *enseignement professionnel* did not peter out, as after 1851, but flourished and developed in new directions.

That this was so was in large part due to the existence of *L'Enseignement professionnel*, a fortnightly journal devoted to the question which was published between 1862 and 1865. It was connected with the working-class side of the campaign for universal education, the *Atelier–Bibliothèque utile* group. One of the editors, Charles Gaumont, had written for *L'Atelier*; Corbon and Leneveux

[1] Ibid., pp. 206–10. [2] Ibid., p. 242, and cf. 221.
[3] *Enquête sur l'enseignement professionnel*, i, pp. v–x.

contributed to *L'Enseignement professionnel*.[1] Many of the ideas of the journal can indeed be found in Corbon's *De l'enseignement professionnel*, published in 1859. Corbon had wanted the 'union of school and workshop', and to this end had advocated manual work as part of education at all levels. The need for manual work was what *L'Enseignement professionnel* preached above all else.

The journal was mainly concerned with workers' education—in its own formulation, with the élite soldiers and corporals rather than the officers.[2] It did not fully accept the 'N.C.O.' idea, for it was contemptuous of clerks and white-collar workers, and criticized the sort of intermediate education which made the worker ashamed to work with his hands. Corbon too had attacked the *écoles d'arts et métiers* for producing technicians and foremen—'a sort of mandarinate of the second rank under the direction of the engineers'—rather than workers.[3] What *L'Enseignement professionnel* wanted was an education for all skilled industrial workers, following the primary school at thirteen or fourteen, and lasting for about three years. It would be a general education, thus differing from the existing *écoles d'apprentissage*, which simply taught a trade; these would survive only for occupations where theory did not matter or for children who had to earn a living at once.[4] The clientele envisaged was thus the working-class élite.

If the education was to be a general one, where did manual training fit in? The *travail manuel* recommended by *L'Enseignement professionnel* was conceived not as a form of craft training but as a general education in manual dexterity which would be relevant to all industrial occupations. It was argued that a few manual operations were the basis of all skills, and that certain tools were 'types' of all the others, so that 'whoever knows how to handle the file and the lathe, or the plane, the saw and the chisel, knows really all that is essential to exercise an infinity of occupations'.[5] As this shows, manual work meant work in wood and metal; the plan was suited to the older artisan industries, and to engineering, but would seem to have little to offer to the factory worker in the textile industries.

[1] A. Cuvillier, *Un Journal d'ouvriers: 'L'Atelier' (1840–1850)* (n.d.), p. 202; cf. *L'Enseignement professionnel*, i (1862), pp. 1–2.

[2] Ibid., i (1863), pp. 51, 67.

[3] Corbon, *De l'enseignement professionnel*, p. 136.

[4] *L'Enseignement professionnel*, i (1863), pp. 95–6.

[5] Ibid., i (1862), p. 18.

The more enthusiastic advocates of manual work, including Corbon, thought it should be included in the education of all classes. For the middle class, it would provide physical exercise and a training to fall back on in adversity. More important, it would narrow the social gap between employer and worker, and give the factory owner or manager first-hand knowledge of the processes which he supervised.[1] *L'Enseignement professionnel* did not fully adopt this line, but it certainly had a deep belief in the moral virtue of manual work and the need to unite the training of hand and brain. It is not surprising that the journal cited César Fichet's work with approval,[2] and Fichet himself re-emerged from obscurity to take part in the discussions. The *école professionnelle* at Mulhouse was a model constantly held up for admiration by *L'Enseignement professionnel*, as was the Institution Rossat at Charleville, a successful private school whose staff included Fichet's pupil Denniée. Neither school was in fact for the working class, but both practised manual work; another often-cited model was a school at Lyons called La Martinière, which did cater for the working class.

The École Turgot, and the example of Pompée, found less favour. Pompée, who contributed to the debate by publishing his *Études sur l'éducation professionnelle en France* in 1863, was a resolute opponent of manual work in general education, and this was a cause of much debate between him and the editors of *L'Enseignement professionnel*, who thought that it was misleading to call Pompée's form of education *enseignement professionnel*; it was rather a form of modern or 'French' secondary education for the lower middle class. Despite these differences, the journal tried to unite all the supporters of educational progress, and was proud of its part in stimulating public opinion.[3] It sponsored a Société pour l'enseignement professionnel from 1864. This included experts in technical education (Perdonnet, Pompée, Tresca, Marguerin—director of the École Turgot—,Fichet, Rossat, and Bader, director of the school at Mulhouse), sympathetic politicians (Wolowski, Lasteyrie, Darimon), left-wing journalists (Sauvestre, F. Morin), and some industrialists (Arlès Dufour, Gouin, and several from Mulhouse). The intention was that the society would help to set up schools and

---

[1] Corbon, op. cit., pp. 146 ff. The influence of Rousseau's *Émile* may be detected here. Hippolyte Carnot wrote to say that he had had his sons taught a trade: *L'Enseignement professionnel*, ii (1864), p. 350.

[2] *L'Enseignement professionnel*, i (1863), p. 50.

[3] Ibid., i (1863), p. 149.

provide teachers and textbooks, as similar societies had done in the early days of primary education.[1] But no more is heard of this society after *L'Enseignement professionnel* itself disappeared at the end of 1865.

Public interest in *enseignement professionnel* eventually waned, but the fact that it spread outside specialized circles in 1862–5 is indicated by the question appearing on the agenda of various conferences and meetings. In 1863, it was discussed by the congress of provincial learned societies—which saw a dispute on manual work between Fichet and Pompée.[2] In 1864, it was studied by the Society of Civil Engineers, which had set up an inquiry headed by Tresca; the engineers proved rather conservative, being satisfied with the existing scientific education provided by the University.[3] The question was also discussed in 1864 by the Société pour l'instruction élémentaire, where Fichet urged the need to act before the religious orders moved in, and by the international social science congress at Amsterdam, attended by Pompée.[4]

Apart from manual work, the main issue dividing the movement was how far the state should take a part in organizing *enseignement professionnel*. Several witnesses before Rouher's commission urged, like Morin and Tresca, that the existing institutions should be reorganized into a national system, and one writer, A. Guettier, wanted to see a complete 'Université des arts et métiers' functioning alongside the University and serving the people as the latter served the bourgeoisie.[5] *L'Enseignement professionnel* criticized Guettier's book for this, and made clear its own surprisingly negative position: industrial education should be left to local initiative, and the role of the state should be confined to encouragement.[6] In practice, this would mean organization by local industrialists.

L'Enseignement professionnel was in any case very hostile to the University. Like Morin and Tresca, it thought the University fundamentally unfitted to deal with the new education, since its instincts were towards uniformity, centralization, and the fossiliza-

---

[1] *L'Enseignement professionnel*, i (1863), pp. 169–71. For members, see ii (1864), pp. 265–6, iii (1865), p. 442.

[2] Ibid., i (1863), pp. 89–93.

[3] *Mémoires et compte-rendu des travaux de la Société des Ingénieurs civils*, 1864, pp. 157–62, 325, 339–54, 433–43.

[4] *L'Enseignement professionnel*, ii (1864), p. 261, iii (1864), pp. 396–9, 411–13.

[5] A. Guettier, *De l'organisation de l'enseignement industriel* (1864), pp. 11–14.

[6] *L'Enseignement professionnel*, i (1863), pp. 74–6.

tion of routine. Moreover, it was the prejudices of the University 'mandarins' which had stifled the growth of *enseignement professionnel*, by devaluing manual labour and producing clerks and petty bureaucrats instead of useful workers.[1] The influence of the classical pattern was a harmful one, but was perpetuated because until now there had been no alternative. Today, however, wrote Jean Macé, the University's system was rejected by the industrial classes at all levels: 'the active bourgeoisie, that which controls production and the movement of commerce' were tired of having their sons return at the age of twenty 'stuffed with Greek and Latin literature' but incapable of helping with the family business.[2] *L'Enseignement professionnel* would have liked to see the classics swept away and replaced by science. 'The goal of modern education . . . can no longer be to form men of letters, idle admirers of the past, but men of science, builders of the present, initiators of the future.'[3] In the journal's general plan for an ideal system, there would be a common education without Latin for all children up to fourteen or fifteen, followed by three specialized forms of secondary education—arts, science, and industry.[4]

But whether *L'Enseignement professionnel* approved or not, the state was preparing to act, and the University was drawing up plans as well as the ministry of commerce. In 1863, Pompée observed that two different approaches were emerging, the ministry of commerce favouring manual work and the ministry of education being against it.[5] In 1864, reviewing the conference of the Société pour l'instruction élémentaire, *L'Enseignement professionnel* similarly discovered two tendencies, one 'economic or industrial', the other '*universitaire* or pedagogic'. 'Some speakers evidently had in view the necessities of work and the needs of the laborious classes, while others were preoccupied . . . with the proprieties of educational theory and spoke chiefly from the point of view of the *classe moyenne*.'[6] This distinction between the practical and academic approaches was valid, and so was their identification with the two ministries, whose rivalry was to complicate the history of technical education for many years. Even the dispute about the role of the state fitted into this pattern: Rouland and Duruy were to follow the University's tradition of

[1] Ibid., i (1863), pp. 41, 115–16.
[2] Ibid., i (1863), p. 187.
[3] Ibid., ii (1864), p. 332.
[4] Ibid., ii (1864), pp. 314–16.
[5] Ibid., i (1863), p. 92.
[6] Ibid., ii (1864), p. 299.

state action and uniformity, while the ministry of commerce was strongly influenced by *laissez-faire* ideas, and was inclined to follow the advice of *L'Enseignement professionnel* and leave action to local initiative. For this reason, the University's 'special secondary education' was to go ahead while the recommendations of Rouher's commission were ignored.

There was also the political side. Money spent on *enseignement professionnel* was money spent on the working class rather than the bourgeoisie, and the Second Empire showed no more inclination to do this than to make primary education universal. Reformers understandably contrasted the fragmentary and haphazard provision of industrial education with the resources lavished on the education of the liberal professions. They also argued that investment in education would benefit the nation as a whole—'Every economist who makes a complete enumeration of the means of developing production and exchange necessarily includes the professional education of the workers.'[1] But even this argument failed to appeal to a regime supposedly inspired by Saint-Simonian ideas.

Perhaps the regime was afraid of the democratic implications of the question, pointed to even in Morin and Tresca's report. Most of the partisans of *enseignement professionnel* saw it as a means of creating an earnest, self-improving and independent-minded working class. *L'Enseignement professionnel* was a non-political journal, but it made its sympathies clear. Commenting, for example, on the Christian Brothers' apprenticeship school of Saint-Nicolas, it found the values promoted there antipathetic to a form of education whose aim should be to inspire enthusiasm for the active life and the conquests of science, and to encourage the legitimate ambitions of the 'bold and intelligent worker'. 'Far from opening up perspectives for them, the aim seems to be to give them a timid outlook and to contract their horizons. In these workshops you can find neither the portrait of a man made famous by science or by some fruitful invention, nor any drawing or picture relating to industry or art.' Only statues of the Virgin were to be seen.[2] This was a criticism with which Duruy would have sympathized, as would many enlightened industrialists. But it was the ideas of the Christian Brothers, willing to co-operate in the task of social control, rather than those of *L'Enseignement professionnel*, which still found

---

[1] *Journal des Économistes*, 2nd series, xxx (1861), p. 373.
[2] *L'Enseignement professionnel*, i (1863), pp. 153–4.

most favour among the propertied classes and in the ranks of the government.

2. THE PROGRESS OF TECHNICAL EDUCATION

After Rouher's commission had published its report in 1865, ignorance could no longer be an excuse for inaction. The two bulky volumes of evidence included details of every worthwhile experiment in industrial education in France, as well as reports on Germany and Britain. The evidence of thirty witnesses was also included. Among them were Pompée, the editors of *L'Enseignement professionnel*, representatives of the Christian Brothers, and the directors of all the prominent industrial schools. The commission's inquiries extended beyond *enseignement professionnel* in the usual sense to cover evening courses, apprenticeship schools, factory schools, and professional education for girls. Their weakness, perhaps, was that they did not try to find out what industry itself wanted. Only five industrialists gave oral evidence, and they were men already conspicuous for their interest in the question. The commission's testing of provincial opinion took the form of asking chambers of commerce for their views, an exercise which produced little of interest.

Perhaps there was no general demand for an expansion of technical education. At any rate, the commission's report, prepared by Morin, was timid when compared with the demands made by Morin and Tresca in 1862. What was needed, it was now said, was not a new system but simply better co-ordination of what existed. Since the teaching ought to be practical and specialized, it would be wrong to create 'a uniform body of doctrines and methods, a regular personnel, in a word a University for industrial education'.[1] Schools should be founded by individual and local initiative, and the role of the government confined to seconding private efforts. In recommending this, it is fair to say that the commission was reflecting the weight of the expert advice given to it.

It chose to ignore, however, the case argued by many of its witnesses for a general form of *enseignement professionnel*. It officially adopted the term 'technical education', and the bill which it prepared for submission to Parliament was concerned only with specialized training—this was probably because Duruy's special secondary education had evolved since the commission had been

[1] *Commission de l'enseignement technique. Rapport et notes* (1865), p. 85.

appointed, and his bill was itself going through Parliament in 1865. The commission's bill also reflected its adoption of *laissez-faire* principles. It did little more than give legal sanction to whatever the founders of technical schools chose to do. The state would simply encourage, by giving subsidies, distributing books and models, and awarding prizes to teachers and pupils. There was, it is true, to be an inspectorate of technical education whose powers would cover all schools, and a Conseil supérieur de l'enseignement technique to give expert advice. A state certificate for technical teachers was also recommended, though there would be no obligation on teachers to possess it. This very embryonic system of state supervision would be presided over by the minister of commerce.

The most radical proposals were not for technical education at all, but for extending the law of 1841 on children's employment. State regulation was to apply to all manufacturing establishments, the minimum age for child workers was to be ten instead of eight, the hours worked would be cut to six for children under thirteen and ten for those between thirteen and sixteen, and compulsory school attendance was to apply to all up to the age of sixteen, not just those under twelve.[1] The intention was presumably that for older children the education would take the form of technical instruction, and the changes would have helped school attendance generally if they had been carried out. But the technical education bill never became law. It was submitted to Parliament only in 1867, watered down still further in committee, and forgotten after 1868.[2] Such interest as the government had originally had in the question had evidently disappeared.

In its report the commission surveyed the existing provision of technical education and discussed the most urgent needs. Here too its conclusions were extremely negative, and almost perverse in the light of the evidence it had gathered. It did identify two areas which needed special attention—commercial education, which was completely neglected, and art teaching, where it recommended the creation of a museum of industrial design as well as improvement at lower levels. But it thought that for workers the encouragement of evening and Sunday courses would generally be enough, and it virtually ignored the needs of the 'N.C.O.s of the industrial army'

[1] *Commission de l'enseignement technique. Rapport et notes*, pp. 101 ff.
[2] *Annales du Sénat et du Corps législatif*, 1867, i, Annexes, pp. 20–30; 1868, xvi, Annexes, pp. 12–23.

and the sort of education for which *L'Enseignement professionnel*
had fought. The biggest gaps, according to the report, were at the
top. The École Polytechnique and École centrale were not producing enough engineers and experts for the needs of industry, and
several more schools should be founded in the provinces on the lines
of the École centrale lyonnaise.

However useful this sector of education was, one might have
thought that its clientele were well capable of looking after their
interests without government support. Nor did its expansion raise
general problems of educational policy, because the parents involved
could afford a full secondary education first. Indeed, at Mulhouse—
and no doubt elsewhere—the industrial bourgeoisie was coming to
appreciate classical education more than in the past and finding it
quite compatible with a higher technical training.[1] The real
problems were at a lower level, where parents could not afford
general education unless it was also practical and useful, and where
some new combination of generality and specialization needed to
be worked out.

It is possible, of course, that the enthusiasts for *enseignement
professionnel* exaggerated the real need for it. They tended—as the
discussions of apprenticeship, of the union of school and *atelier*, and
of manual training showed—to think that the typical worker should
be a skilled craftsman, and to ignore the real nature of factory
employment. *L'Enseignement professionnel* itself had to admit that
the opportunities for skilled workers and foremen were limited, and
that the *écoles d'arts et métiers* were already turning out as many as
could find jobs.[2] Bader, the experienced director of the *école
professionnelle* at Mulhouse, told Rouher's commission that the
employers themselves were reluctant to take on workers from
industrial schools, to whom they ascribed 'excessive pretensions'.
They preferred to train their workers on the job and promote
foremen from below, giving more weight to experience and character
than to technical knowledge.[3] A preference for learning on the job,
seen by French observers as one of the characteristics of the English
approach to education, certainly existed also in the French industrial
world.

Nevertheless, specific and localized demands for technical

[1] Oberlé, *L'Enseignement à Mulhouse*, pp. 145–7, 166–7, 252.
[2] *L'Enseignement professionnel*, i (1863), p. 67.
[3] *Enquête sur l'enseignement professionnel*, i, pp. 249, 261.

education did arise, and were met as in the fifties by local initiatives. The existing *écoles professionnelles* continued to flourish, and municipalities now turned their attention also to apprenticeship schools: Le Havre opened one in 1867, and Besançon had created one for the local clock- and watchmaking trade. In Paris, the chamber of commerce opened a commercial school in 1863, which took pupils from the age of eleven and gave them a three- or four-year course; in 1869 the chamber took over the old-established École supérieure de commerce, which taught at a higher level. The very successful École Turgot was also biased towards commerce—of 1,850 boys leaving between 1869 and 1877, 1,040 went into commerce[1]—and in 1868 the municipal council founded a second school of the same kind, the École Colbert.[2]

Employers too played their part, either by organizing training within their factories to replace apprenticeship (as with the Chaix printing firm at Paris), or through schools or evening courses run by *sociétés industrielles*. There were active *sociétés industrielles* at Amiens, Reims, Nantes, and Mulhouse. Mulhouse was unique in the range of educational institutions provided. The town already had the *école professionnelle* (now, it seems, taking its pupils from the same social strata as classical education),[3] and the much less successful *école préparatoire* for applied science founded by Fortoul. In the sixties it added a school of chemistry (1866), a school of mechanical weaving (1861), a school of spinning (1864), and an *école supérieure de commerce* (1866). These developments were a direct result of technical changes in the cotton industry and of the acute consciousness of international competition possessed by the Mulhouse employers.[4] The activities of the enlightened bourgeoisie of Mulhouse might seem to justify the faith of contemporary opinion in private initiative if they were not so exceptional. The institutions of Mulhouse were often cited as models, less often imitated. It was a one-industry town where new educational needs could be identified with precision, and was fortunate in having teachers of talent at its disposal. Elsewhere, there was genuine difficulty in seeing just what sort of education was needed, for which

[1] Gréard, *Éducation et instruction. Enseignement primaire*, p. 158 n. 1.
[2] The Paris municipality also ran the Collège Rollin, an ordinary classical college, and the Collège Chaptal, which gave a full-length secondary education based on modern subjects.
[3] *Enquête sur l'enseignement professionnel*, i, pp. 248–9.
[4] Oberlé, op. cit., pp. 211 ff.

classes, and in preparation for what jobs. This was reflected in the confusion which surrounded the debates on *enseignement professionnel*; and this confusion was by no means absent when the University unveiled its new special secondary education, announced as suitable for the industrial, commercial, and agricultural classes throughout France.

CHAPTER ELEVEN

Special secondary education

1. BEFORE DURUY

Special secondary education was embodied in a law pushed through by Duruy in 1865. Both the novelty of the reform, however, and the extent to which Duruy was responsible for it, have often been exaggerated, not least by Duruy himself in his memoirs. In the first place, this form of education was not an innovation, but a development of the special courses which already existed in the lycées and colleges. In the second, Duruy took over a project which had already been worked out before he became minister. Duruy made many important and original additions, but the reform was fundamentally the work of Rouland—or more precisely of Jean-Baptiste Dumas, still the most powerful scientific figure within the University.

The idea of developing the special courses into a proper system of *enseignement professionnel* was a fairly obvious one, and it was suggested even before 1860 by a number of *conseils académiques*.[1] These courses had not been killed by bifurcation, and in many towns they offered a serious education. At Le Havre, for example, they had 100–120 pupils, and a chair of 'Rhétorique française' had been created in 1858.[2] At Bayeux, the school announced a re-organization of its courses in 1861: they would be taught by the professors of the college instead of by inferior masters, and would enjoy the same status as classical education; the social advantages of educating for all professions together were pointed out.[3] At Saint-Amour (Jura) the college offered both a *cours de français*, of a more literary type, and a practical *école professionnelle*.[4] Many pupils of the special courses aimed at entry to the *écoles d'arts et métiers*, and

[1] Minutes of *conseils académiques* in A.N. F17 4350 (1858: Aix, Caen), 4351 (1859: Caen, Lyons), 4353 (1860: Douai, Toulouse), 4354 (1861: Bordeaux, Caen, Douai, Lyons).

[2] Anthiaume, *Le Collège du Havre*, ii, p. 319.

[3] A.N. F17 9099, prospectus of college of Bayeux, 31 Aug. 1861.

[4] C. Saint-Marc, *Collège de Saint-Amour. Distribution solennelle des prix pour l'année 1858. Discours* (1858), pp. 11–12.

this involved a craft test. Schools therefore had to arrange manual training, and in some places themselves had workshops. At Pont-à-Mousson, in Lorraine, there was 'a *workshop*, where on rainy days the pupils can practice manual exercises under the supervision of a worker'. This was a carpenter's shop, and was obviously designed for amusement as much as practical training, but workshops existed also at Remiremont and Saint-Dié in the same area.[1]

A more serious experiment took place in the small industrial town of Castres, in the Tarn. In 1861, three courses were started, in 'mechanical arts', industrial and agricultural chemistry, and spinning and weaving, with workshops for manual training. The buildings and equipment, paid for by the municipality, were said to be 'worthy of a faculty of science'.[2] This experiment was closely watched by the central administration, which assembled a special team of teachers with practical experience. The principal of the college was Ferdinand Roux, later chosen by Duruy to be head of the *école normale* for special education at Cluny. Roux was a native of Alès (Gard), as was Dumas; in the fifties, Roux had been principal at the college of Alès, and had experimented with special education there with Dumas's encouragement.[3] But Dumas was not the only familiar figure involved: the teachers sent from Paris to Castres seem to have been chosen by General Morin. One had been his private secretary, and two others had taught at the Conservatoire des arts et métiers. These last two were also natives of Mulhouse—the world of industrial education was a tight one. Finally, the deputy for the Tarn was the Saint-Simonian banker Eugène Péreire, and he also took an interest in the school, offering to find jobs for the best pupils, and using his political influence to advance Roux's career.[4]

The University thus had its own experts on *enseignement professionnel*, and what is more it had experience of manual work in education. In 1861 Roux published a pamphlet in which he expounded a theory of manual work almost identical with that of *L'Enseignement professionnel*—certain skills are basic to all crafts,

[1] A.N. F¹⁷ 4356, minutes of *conseil académique* of Nancy, 1862.

[2] Ibid., report of *inspecteur d'académie* of Tarn to *conseil académique* of Toulouse, 1862.

[3] A. Ducourneau, *De l'enseignement secondaire spécial au collège d'Alais* (1866), p. 5; A.N. F¹⁷ 8212, file on Alais (the contemporary spelling).

[4] On Castres: A.N. F¹⁷ 8302, file on Castres; F¹⁷ 2650, quarterly report of rector of Toulouse, 10 Jan. 1863; F¹⁷ 6849, replies to circular of 16 July 1864, *inspecteur d'académie* of Tarn and principal of Castres; F¹⁷ 4354, minutes of *conseil académique* of Toulouse, 1861.

certain tools are *outils types*. He differed from *L'Enseignement professionnel* in wanting to give his form of education to the industrial and commercial class rather than the workers, and in regarding it as truly secondary. 'Industrial' secondary education was exactly parallel to classical education, though in a different intellectual field, and should be given in the same schools under the direction of the University.[1]

In 1862, Rouland published a report on 'commercial and industrial education', and set up a commission of experts to make detailed proposals. The vigour of Rouland's action on this occasion suggests some encouragement by Napoleon III. In the report, Rouland referred to the 1860 treaty, the 1862 exhibition, and the way education could increase the productive forces of the country. He declared that a new type of education was needed for 'the children of those thousands of families who have achieved prosperity through labour and thrift', for that *classe moyenne* which had earned the government's attention 'by its numbers, its utility, and its spirit of order, prudence, and perseverance'.[2] By this he meant not so much salaried white-collar workers as the independent farmer or small businessman, the man who ran his own enterprise and wanted his son to follow him. There was an ambiguity about the status of the new education which was to persist. Sometimes it was contrasted with education for the liberal professions; at other times, its equality with classical education was stressed. It was described as 'French' or 'modern' secondary education, and the ideal of a full secondary education based on modern subjects was very clearly put forward. It was even said that some Latin might be included, and there was no mention of manual work. It would be given in the lycées and colleges, but where appropriate separate schools might be set up, 'veritable modern colleges, analogous in some respects to the *écoles centrales* at the beginning of the century'.[3]

The most controversial part of Rouland's report was his assertion that the University had a right to move into this new field and keep up with the demands of the age, although there was some recognition of the argument that University methods were unsuitable: the experts were to consider how special teachers should be trained,

---

[1] F. Roux, *De l'enseignement professionnel en France* (1861), *passim*. Cf. his *Histoire des six premières années de l'École normale spéciale de Cluny* (1889), pp. 87–94.

[2] Speech of 1862 in Rouland, *Discours et réquisitoires*, ii, p. 154.

[3] Report to Emperor, 14 June 1862.

and Rouland was prepared to extend the École Normale or to create a new school for the purpose. He justified the University's role by a modern analogy: 'Every time a new railway branch penetrates into a previously neglected region, it brings life, activity, prosperity. . . . Surely the University has the right in its turn to say that every time a new layer of the population is initiated by the study of letters and science into the sentiment of beauty and the knowledge of truth, there too life and activity are penetrating.'[1] Education, observed Rouland, was as solid an investment for the state as railways. The basic idea here was one also found in 1852: the University's education has a vital moral function because it always includes a general element based on literature and abstract science.

The chairman of the commission of experts was Dumas, and most of the members were teachers and officials, with only a few outside experts and hardly any representatives of industry. It worked fast, and by December 1862 Rouland was able to present a bill to the Conseil impérial. This provided for four years of *enseignement intermédiaire*—at a later stage this became *professionnel*, before the traditional but misleading term *spécial* was finally chosen. The course would be based on French, modern languages, modern history and geography, mathematics and science, 'the elements of legislation and industrial economy', 'technology and rural economy', drawing, book-keeping, and calligraphy. At the end there would be an examination and leaving certificate. The new education would be given in the lycées and colleges, but municipal councils could vote to convert their colleges wholly to the new organization.[2]

This project, which differed only in detail from Duruy's law of 1865, was approved by the Conseil impérial and signed by Napoleon III, and was about to be submitted to the Conseil d'État in June 1863 when Duruy succeeded Rouland.[3] Duruy's memoirs give the impression that special education was his sole invention, based on his experience as an inspector-general.[4] In fact he took over a fully worked-out scheme, and there is no necessary link between special education and the more democratic orientation of the ministry under Duruy.

2. DURUY TAKES OVER

Although Duruy did not invent special secondary education, he

[1] Ibid. [2] A.N. F¹⁷ 12957, minutes of Conseil impérial, 18 Dec. 1862.
[3] A.N. F¹⁷ 8702, anonymous note of 1863 on development of the plan.
[4] Duruy, *Notes et souvenirs*, i, pp. 167–8, 252 ff.

added so much that it bore his personal stamp. The bill prepared by Rouland did not become law until 1865, but Duruy used the interval to good advantage by carrying out the careful inquiries characteristic of his ministry. He modified the project in ways which reflected the current debates on *enseignement professionnel*, and learnt from his own initial mistakes. After 1865, he continued to experiment by turning three schools—at Mont-de-Marsan, Alès, and Napoléonville (Pontivy)—into 'special' schools which concentrated on the new form of education and which also served as testing grounds for some of his other new ideas. In 1866, he opened the École normale spéciale at Cluny, directed by Ferdinand Roux, to train suitable teachers.

Duruy's first action, in 1863, was to introduce a complete new syllabus for special education. This was possible without legislation, since the special courses already existed in the schools, and took on a new importance now that Duruy was phasing out bifurcation and looking to special education to take over part of its functions. This syllabus differed in some respects from that outlined in Rouland's bill.[1] 'Technology' disappeared, but the literary element was strengthened. In the French course, literary history was introduced, including an introduction to classical literature, for 'it would be shocking for these young people to leave our lycées without having heard speak of the finest geniuses of Greece and Rome'. At the other end of the time-scale, the syllabus included the Romantics—Lamartine, Hugo, and Vigny—and the modern historians—Thierry, Guizot, and Thiers. And, as for classical pupils, the history course was brought down to the Second Empire.

Duruy's choice of modern authors was controversial. An even bolder innovation was a course in ethics (*morale*), which was to be the 'special' equivalent of philosophy. It was based on the theme of man's duties—to himself, to his fellow men, to the family, to the state, and to God. Formal respect for religious orthodoxy was preserved, but this was plainly conceived as a course in secular morality, and bears a marked similarity to the famous programme of moral instruction devised by Jules Ferry for the Third Republic's primary schools. Privately, Duruy made it clear that he saw special education as an anticlerical weapon: 'The clerical party knows that I am touching it on the quick with special education, which will spread . . . *the applied sciences* among the people. . . . All my efforts

[1] Circular and programmes of 2 Oct. 1863.

are devoted to the revival of the lay spirit . . . to which special education will give a philosophical direction.'[1]

In making sure that special education did not neglect literary and moral instruction, Duruy was yielding to his instincts as an *universitaire*. His syllabus created something almost on a level with classical education. But this was really a miscalculation. The course lasted four years (plus a special class for those aiming at the École centrale and similar schools), with a certificate at the end (the *diplôme ès arts*—the word baccalaureate was carefully avoided). The syllabus assumed that pupils would stay for the whole of the course, for the most practical subjects, the natural sciences, were taught fully only in the third and fourth years, and literature and history were taught chronologically so that the most interesting parts came at the end. Ethics was also reserved for the fourth year. But, as Duruy's inquiries over the next few years revealed, most boys likely to use special education could not afford to stay for four years, and in 1866 he had to revise the syllabus radically.

The clientele of special education consisted overwhelmingly of 'small shopkeepers, workers, small rural proprietors and peasants',[2] and this was shown in detail by the extensive questionnaire on secondary education sent out by Duruy in 1864, which produced lists of parents' occupations.[3] Except in a few towns where special education had been developed to a higher level, middle-class parents who could afford it used classical education whether they were themselves lawyers, officials, merchants, or industrialists. In the larger towns, this social division was very apparent: the special pupils were called 'the grocers' (*épiciers*) in schoolboy slang, although the inquiry showed that actual segregation of pupils was rare. In smaller towns, the background of classical and special pupils was less distinct, and the former might be outnumbered; but at this level a large number of pupils came from peasant families. It was often said that special education appealed especially to peasants seeking extra education for their sons before they returned to the farm, while the ambitious urban lower middle class were more interested in the classics.

[1] Letter to Mme Cornu, printed in *La Dépêche* (Toulouse), 5 May 1904. Duruy's ethics course was in addition to conventional religious instruction, not a replacement.

[2] A.N. F17 8702, summary of replies to circulars of 25 Jan. and 29 Mar. 1865: colleges, academy of Lyons.

[3] Cf. Anderson, in *Past and Present*, no. 53 (1971), pp. 132–4.

The official emphasis on industry in discussion of special education was therefore somewhat wide of the mark, and so was the idea of an education parallel in status and prestige with the classics. 'An inadequate early education, rusticity of manners, limited intelligence: that is in general what the pupils of special education, of all ages, bring us.'[1] Duruy's ambitious syllabus was not for them, and officials generally reported that while a demand for education above the primary level certainly existed parents' conceptions of it were narrow: 'The spirit of the families is generally positive and self-interested. They send a child to the college so that he will know a little more than those who stay in the village, and they ask no more of us than knowledge which has a material and as it were palpable utility.'[2] The demand for the new sort of education, far from expressing itself urgently, would have to be stimulated: 'the need for this education has not yet penetrated enough into the ideas of the inhabitants of the small towns, and it is only in the long term that parents will feel the necessity for it.'[3]

Duruy's own uncertainty about the level aimed at is perhaps shown by one of his questions in 1864—will the development of special education attract a new clientele into the schools, or will it be at the expense of the classics? Officials were divided in their replies; many did not anticipate any influx of new pupils, and those who did stressed that fees must be kept low to compete with the primary schools and the *pensionnats* of the Christian Brothers, who were seen as strong competitors in this field.

Another set of problems arose from the attitudes of the municipal councils, on whose co-operation Duruy was depending. Those which ran *écoles professionnelles* were naturally unenthusiastic about competition from the lycées, and councils would generally have preferred an extension of higher primary education, as that would have remained under their control.[4] Councils were also unresponsive to the idea of converting small colleges into schools giving only special education; they wanted to 'keep a little Latinity' for the sake of prestige.[5] In larger towns, it was feared that the development of

[1] A.N. F17 4361, report of *inspecteur d'académie* on special education at Lille to *conseil académique* of Douai, 1866.

[2] A.N. F17 8702, report on Lunéville included in reply of rector of Nancy to circular of 29 Mar. 1865.

[3] A.N. F17 8702, vice-rector of Paris (Mourier) to Duruy, 12 Nov. 1863.

[4] Mourier, *Notes et souvenirs*, pp. 225–7.

[5] A.N. F17 8702, replies of rectors to circular of 25 Jan. 1865, colleges, Paris.

special education in the lycées would lead to social dilution. At Dijon, the municipal council was very hostile to it because it would bring 'far too vulgar elements of the population' into the lycée. The rector sympathized with this attitude, and like several of his colleagues feared that the result might be to drive the richer parents into the arms of the Jesuits.[1]

In inquiries in 1865, officials were especially asked to sound local opinion. The general impression was of apathy, and willingness to accept what the administration decided. Even in industrial areas, there was no strong support. In the north, it was said that 'the industrialists, merchants and landed proprietors who sit on our municipal councils have no reason to encourage this education', for it was not specialized enough for their purposes. In any case, much of industry 'seeks profit rather than progress', and rather than have men with scientific training prefers to take boys straight from primary school who do not expect to be paid so much.[2] The rector in this area wanted more courses with an evident relevance to local industry, and this desire was generally expressed throughout the country: there should be courses in agriculture, in viticulture, in the chemistry of the perfume industry (Grasse), in carpet design (Aubusson), in navigation, and so on. Public opinion clearly regarded special education as akin to *enseignement professionnel* rather than true secondary education, with the main purpose of giving a practical and useful education to those who could not afford to study the classics.

Duruy did try to respond to the demand for greater specialization, and encouraged local variations in the syllabus. He also introduced for each school a *conseil de perfectionnement* composed of local notables and industrialists, who would advise on local modifications and help to find jobs for pupils. In Paris, a Conseil supérieur de perfectionnement—actually dominated by officials and scientists, headed by Dumas—was supposed to co-ordinate these efforts and give expert advice to the minister.[3] This attempt to stir local opinion out of its apathy was not very successful. The reports of the councils show that many deliberated conscientiously, and made detailed suggestions, but their zeal began to flag after the first year,

[1] A.N. F^{17} 6845, reply of rector of Dijon to circular of 16 July 1864.
[2] A.N. F^{17} 8702, reply of rector of Douai to circular of 29 Mar. 1865, and cf. reply to circular of 25 Jan. 1865 (lycées).
[3] Circular of 7 Sept. 1864, law of 21 June 1865, *arrêté* of 6 Mar. 1866; decree of 26 Aug. 1865.

and they often ceased to meet. Some, 'composed no doubt of persons with little devotion to the University', refused to meet at all—one of the hazards of trying to rely on local initiative.[1]

Duruy also became interested in manual work. In 1863, he had ruled it out as a part of special education, but in 1864 he asked about it in his questionnaire. It was not properly organized anywhere except Castres—the experiments in Lorraine had been given up— but officials were not hostile to the idea. They feared, however, that it would be unacceptable to parents who sent their sons to the college to learn middle-class manners rather than to dirty their hands, and would accentuate the social division between special and classical pupils. Manual work was not included in the new syllabus which Duruy issued in 1866, but in the accompanying circular he did encourage its development.

This new syllabus[2] shows that Duruy had listened to criticism, and realized that his original ideas were too advanced. A preparatory year was added to the original four years, to help those who came direct from the primary school. Literary subjects still shared the time about equally with science, but it was now acknowledged, by making each year self-contained, that most pupils would not complete the course, and science was taught at all levels. The ancients were dropped from the literature programme, and history was reorganized with more concentration on France. New subjects were also introduced, including gymnastics, economics (was it not 'the philosophy of the industrial professions'?), and the 'history of industrial inventions'. This was to include self-help biographies, and so form 'a course of practical ethics, a true morality in action'. The moral instruction programme of 1863 was also retained and elaborated.

Duruy's instructions, in both 1863 and 1866, laid great emphasis on the practical approach. Industrial drawing occupied a large place, and chemistry teaching was to include practical experiments (*manipulations*).[3] Special education was to be concrete and 'applied' where classical education was abstract and speculative. Duruy had a clear vision of what a modern secondary education might be— practical, secular, and concerned with France rather than the ancient world, yet still fully liberal and general. Thus he was able

[1] A.N. F[17] 8711–14, annual reports of *conseils de perfectionnement*, 1866–9; F[17] 8714, note of 13 Apr. 1869.

[2] Circular and programme of 6 Apr. 1866.   [3] Circular of 9 June 1864

to take special education as the basis of his scheme for girls, and also thought it ideal for French education abroad. Duruy was especially interested in extending French influence in the Near East: he founded the first French lycée abroad at Constantinople, and persuaded the Egyptian government to send pupils to his École normale spéciale at Cluny.

But this kind of modern education could only have found a clientele if it had been given equal status with the classics. This status was denied to special education because it did not lead to a baccalaureate. Duruy himself continued to distinguish between the liberal and the practical professions, and to stress that special education would not harm the classics because the latter would continue to nourish the 'aristocracy of intelligence'—a poor compliment to special education, as *L'Enseignement professionnel* pointed out.[1] Duruy also failed to distinguish clearly between the different levels of wealth and status within the 'industrial classes', and sometimes spoke as if special education could extend to the whole of the producing class. Outlining his plans to Napoleon when taking office, Duruy observed that France had 24 million citizens engaged in agriculture, 12 million in industry and commerce; special education would provide for them a 'French secondary education'.[2] He also liked to speak of it as the 'secondary education of the people'. In 1867, he said that the Empire, as a regime based on popular assent, had the duty to 'widen the base of our system of education, to make it more practical, and to extend to every level of the people (*la démocratie*) the civilizing and liberal influence which the preceding governments have exercised in favour of the bourgeoisie'.[3] Just as every soldier has a marshal's baton in his knapsack, so in the industrial army special education would allow the able worker to rise to the top.[4]

All this exaggerated the democratic implications of special education. If Duruy had wished to help the industrial working class, it would have been better to develop primary education and revive the higher primary schools. That, at least, was the opinion of the democratic press, and the line taken by Simon in the debate on

[1] *L'Enseignement professionnel*, iii (1865), p. 546. The review welcomed special education, but did not see it as meeting its own demands. It was in fact closer to Pompée's ideas, and Pompée became an influential adviser of Duruy.

[2] Duruy, *Notes et souvenirs*, i, p. 197, and cf. pp. 252–3.

[3] *L'Administration de l'instruction publique de 1863 à 1869*, p. 491.

[4] Circular of 2 Oct. 1863.

Duruy's law.[1] As long as special education was attached to the lycées and colleges, access to it from below was difficult. Although Duruy intended it to be open to primary pupils, he took no measures to encourage regular transfer or to co-ordinate the two systems. The financial barriers were especially significant: primary schools were cheap or free, but the fees for special education were no lower than those for secondary education proper, and critics said that even for day-boys the fees were beyond what most of the class Duruy claimed to be aiming at could afford.[2]

If special education had been developed as an extension of the primary school, it would be inviting to pupils, would encourage them to stay on, and would raise the general standards and per-spectives of primary education. But in the lycées, it was said, special education would either suffer through always being con-sidered inferior, and be 'strangled between rhetoric and logic, between Greek and Latin',[3] or weaken classical education itself by attracting pupils away.

On the other hand, there might be a democratic argument for keeping special education within the secondary sector. It did at least mean that different elements of the middle class used the same school, and that poorer pupils' ambitions were encouraged by contact with middle-class children. In the lycées and colleges, they were on the bottom rungs of the middle-class career ladder; in a higher primary school, biased towards a limited range of jobs, talent would have less opportunity to rise. The traditions of the University favoured social mixing, and in the early stages Duruy stressed the advantages of having both kinds of education in the same school; 'the lycée is a national institution, and one of the symbols of that equality to which our country is so attached.'[4] But the long-term implication of his plan was that classical and special education would be separated. He wanted to convert as many colleges as possible, and even some lycées, to give special education only, and to concentrate the education of the élite in a smaller number of schools.[5] He also used the traditional arguments about

[1] Parliamentary debate, 30 May 1865, reported in *Journal général de l'instruction publique*, xxxiv (1865), pp. 350–4; cf. Simon, *L'École*, pp. 357–8.

[2] e.g. *Le Siècle*, cited in *Journal général de l'instruction publique*, xxxvi (1866), pp. 269–70.

[3] *Journal des Économistes*, xxxv (1862), p. 502.

[4] Circular of 2 Oct. 1863.

[5] Albert Duruy in *Revue des Deux Mondes*, 3rd period, lxi (1884), p. 873.

diverting 'unsuitable' pupils from the classics and relieving pressure on the professions.

Duruy's policy on state scholarships fits into the same pattern. He was able to raise the amount spent on them from 860,276 francs in 1863 to 1,038,522 in 1869,[1] but he did not change the basis on which they were awarded. The republican idea of using scholarships for the systematic encouragement of social mobility seems never to have been a part of Duruy's thinking. If anything, he restricted the contribution to mobility which they could make, for he began to give state scholarships for special as well as classical education, and in the colleges as well as the lycées; in 1867, 22 of 170 *bourses* awarded were for special education.[2] The old policy, he explained, had forced parents to make sacrifices in order to get their sons into the liberal professions when they left the lycée; now they would be directed towards careers more in line with the parents' own modest status.[3] But those of exceptional ability would still be able to transfer to the classics—the idea of a small élite within the bourgeoisie, an 'intellectual aristocracy', ran through all Duruy's plans.

Duruy developed special education rather than higher primary schools mainly because he found a scheme already prepared, and because it was the cheapest and least controversial way of expanding education in a new direction. He was also influenced by the failure of the higher primary schools after 1833, which had shown that parents preferred the prestige of secondary education. But he could legitimately be criticized for neglecting the links between primary and secondary schools, and for failing to remove the financial obstacles which faced poorer families. Perhaps there was really a need for two forms of 'intermediate' education—one for the lower middle class, on the same lines as special education, and one of higher primary type. In any case, it was the peasants and lower middle class who continued to be the main users of special education after its reform by Duruy, and its main fault in their eyes was to be too general, too literary, and perhaps too concerned with the supposed needs of industry. The time for a more ambitious experiment had not yet come. In later years, however, the nature of special education and the direction in which it should move became

---

[1] Nicolas, *Les Budgets de la France*, Table 22.
[2] A.N. F¹⁷ 7481, note for minister, 8 Oct. 1867.
[3] Circular of 6 Apr. 1866. Cf. *arrêté* of 26 Dec. 1868, and A.N. F¹⁷ 8702, Duruy to de Lesseps, 3 June 1866.

controversial issues, and it ended up (in 1891) as a modern branch of education fully parallel with the classics. The sort of families which had used special education in the sixties found themselves directed away from the secondary sector and into the revived higher primary schools. The logic of the French educational system seemed to have no room for an education which was secondary in spirit but too short and practical to fit into the traditional secondary pattern.

3. THE LAW OF 1865 AND ITS APPLICATION

While Duruy was carrying out inquiries and experimenting with syllabuses, the bill on special education was passing through the legislative machinery, and became law on 21 June 1865. The final version did not differ fundamentally from the draft of 1862, but included some additions like the *conseils de perfectionnement* and a special teachers' certificate. The law gave private schools rights similar to those under the *loi Falloux*, thus giving the Christian Brothers' *pensionnats* and similar experiments complete freedom of action. There was also a clause affecting primary schools: drawing, modern languages, book-keeping, and geometry were added to the list of extra subjects which primary education might include. This was a concession to the demand for a revival of higher primary education, giving more scope to councils who wished to open that type of school.

In the debate, as we have seen, Simon voiced some of the criticisms of Duruy made on the left, though as he said he was really 'the supporter and friend of those whom I seem to attack'.[1] The discussion was well informed but not passionate, and the bill was eventually passed unanimously. But Parliament failed at the same time to provide the credits which Duruy asked for; Rouland's original plan had envisaged spending 1,800,000 francs on establishing new courses and buying scientific equipment. None of this was made available, and Duruy was thrown back on his own considerable resources of energy and ingenuity. It was a serious blow, because it prevented Duruy from making striking innovations and improvements which could stimulate public interest in the new form of education, and meant that it was little different from the old special courses. The episode, like the history of technical education, shows that the politicians and officials of the Second Empire had little interest in this form of social investment.

[1] *Journal général de l'instruction publique*, xxxiv (1865), p. 352.

Duruy's most original contribution to special education was perhaps the École normale spéciale which he founded to train teachers and to demonstrate the University's ability to adapt itself to new ideas. The plan went back to 1864; Duruy chose to site the school at Cluny because the old monastic buildings there were available and the local council was willing to help. It opened in 1866, and the existing municipal college was turned into a *collège annexe* where pupils would practise teaching. Ferdinand Roux came from Castres as director, bringing some of his teachers with him. He was an obvious choice as one of the few experts on *enseignement professionnel* working within the University, and also as an exponent of manual work, for Duruy planned from the start that the École normale spéciale would have workshops.[1] They were duly installed, though the relevance of Roux's ideas at this level of education was uncertain.

The teaching had a strong scientific emphasis, and led in two years to the new *brevet de capacité* for special education, or in three to the 'special' *agrégation* which Duruy created so that these teachers could have the same status and salary as their classical colleagues. But there was some conflict between Duruy and Roux about how Cluny should develop. Duruy tried to prevent the teaching becoming too theoretical and literary, insisting that practical men were required, not 'professors in yellow gloves', and that unlike the École Normale Supérieure Cluny should remain an establishment for professional training and not cultivate science and learning for their own sake.[2] Roux did, however, persuade Duruy to maintain Latin in the *collège annexe*, arguing that it must always be available to help exceptional talent move up the social ladder.[3] Duruy also encouraged Roux in his desire to develop the modern languages, accepting that they 'play the part in special education of the dead languages in classical education'.[4] Cluny eventually had three sections—applied science (the largest), literature and economics, and modern languages—and had a significant part in Duruy's plan to improve language teaching. The language students spent their last year abroad under exchange arrangements made with schools in England and Germany; this collapsed when

---

[1] *L'Enseignement professionnel*, ii (1864), p. 370.
[2] Roux, *Histoire des six premières années*, pp. 36–7.
[3] Ibid., pp. 122–9, 132. Cf. A.N. F¹⁷ 8741, Roux to Duruy, 12 Oct. 1867.
[4] Roux, op. cit., pp. 129–34.

H

war broke out in 1870, but must have been one of the earliest schemes of the kind.[1]

The school at Cluny was for a time Duruy's consuming interest, and he corresponded daily with Roux. It was also an example of his administrative talents, for it was established with minimal resources. Parliament did not vote a special credit until 1868, and the school was financed by appealing to local authorities and (for books and equipment) to other University institutions and private companies. There was a pioneering atmosphere, and much enthusiasm among the students. In the long run, Duruy's personal identification with the school harmed it, and it had enemies in the University from the start. In 1872, it lost its administrative autonomy and Roux resigned, and in 1891 it disappeared when special education was itself reformed.

Most of the pupils at Cluny were qualified primary teachers, some of them already teaching in the special courses of secondary schools, and they were financed mainly by scholarships from the departments. The great majority passed their examinations, and continued to teach after graduating; by 1877, Cluny had supplied 119 teachers to lycées, and 186 to colleges.[2] But they met much hostility in the University, which was accustomed to seeing the special courses as primary in nature, and reluctant to accept as equals men who had not themselves been to a secondary school.[3]

There were three other schools in which Duruy took a special interest—the model lycées at Mont-de-Marsan in the south-west and Napoléonville in Brittany, and the college at Alès. Only Alès was an industrial town; Napoléonville and Mont-de-Marsan were small lycées in backward areas, which it was hoped special education would revivify. Mont-de-Marsan was used chiefly to try out Duruy's ideas on the reform of classical education: a complete course lasting only five years was introduced, together with crash courses which would give exceptional pupils from special education enough Latin to pass the baccalaureate in one or two years—an idea with fairly radical implications.[4] In all three schools, the classics were main-

---

[1] Roux, op. cit., pp. 182–4, 198–207, 226 ff.

[2] J. Lougnon, *L'École normale d'enseignement secondaire spécial de Cluny. Statistique des douze premières promotions* (1880), p. 8.

[3] Roux, op. cit., pp. 195–7.

[4] *Bulletin administratif du ministère de l'instruction publique*, new series, viii (1867), pp. 880–2; A.N. F¹⁷ 8702, Duruy to mayor of Mont-de-Marsan, 27 Apr. 1866.

tained as a result of local pressure, and all reverted to the conventional pattern in later years.

Napoléonville was to specialize in agriculture, a subject generally neglected by experts on *enseignement professionnel.* Duruy had suggested this when inspecting the school in 1862, and managed to persuade the department to create forty scholarships for day-boys. A model farm was attached to the school, but the opening of this was delayed by the apathy of the ministry of agriculture, while the Frères de Ploërmel succeeded in creating a rival establishment with the aid of a local farmer.[1] It is perhaps significant of the way Duruy saw special education as an anticlerical weapon that Napoléonville was a traditional centre of liberalism in a Catholic area. There were also some conflicts in the other towns. At Cluny, the parish priest opened a campaign against the school, alleging that its pupils were to be seen sitting in cafés and attending dances; but Roux succeeded in winning over the bishop.[2] Alès (like Castres) was a town divided between Catholics and Protestants, and in 1867 only 68 of 140 pupils were Catholic. The *frères* had a school next door, and the principal complained that they imitated the college slavishly, setting up their own workshops and looking over the wall while the University's pupils did their gymnastics in the courtyard (he had ordered the heightening of the wall).[3] The presence of this pilot college at Alès was due largely to Dumas's interest in his native town; he continued to take a hand in special education, although the advent of Duruy had displaced him from his position of power, and the abolition of bifurcation had caused some coolness between the two.

Duruy's willingness to experiment with innovations on a small scale contrasted with the usual attitude of the University, and meant that his reforms would be solidly based when they took their final form. The experiment in special education was cut off half way by Duruy's dismissal, and it is difficult to say how it might have developed if he had stayed. Some of his policies—notably the training of teachers and the improvement of premises and equipment—could in any case bear fruit only in the longer term. If we look at what happened to special education in the Duruy period, its success seems limited.

[1] A.N. F17 6806, correspondence of 1867; F17 7962 (especially report of Duruy and Roustan, 24 Mar. 1862), 7964, 7965, file on Napoléonville.
[2] A.N. F17 8741, correspondence of 1867, especially Vieille to Danton, 2 June 1867.
[3] A.N. F17 8212, principal to Duruy, 14 Nov. 1867.

In 1863, there were 4,386 special pupils in the lycées, 8,926 in the colleges. After the reorganization, the numbers grew as follows:[1]

	Lycées		Colleges	
1865	5,002	(15%)	11,880	(36%)
1867	6,384	(18%)	10,825	(33%)
1869	7,034	(19%)	11,429	(34%)
1876	8,696	(21%)	14,012	(37%)

This suggests significant though not spectacular growth, especially in the lycées, where special education was less developed before. Did this growth also mean that the level of special education rose? The figures suggest not, for in 1876 as in 1865 the great majority of pupils were in the lower forms:

| | 1865 | | 1876 | |
	Lycées	Colleges	Lycées	Colleges
Preparatory class	424	3,057	2,599	4,471
1st year	1,718	3,521	2,791	4,425
2nd year	1,634	3,015	1,968	3,245
3rd year	954	1,765	1,075	1,451
4th year	272	522	263	420

Pupils were staying for only a few years, as with the old special courses, and in many places Duruy's elaborate programmes must have remained a dead letter. Few were reaching the end of the course (fewer in 1876 than 1865) or taking the diploma; in the Paris region, there were only 2,130 candidates for the diploma between 1865 and 1880, of whom 653 passed. 22 per cent of the candidates came from Catholic schools.[2]

The success of special education naturally varied according to the character of different areas. It was only moderate in the academy of Paris,[3] but seems to have been greatest, as might be expected, in the north and east. In the Meurthe, special education attracted new

---

[1] 1863: *Journal général de l'instruction publique*, xxxii (1863), p. 887. 1865: *Statistique de l'enseignement secondaire en 1865*, Tables 12, 20. 1867: *Bulletin administratif du ministère de l'instruction publique*, new series, viii (1867), p. 675. 1869: Rohr, *Victor Duruy*, p. 131. 1876: *Statistique de l'enseignement secondaire en 1876* (1878), Tables 15, 23.

[2] O. Gréard, *Éducation et instruction. Enseignement secondaire*, i, pp. 60–1.

[3] Ibid., i, Appendices 12–15, 18–23; A. Mourier, *Conseil académique de Paris. Exposés . . . Sessions 1862–1878* (1879), pp. 69–71.

pupils to the colleges, and in 1867 and 1868 special pupils out-numbered classical; in the Vosges, numbers were about equal.[1] At Mulhouse, the new programme was applied in the old *école professionnelle*. At Lille, where the lycée offered all four years of special education, a chemistry laboratory was set up, where the pupils themselves worked at the bench—this was reported as a great innovation.[2] In Alsace and Lorraine, a few towns—Forbach, Sarrebourg, Sainte-Marie-aux-Mines—agreed to set up colleges exclusively devoted to special education, and Duruy planned that the college at Rouffach should specialize in agriculture. Otherwise, the towns prepared to abandon the classics were mostly small ones in the centre or south: the list includes Lectoure, Parthenay, Tournus, Montélimar, Bayonne, Thiers, Cognac, Le Vigan, Saint-Nazaire, Saint-Servan, Manosque, Béziers, and Pézenas.[3]

It was in such small towns, where special education was really more important than classical, that Duruy's reform was most useful.[4] In larger towns, its development was hampered by its being given in the lycées, where it naturally took second place to the classics even in industrial or commercial centres. In some towns, as at Lyons, special education was already well developed, and Duruy's reform led to no increase in numbers.[5] At Bordeaux, special education was evidently used by the richer parents, as it sent boys on to the faculties and *grandes écoles*.[6] Here the municipal council voted for the creation of a separate special lycée. This would have been a significant step: no provincial town (except for the special case of Mulhouse) had more than one state secondary school, but their multiplication would open the way to greater educational and social differentiation.

Thus special secondary education took over the role of the old special courses without fundamental change. In most places, it gave a practical education to boys who stayed for only a year or two, while in a few, like Lille or Bordeaux, it was more ambitious, and

---

[1] A.N. F^{17} 9375, quarterly reports of prefects, Meurthe, 31 Dec. 1867, 11 Apr. and 7 July 1868; Vosges, 4 Apr. 1868.

[2] *Revue de l'instruction publique*, xxviii (1868), p. 401.

[3] *Bulletin administratif du ministère de l'instruction publique*, new series, vii (1867), pp. 224–5, viii (1867), p. 678.

[4] Cf. L. Gérard-Varet, 'Le Régime Victor Duruy: un collège de province de 1865 à 1880', *Revue universitaire*, 37e année, ii (1928), pp. 109–15.

[5] M. Chabot and S. Charléty, *Histoire de l'enseignement secondaire dans le Rhône de 1789 à 1900* (1901), pp. 197–8.

[6] *Le Centenaire du lycée de Bordeaux (1802–1902)* (1905), p. 390.

might offer parents a genuine alternative to the classics and a substitute for Fortoul's scientific sections. Special education was more efficient than the old courses, because it had a carefully worked-out syllabus, a diploma to give pupils something to work for, and greater official recognition and prestige. The other side of this was that the new status might frighten away those with limited demands, and that the new syllabus might inhibit the adaptation to local needs which had been possible under the old unregulated arrangements. As we have seen, there were ambiguities in the scheme which reflected a vagueness in Duruy's thinking. His reforms in special as in classical education were really more notable for the original and interesting ideas attached to them than for their fundamental radicalism.

CHAPTER TWELVE

University reform

The history of higher education in our period is rather negative. It remained in 1870 what it had been in 1848, and what Napoleon I had made it: a collection of individual schools and faculties, unconnected with each other and successful only when they concentrated on professional training. There were only a few significant changes, but there were some intimations of further change. In particular, the shadow of German competition in the sixties began a movement for university reform whose spokesmen included Pasteur and Renan. After 1870, this movement was to have great significance, but in the sixties few people listened; one who did, however, was Duruy, and higher education did not escape his reforming zeal.

In Germany, the university system provided a general education which completed that given in the secondary school and which was part of the common experience of the middle class. In France, there was nothing of the kind. The faculties of letters and science, which might have given it, were indeed numerous, and eight new ones had been created in 1854, so that there were sixteen of each in the sixties. But the number of full-time students attending them was derisory. The *licence*, the examination for which the faculties prepared, was awarded in 1865 to 90 students in letters and 100 in science.[1] And although candidates had to register in the faculties, they did not have to attend any courses. The *licence* in letters, in particular, could easily be prepared for by private study, as it was essentially a classical examination similar to the baccalaureate. Most of those who took the *licence* were teachers or men already working as *maîtres d'études*; there was no other profession for which it was a valuable qualification.

About half the candidates in science, and a third of those in letters, were in Paris. The Paris faculties were the only ones with any real life, and there was usually no difficulty in attracting distinguished men to their chairs. It was customary for professors at

[1] *Statistique de l'enseignement supérieur*, p. 12.

the Sorbonne also to hold posts in other institutions, or to pursue careers in literature or journalism, or, like Dumas, to help form educational policy. In the provinces, it was a different matter, and it was difficult to attract and keep able men. The possibilities for research were limited outside the capital, and the main task of professors was conducting baccalaureate examinations—an unstimulating duty, and a time-consuming one when the examination was still mainly oral. The professor was also obliged to lecture twice a week, but the absence of students created a problem. If he gave serious and solid lectures, he was likely to find himself talking to an empty hall. Most professors, therefore, tried to create an audience by giving more superficial lectures which would attract members of the general public. Lectures were given in the evenings, often to a fashionable audience including officers of the garrison and upper-class ladies. To appeal to such an audience, lectures in history, philosophy, or literature had to be polished, diverting, or instructive, but could hardly be scholarly; professors of science had to emphasize the popular or practical side of their subjects, sometimes, it seems, gaining a serious audience of young employees of industry or even workers.[1]

Renan, in an article published in 1864, analysed the effects of this system on French intellectual life. Since professors did not have an audience of serious students, attending continuously and prepared to work for themselves, they could not enter on difficult subjects or try to teach methods and principles. Their reputations, and often their social success, depended on holding their audience, and thus on the cultivation of style, elegance, and oratorical brilliance. The preference given to form over content was already a weakness of the French national character, in Renan's view, and it prevented the faculties being devoted like the German universities to the solid pursuit of science and learning. Renan himself was a distinguished representative of the new German science of philology, and would have liked to see the traditional term 'letters' replaced by 'historical and philological sciences'.[2]

From time to time, attempts were made to provide the faculties with students. Fortoul had a real interest in the improvement of the

---

[1] *Statistique de l'enseignement supérieur*, pp. 9–11; K. Hillebrand, *De la réforme de l'enseignement supérieur* (1868), p. 99; Taine, *Journeys through France*, pp. 6, 111–12, 144.

[2] *Oeuvres complètes de Ernest Renan*, i, pp. 80 ff.

faculties arising from his own experience in the provinces before 1848. His solution to the problem was to make it compulsory for law and medical students to attend courses in the faculties of letters and science respectively, and to revive the idea (tried by Salvandy before him and Duruy after) of placing *maîtres d'études* who were studying for the *licence* in the lycées of faculty towns so that they could attend lectures. Neither provision had any lasting effect. Fortoul also tried to make the teaching more regular by making professors submit their lecture programmes to the ministry, and by imposing a three-year cycle in the teaching of each subject.[1] Thus the professors of history had to teach ancient, medieval, and modern history in successive years. Fustel de Coulanges, opening his lectures at Strasbourg in 1862, made a virtue of this necessity, arguing that 'this regulation, beneath its laconic and imperious form, teaches us a great and very profound truth: that history is not entertainment but science, and that its aim is . . . to have us know man completely in all the phases of his existence'.[2] In fact, the regulation showed how the inadequacy of the faculties made superficial teaching inevitable. Provincial faculties of letters had only five professors—philosophy, history, ancient literature, French literature, and foreign literature—and there were no assistants or tutors to share the teaching. Science faculties had five or six professors, which meant that, for example, one professor had to handle zoology, botany, and geology. In Paris, there were eighteen chairs in science and eleven in letters, but even there the whole of foreign literature was given to one professor. Only one wholly new chair was founded under the Second Empire, that in physiology created in 1854 for Claude Bernard; Fortoul also introduced the teaching of comparative grammar, but this was by the suppression of Cousin's chair in the history of philosophy.

The reasons why France failed to develop a true university system are not difficult to understand. The universities had been decaying institutions before 1789, and their tradition was not strong enough to reimpose itself afterwards, while the position of the lycées became strongly established. The social groups who filled universities in other countries had learned to do without them in France, or had found other ways of meeting their needs. Oxford and

---

[1] Decrees of 10 Apr. 1852, 17 Aug. 1853, *arrêté* of 7 Mar. 1853.

[2] F. Stern (ed.), *The Varieties of History, from Voltaire to the Present* (1957), p. 181.

Cambridge, for example, were based on the patronage of the landed class and the training of the Anglican clergy. In France, the upper class used the law faculties, but there was nothing to attract them to the faculties of letters; Catholic universities, which could have tapped this clientele, were not legalized until 1875. The training of the Catholic clergy, of course, bypassed the faculties altogether. There were five faculties of Catholic theology, but they had no real function. The two faculties of Protestant theology, however, were used to train the Protestant ministry, and that at Strasbourg, because of the opportunities for intellectual exchange with Germany, was a centre of religious thought and scholarship.

What about the middle class? Why should the faculties not continue the work of the lycées, training men for the professions and the civil service as their counterparts did in Germany or Scotland? To some extent they did: but the French idea that general education stopped with the baccalaureate meant that it was the professional faculties of law and medicine which flourished. Of 4,895 law students in 1867, 2,052 were aiming at the bar and magistracy, 1,054 at other legal professions, 659 at the civil service, and 136 at commerce or industry, while 994 declared that they were simply completing their general education.[1] But the actual teaching of the law faculties was narrowly professional; mastery of the detail of the codes was the aim, and there was little theoretical teaching. The same kind of criticism was heard of the medical faculties.[2]

There were eleven law faculties in 1865, two of them newly created. The law students formed the only real student body in most faculty towns, and outside Paris student life lacked vitality. Poitiers, where the politician Waldeck-Rousseau was a student in 1864–6, was typical of the smaller towns: the three faculties together had only about twenty teachers and 300 students—fewer than most lycées.[3] Medical education was organized slightly differently: there were only three faculties (Paris, Montpellier, Strasbourg), but twenty-two towns (in 1865) had 'preparatory schools' which awarded certain minor medical qualifications, and where students could start the full course which they later completed in a faculty. In 1865, there were some 2,900 students in the faculties

---

[1] *Statistique de l'enseignement supérieur*, p. 7, n.
[2] Hillebrand, *De la réforme de l'enseignement supérieur*, pp. 85–95.
[3] P. Sorlin, *Waldeck-Rousseau* (1966), p. 82.

and schools.[1] Neither legal nor medical education was cheap; fees and living expenses accounted for about 1,000 francs a year in the provinces, 1,500 in Paris.[2]

Other forms of professional education were, of course, provided by the *grandes écoles*, whose separate existence was an obstacle to the rational organization of higher education. Those who wanted to see more students in the faculties sometimes suggested that the *grandes écoles* should only take students with the *licence*, but this was never a practical proposition. The significant *grandes écoles* were the Polytechnique, the École centrale, and the École Normale. The first two between them met much of the middle-class demand for training in engineering and technical subjects, and as we have seen they had their provincial imitators. The École Normale, though it only trained a small élite, did something to compensate for the deficiencies of the faculties. It was the only institution where scientific and literary subjects at a high level were taught to students in a personal way. The *conférence*, a kind of seminar, was used rather than formal lectures, and the teachers, who included many of the University's leading names, were able to have a real personal influence.

The vicissitudes of the École Normale under the Empire are well known, mainly because a brilliant generation of students—Edmond About, Francisque Sarcey, Taine, Gréard, Émile Levasseur, Prévost-Paradol—entered the school in 1848 and 1849, suffered from Fortoul's oppression, and described the experience in their letters and memoirs. A new authoritarian regime had in fact started in 1850, when the Catholic Michelle replaced the liberal Dubois as director. Fortoul reinforced Michelle's insistence on religious and political conformity, and tried to make the school an institution for training teachers rather than pursuing learning. The official view at this time was that 'the proper mission of universities is to teach the most undisputed parts of human knowledge; it is not to encourage the inventive spirit, nor to propagate discoveries that are not fully verified'.[3] Fortoul did, however, set up a higher division at the École Normale, where selected students could stay on for two years to do research and prepare a doctorate; this lasted only a few years.[4]

---

[1] *Statistique de l'enseignement supérieur*, p. 5.
[2] Sorlin, op. cit., p. 86.
[3] Jourdain, *Le Budget de l'instruction publique*, p. 216.
[4] Decree of 22 Aug. 1854, *arrêté* of 22 Dec. 1855.

In 1857, Michelle was replacea by Désiré Nisard, with Pasteur as his deputy. Nisard was intellectually conservative and politically docile, and there was little change in the atmosphere. In 1867, however, a crisis arose when the students sent an address to Sainte-Beuve congratulating him for his speech defending freedom of thought in the affair of the library at Saint-Étienne. Duruy disciplined the students, and took the opportunity of dismissing Nisard and Pasteur and remodelling the school.[1] (It is typical of the favourable treatment of Duruy by historians that the dismissal of Pasteur has never been held against him.) The new director was Francisque Bouillier, a somewhat old-fashioned philosopher of the Cousinian school, and a conservative who resigned when the Empire fell.[2] It was not until the seventies, when Ernest Bersot was director, that the school entered on a period of confident revival and became once more the spiritual centre of the University.

How to restore vitality to the faculties and provide them with students was one aspect of university reform. Another much-debated question was whether the independent faculties in each town should be grouped together to form universities on the German pattern. There were two schools of thought. Those who knew Germany, and who were mainly interested in the promotion of science and learning, thought that the French provinces could not support more than four or five universities, and wanted to see efforts concentrated in those towns that already had some intellectual life, like Lyons or Strasbourg. This was the view of Renan, of Guizot, and of Cousin, who had made plans when minister for a 'Breton university' at Rennes. Politicians and administrators, on the other hand, thinking of the needs of the baccalaureate, and unwilling to offend local pride by abolishing existing faculties, were more inclined to build up university centres by new creations. Under the July monarchy, Salvandy, an active reformer of higher education, had doubled the number of faculties of letters.[3] Fortoul followed the same path in his law of 1854. Official statements at the time spoke of creating *foyers* of culture in the provinces, of the universities of the ancien régime, and of the English and German

[1] Nisard, *Souvenirs*, i, pp. 76–84, ii, pp. 63–7. Nisard and Duruy were old enemies.

[2] F. Bouillier, *Souvenirs d'un vieil universitaire* (1897), pp. 35–7.

[3] L. Trénard, 'Les Facultés des Lettres sous la Monarchie de Juillet', *Actes du 89e Congrès National des Sociétés Savantes. Lyon 1964. Section d'histoire moderne et contemporaine* (1965), ii, pp. 678–80, 690–1.

examples. But it was administrative neatness which dictated the new pattern: each of the new 'large' academies was to have faculties both of letters and science. The utility of new science faculties at Lille and Marseilles seemed justified by industrial interests, but the same could hardly be said of those at Clermont and Poitiers.

A town that received two new faculties was Nancy, and in this case Fortoul was responding to a genuine local demand. There was a long-standing local campaign, led by Guerrier de Dumast, an amateur scholar and indefatigable pamphleteer, for the revival of the glories of the old University of Lorraine. The campaign was supported by the municipal council, whose pressure in 1852 had ensured that Nancy became the seat of a new academy; they now got their faculties, and in 1864 a law faculty was added, though only after the town had agreed to bear all the expenses. The new faculties were housed in the 'palais des facultés', built by the town and opened in 1862; there were very few towns (only two others in 1865)[1] where the faculties were in adequate buildings designed for the purpose. All this local zeal, however, could not provide students for the faculties of science and letters, though the law faculty had 180 by 1868. Some of them lived in a students' hostel provided by the liberal-minded bishop Lavigerie, which was perhaps the first venture of its kind.[2]

The expansion of the faculties in 1854 arose from administrative motives and (in the case of Nancy) from regional pride and the liberal Catholic belief in 'decentralization'.[3] But in the sixties, quite different motives for university reform were to appear. Behind Renan's critique of the French system was the idea that the universities should be centres of research as well as teaching, and that the health of science and scholarship were matters of national concern. After France's defeat in 1870, he was to develop this argument, showing that the universities gave the German educated class a seriousness and solidity, an openness to new ideas and respect for truth, which were lacking in France. The promotion of science and

[1] *Statistique de l'enseignement supérieur*, Table C.
[2] O. Voilliard, 'La Faculté des Lettres et le mouvement intellectuel en Lorraine avant 1870', *Annales de l'Est*, 5th series, v (1954), pp. 187–209; A. Logette, *Histoire de la Faculté de Droit de Nancy* (1964), pp. 64–88, 93–5, 175–6, 193–4.
[3] Cf. C. Lenormant, *Essais sur l'instruction publique* (1873), pp. 183 ff. (written in 1845).

learning was, therefore, a direct duty of governments concerned with France's power and European influence.

This was a new idea in France, where the faculties were regarded by the public mainly as examining machines, and where higher education largely paid for itself through fees rather than forming a field for public investment. One of the first to protest about the neglect of science was Pasteur, in a pamphlet published in 1858. In this he complained that the state spent nothing on laboratories, and described the deplorable conditions in which scientists at Paris had to work. The faculty of science was virtually without laboratories, though one for physics had just been created; Claude Bernard had no laboratory at the Sorbonne, and had to work in a damp basement at the Collège de France (an institution of learning independent of the faculties); the only good laboratories were at the École Normale, which had now become the main centre for scientific research. It was Dumas, who had been pressing for better facilities since the forties, who was mainly responsible for what progress there had been. But even where a laboratory was provided, there were inadequate funds for technical assistance; Pasteur cited the case of an academician who had to wash his own equipment.[1] If these were the conditions in Paris, those in the provinces may be imagined. Both laboratories and libraries lived in penury, even in relatively lively centres like Strasbourg.[2]

Traces of the ideas of both Renan and Pasteur may be found in Duruy's policies on university reform. His ideas were bold and original; whereas his plans for primary education were riding on a wave of public opinion, little was being said at the time about the reform of the faculties. Duruy's plans were set out in the statistical report on higher education which he published in 1868—for it was only in the last year or two of his ministry that he turned to this subject. In this report, he declared that the foundations of the system were sound; what was needed was not an organizational upheaval, but adaptation to meet new needs, and the commitment of adequate resources. He wanted to see the faculties filled with

---

[1] L. Pasteur, *Pour l'avenir de la science française* (1947), *passim* (includes his *Le Budget de la science* of 1858); cf. Liard, *L'Enseignement supérieur*, ii, pp. 272–4, and O. Gréard, *Éducation et instruction. Enseignement supérieur* (2nd edn., 1889), pp. 50–1, 62–3.

[2] Y. Laissus, 'L'Université de Strasbourg il y a cent ans d'après les papiers d'Adolphe Brongniart', *Comptes rendus du 92e Congrès National des Sociétés Savantes. Strasbourg et Colmar 1967. Section des sciences* (1969), i, pp. 181–2.

serious students, and his definition of higher education—that it should not just present facts but train the student in the methods of the various sciences—was close to Renan's, and incompatible with the old French tradition.[1]

Where were the students to come from? Duruy saw that prospective teachers formed the only large reserve of potential students, and that their social background made scholarships essential if they were to be able to study full-time for the *licence*. Duruy's idea of higher education scholarships could not be carried out because of lack of money, but it was to be introduced under the Third Republic, and eventually to provide the faculties of letters and science with the bulk of their students. In the short term, Duruy tried like Fortoul to regularize the attendance of *maîtres d'études* at courses in the faculties. Duruy also looked forward to the reconstitution of universities, and in a bill which he introduced in the Senate in 1870, when out of office, he outlined a programme which was only to be achieved gradually between 1885 and 1896: the faculties were to be financially autonomous, and to draw up their own courses; they were to be linked by a Conseil des Facultés in each academy, elected by the professors; and in towns with at least three faculties, this council was to be turned into a University named after the town.[2]

Duruy thought research as important as teaching, and was one of the few official figures to appreciate the importance of science for France's economic and military strength. Following Pasteur, he insisted that the distinction between pure and applied sciences was false, and that theoretical research was vital in the long run to industrial prosperity. He approached the question in a strongly nationalist way, describing laboratories as the 'arsenals of science', and writing to Napoleon: 'I venture to request the Emperor to read this description of the physico-chemical laboratory which the Prussians are building at Bonn. It is heart-rending for your minister of education, and menacing for French science.' Duruy evidently succeeded in awakening Napoleon's interest, for in 1868 the Emperor called a meeting of leading French scientists to advise him on what should be done.[3] But Duruy failed to get the 'science

[1] *Statistique de l'enseignement supérieur*, p. xxxiii; cf. Hillebrand, *De la réforme de l'enseignement supérieur*, p. 98.

[2] Duruy, *Notes et souvenirs*, ii, pp. 59–75.

[3] *Statistique de l'enseignement supérieur*, pp. x, 711; Duruy, *Notes et souvenirs*, i, p. 312; Pasteur, *Pour l'avenir de la science française*, pp. 36–7.

budget' which he wanted, and as with Cluny and other ventures he had to resort to hand-to-mouth expedients. A new meteorological observatory, for example, was incongruously installed in a Tunisian pavilion left over from the 1867 Exhibition (rebuilt in the parc Montsouris, where it still stands).

Duruy's chief contribution to the promotion of science and scholarship was the École pratique des hautes études, created in 1868. This was not a distinct institution so much as a flexible administrative framework for channelling money to where it was needed. Laboratories attached to the school had directors who received an annual grant, and students who might also be subsidized by the state. The aim was both to advance knowledge and to train researchers. Duruy thought that 'to make the French understand a new idea, you have to find a name which catches their fancy'.[1] The new idea was the necessity of laboratories, including 'laboratories' of history and philology. The school had four sections—mathematics, physics and chemistry, natural history and physiology, and history and philology; new sections were added later, but the school still functions today in the way Duruy envisaged, and has proved the most fecund of his innovations. Duruy himself wanted to see a fifth section devoted to economics, a science in which he had great faith. He planned to create a chair of economics in every law faculty, though he was able to achieve this only in Paris.[2]

Duruy not only tried to reform the existing institutions of higher education, but also tackled the controversial question of 'liberty of teaching'. Higher education was unaffected by the *loi Falloux*, and the state still had a monopoly. From 1867, with encouragement from Rome, Catholics opened a campaign for the legalization of Catholic faculties.[3] In the conflict over this, which continued throughout the seventies, the main point at issue was the awarding of degrees (*collation des grades*): Catholics claimed that private institutions should be able to award degrees recognized by the state as equivalent to its own, but even the most liberal politicians would not go more than half way to meeting this demand. Control over entry to the professions was seen as something too vital for the state to surrender.

---

[1] G. Monod, *Portraits et souvenirs* (1897), p. 128.

[2] Cf. É. Levasseur, *Résumé historique de l'enseignement de l'économie politique et de la statistique en France* (1883), pp. 26–32.

[3] L. Grimaud, *Histoire de la liberté d'enseignement en France* (1898), pp. 451 ff.

Duruy had suggested liberating higher education to Napoleon as early as 1863, partly because he believed that it was necessary in a liberal state, partly because he thought competition would help revivify the faculties and expose the intellectual weaknesses of the 'men of darkness'.[1] In 1867, he submitted proposals to a committee of the Conseil impérial composed in the majority of Gallican magistrates. Duruy's account of the debate is illuminating evidence of official attitudes, and shows the gap between him and most administrators. The critics of the project were preoccupied by the political dangers and the threat to the interests of the state, and obsessed by the idea that the Jesuits (and to a lesser degree the 'reds') would exploit freedom to increase their hold over France. Duruy, arguing that 'it is not a question here of *state interest*, but of knowing whether in a free society the most important of all liberties is to be enjoyed', was talking a different language from Troplong, who asked 'Where are your means of surveillance, of information and of repression?'[2]

In view of this opposition, Duruy dropped his proposals. The question returned to the political agenda in 1870, under the 'liberal Empire' government, which was favourable to Catholic interests. The principle of 'liberty' was conceded, and a commission headed by Guizot worked out a compromise on *collation des grades*: degrees could be obtained either from the state faculties or from special independent examining boards. Duruy took the opportunity to present his own scheme to the Senate. This reserved *collation des grades* to the state, so that students wanting a qualification valid for public employment would have to be examined by the University. Duruy would also have forbidden private institutions to call themselves 'faculties' or to use the state titles for the qualifications they awarded.[3] When Catholic universities were eventually legalized in 1875, Guizot's compromise was accepted; but this was in turn reversed in 1880, and the eventual settlement was nearer to Duruy's idea of freedom for private education combined with no surrender of state privileges.

Though Duruy was unable to introduce legislation on this question, he opened one chink in the armour of state monopoly. For the first time, permission was given for individuals to run 'free

[1] Duruy, *Notes et souvenirs*, ii, p. 2.
[2] Ibid., ii, pp. 21–38; cf. Rohr, *Victor Duruy*, pp. 121–3.
[3] Duruy, *Notes et souvenirs*, ii, pp. 42–59.

courses' at university level.[1] These courses, a higher version of the evening courses for adults given in the primary schools, proved extremely popular. There were 20 in 1863, 300 in 1864, 1,003 by 1866. In Paris, a special room was opened at the Sorbonne to accommodate them, but they were equally successful in the provinces. The favoured subjects were science (illustrated with lantern slides, then a novelty), literature, and history; courses in economics were especially encouraged by Duruy. The speakers included professors in the faculties and lycées, public officials, doctors and lawyers, writers and artists.[2] These lectures were naturally popular with a public starved of open discussion— Napoleon III's liberalization of the laws on the press and public meetings did not come until 1868. Duruy had to keep a very close watch to ensure that the courses did not become a front for political opposition, and that veiled allusions to Poland or Garibaldi did not creep into lectures on literature and history. He used his power to refuse permission freely against liberal and democratic politicians, including his friend Simon.[3]

The episode illustrated once more the difficult position of a liberal minister in a not very liberal Empire, and more dilemmas of conscience arose in the field of higher education than anywhere else. As we have seen, Duruy was obliged to confirm Rouland's dismissal of Renan from the Collège de France for questioning the divinity of Christ. In 1865, he took severe disciplinary action against some students who had attended a free-thought congress at Liège. But the worst problems arose from Catholic attacks on the 'materialism' of the faculties. The Catholic campaign for 'liberty' rested partly on the claim that the state was allowing atheism to be taught in its own institutions, especially in the medical faculties. The medical faculty of Paris was indeed becoming a stronghold of positivist doctrine, and Catholic alarm is understandable in view of the social and intellectual influence which doctors could have; they were to form a substantial element in the local political personnel of the Third Republic. Dupanloup saw the faith of rural France being undermined by the missionaries of atheism sent out from the faculties—'it is through higher education that impiety arrives in the

[1] His long-term plan was that qualified individuals would be able to attach themselves to the faculties like the German *Privatdozenten.*

[2] *Statistique de l'enseignement supérieur*, p. xlii; *L'Administration de l'instruction publique de 1863 à 1869*, pp. 215–18; Mourier, *Notes et souvenirs*, pp. 338–9.

[3] Duruy, *Notes et souvenirs*, ii, pp. 5–14.

hamlets'—and also described the distress of Catholic parents 'whose sons are pious and good when they leave for Paris, but who return to them without beliefs'.[1]

A petition on higher education was organized by Catholics in 1867, and debated by the Senate in 1868. Duruy refers to the 'alliance of the cardinals in the Senate to frighten the timorous members of that venerable assembly'.[2] The Catholic speakers, as well as attacking the laxity of the minister, sought to link the state of the faculties with the growth of socialism and political radicalism, which was not implausible at a time when the Latin Quarter was becoming a hotbed of opposition. Cardinal Donnet put the matter simply: materialism meant atheism, and atheism meant the end of morality. 'What will become of societies then? What will become of the family and property?'[3]

The most notable speech in this debate was made by Sainte-Beuve. He began by claiming that he was speaking for a 'diocese' as extensive as any represented by the bishops, that constituted by those in every country who believed in science and freedom of thought. He went on to defend the rights of science, and to denounce the 'clerical party' and its 'aggressive and encroaching attitude'. Michel Chevalier also spoke on the freedom of science: it could not flourish if outside authority was allowed to dictate to it; this included religious authority, and Chevalier was sceptical about the chances for intellectual freedom in Catholic faculties.[4] Most of the senators would not have gone this far, but they did reject the petition. The prevailing mentality in the Senate was the same as that which had condemned Duruy's 1867 project: social and political authoritarianism combined with a strong resistance to Catholic incursions on the state's powers and distaste for the extravagant language of prelates like Dupanloup.

Duruy's own position in the debate was difficult, since he both tried to deny the existence of materialism in the University, asserting that it was essentially 'spiritualist' and pointing to his restoration of philosophy in the lycées, and claimed that he acted severely whenever atheistic tendencies appeared. In fact, he annulled in 1868 a 'materialist' thesis which had previously been

[1] F. Dupanloup, *La Liberté de l'enseignement supérieur* (1868), pp. 21, 30.
[2] Duruy, *Notes et souvenirs*, i, p. 359.
[3] *L'Enseignement supérieur devant le Sénat* (1868), p. 127.
[4] Ibid., pp. 118, 272.

accepted by the medical faculty. Duruy was himself not a positivist, but he thought that all opinions were permissible in the University provided that the orthodoxies were respected in the classroom. He cannot have enjoyed the repressive actions into which his position forced him, but he would certainly have lost that position if he had openly defended atheism.

True freedom of thought in higher education raised questions about the future of the Second Empire and the limits of its liberalization. In a country where higher education was directly controlled by the state, could intellectual vitality and the maintenance of political order be reconciled? Was it possible to teach philosophy, history, or economics at the highest levels without going outside the boundaries of 'science' and raising political questions? If higher education were to be expanded and liberalized, would this inevitably mean political reform, or might it provoke disorder and political reaction? These were questions familiar in countries like Russia, and in the fifties Napoleon III had maintained oppressive attitudes which stifled freedom even in the secondary schools, and had faced a sullen and sometimes defiant intelligentsia. On 17 December 1851, Jules Simon had denounced the *coup d'état* as a violation of justice from his lecture-platform at the Sorbonne: 'Gentlemen, I am here as a professor of ethics. I owe you a lesson and an example. . . . If there should be no more than one paper in the ballot-box to pass condemnation, I claim it in advance. It will be mine.'[1] Simon was dismissed. Much had changed by the time of Duruy, but it was still impossible for professors at the Sorbonne to speak as their conscience dictated.

But if authoritarian government was fatal to intellectual freedom, would democracy be any more tolerant? Renan raised this question in 1864, asking whether science and high culture, 'aristocratic' by nature and inaccessible to the masses, could survive in the modern world. He was optimistic, relying on the instinct of the 'people' to see the value of science and freedom even if they did not understand the details, just as, he thought, popular instinct would seek the highest in art and literature. 'The great experiment which France has been carrying out since the end of the last century continues in the intellectual as in the political order. The result of this experiment is quite uncertain, but to have attempted it will be a

[1] J. Bonnerot, *La Sorbonne. Sa vie, son rôle, son oeuvre à travers les siècles* (1927), p. 44.

certain title to glory. In politics, can democracy in the French manner constitute a strong and lasting society? In the intellectual order, can it constitute an enlightened society, one not dominated by charlatans, where knowledge, reason and superiority of mind will have their place, their legitimate authority and their reward? That is what we will know in a hundred years time, and we will know it thanks to France.'[1] Renan's optimism seems to have been justified, though perhaps not for the reasons he suggested. The succeeding years saw the revival of higher education and the flowering of science and independent thought. There were many causes, but among them was the disappearance of the Second Empire. As with universal education, the political structures and mentalities which the regime sustained were real obstacles when progress demanded intellectual boldness, openness of mind, and the willingness to take risks.

[1] *Oeuvres complètes de Ernest Renan*, i, pp. 69–71, 96.

Conclusion

Superficially, there were more changes in middle-class education than in primary during the period 1848–70. Yet for all the reforms accomplished or planned, the nature and functions of the former did not change fundamentally, whereas in primary education the 1860s can be seen as a period of silent revolution, when the system which had developed on the basis of the law of 1833 emerged into modernity.[1] In some areas, school attendance was already as high as it was to be after compulsion was introduced; in France as in other countries, the laws which made education free and compulsory were completing the work of several decades rather than initiating a vast transformation. Progress in France had not been particularly fast by Western European standards. Despite the French tradition of centralized state action, the development of French primary education was closer to the English than the Prussian pattern: the pace of educational legislation was much the same in England and France, and illiteracy was greater in France than England throughout the century.

The laws of the Third Republic were to fill in some important gaps, notably between town and country (by universalizing the abolition of fees) and between provision for boys and girls (by favouring the lay schoolmistress and training her in secular ideas). They were also, of course, to impose on education a new democratic, nationalist, and anticlerical ideology, to exclude religious teaching from the schools, and to put an end (though only gradually) to the employment of nuns and Christian Brothers in public schools. This created a situation which many Catholic parents found unacceptable, and drove them to use private schools; whether this was a greater invasion of liberty of conscience than the previous system of compulsory religious instruction is a matter of opinion. The new religious settlement was imposed as a matter of national policy by the Third Republic, whereas previously local councils had been able to choose between lay teachers and the religious orders: Ferry's laws were, among other things, centralizing measures, which

[1] Cf. Prost, *Histoire de l'enseignement en France*, pp. 114, 123, 142.

concentrated decision-making and expertise in the ministry at Paris in a way which was only beginning to develop in the sixties.

It is significant that even the enacting of free and compulsory education had to await the full takeover of power by the republicans around 1879. Although this reform had been on the agenda since 1848, and the failure to achieve it seemed increasingly anomalous, neither the Second Empire nor the conservative governments of the seventies ever looked like carrying it out. Even the defeat of 1870-1, which set off a mood of national self-criticism and regeneration, could not give the necessary impetus. As the Second Republic shows, it seems that only democratic republicanism could provide men with the idealism and will to make universal education a reality. For republicans, indeed, it was the first social priority; but the notables of the Second Empire—officials, parliamentarians, even the University administration—had not advanced beyond the views held by liberals under the July monarchy. Unlike more confident governing classes—such as Britain had in the sixties— neither conservatives nor old-style liberals in France could nerve themselves to take a leap in the dark. This was underlined by Duruy's unsuccessful struggle to win over the regime which he served. Duruy's ministry, like the events of 1848, also showed that in the historical conditions of nineteenth-century France the men who eventually made education universal would also be anticlerical. Anticlericalism, with its divisive social effects, was an integral part of the reforms of the eighties, not an unfortunate aberration.

Duruy had urged Napoleon III to place himself at the head of progress by making education free and compulsory. That he failed to do so leads to some general reflections on the nature of his rule. The Second Empire rested on universal suffrage, but it was perhaps not really the case that universal education was its obvious corollary. It was not just that an educated electorate might prove less docile, but that the bulk of the regime's electoral clientele were peasants. Duruy's own inquiries in 1864 showed that while the peasantry were coming to appreciate the practical value of education they were still likely to resist the idea of compulsion. The urban workers certainly wanted it, but by 1870 they were already alienated from the Empire and only radical measures, including secularization, could have won back their support. Napoleon's educational policies do not substantiate the idea that he was a special friend of the working class, but rather suggest that the regime was bourgeois through and through. At no time did it adopt any policy (like a democratic scholarship system) which might threaten the interests of the established classes or even increase social mobility. The priorities were especially clear when it came to spending money. The privileged status of secondary education was maintained, and projects of wider benefit were denied funds or cut down—a policy willingly pursued by Fortoul, forced against his will on Duruy. In educational matters, the Empire was always willing to defer to the parsimonious inclinations of its Parliament.

The Second Empire has a reputation as an efficient regime which used the power of the state to promote industrial progress. The fact that one of its first reforms was the strengthening of scientific education in the lycées is certainly significant, and Fortoul's policies show the blend of technocracy and authoritarianism characteristic of the regime, and distinguish it from traditional conservative governments, which from the Restoration to Vichy made their mark by restoring or reinforcing the classics. Both bifurcation and special secondary education had serious merits, though both, it may be noted, were based on developments before 1848 and on the ideas of men like Dumas rather than on any new inspiration provided by the Empire. In particular, Saint-Simonism had little to do with them: its influence on the Empire has often been exaggerated, and it had more impact on education under Carnot.

Both reforms also had their limitations, suffering especially from being constricted within the existing schools. Perhaps the greatest unfilled gap in the system was 'intermediate' education, and it remained unfilled in 1870. The growth of an 'intermediate' class of clerks, minor officials, skilled workers, and shopkeepers was certainly a feature of the age, but the Empire did little to meet its needs, and the efforts it made were often based on confused ideas. Special secondary education appealed as much to a traditional clientele of peasants and small-town artisans as to this new class. Higher primary education, which might have done more to help the urban working class, decayed after 1850 and was not revived. In the field of technical education, the government did virtually nothing, leaving all to local and private initiative. The Empire's general industrial and commercial policies simply failed to take account of education and to appreciate how it could contribute to the nation's prosperity.

There were, it is true, some reasons for this rather inadequate performance. One was that although there was much talk of science and its place in education, its practical value was uncertain. Careers based on theoretical science were few, and the growth of salaried technical and managerial jobs was only just beginning. Until wider career opportunities appeared, parents were unlikely to be seduced from the powerful classical tradition. It was, no doubt, the prestige of the secondary school and the baccalaureate which attracted them rather than a love of the classics themselves; but the idea of a full modern education of equal status with the classics, though present in both Fortoul and Duruy's reforms, failed to establish itself, and was not to do so until the end of the eighties. The development of science was also distorted by the peculiarly French link between science and military careers; bifurcation tried to break this down by associating scientific education with industry and medicine, but was ahead of its time.

A second obstacle, both to the development of technical education and to making primary education compulsory, was the great strength of *laissez-faire* ideas. These were the orthodoxy of the age, and the real economic ideology of the Empire. Nor was it only a matter of theory: the history of these years suggests that individual enterprise and initiative did exist in France and were capable of achieving much, and that local opinion was often hostile to state intervention. The organization of technical schools and courses in industrial towns, the educational campaigns emanating from the industrialists of Alsace, the activities of Jean Macé and the Ligue de l'Enseignement, the public library movement, and the burgeoning of evening courses under Duruy's impulsion are all evidence of this individual energy.

Perhaps the greatest voluntary efforts were those of the Church, for the institutional action of bishops and priests was seconded by the devotion and the financial sacrifice of laymen. The work of the teaching orders, the foundation of charitable schools, the patronage of apprenticeship, the political and press campaigns conducted nationally and locally[1] added up to a formidable body of activity. It was, of course, inspired by an educational ideal of a religious nature, an ideal which tended in this period to reassert traditional spiritual values against the materialism and egoism of nineteenth-century life. In social terms, Catholic education at all levels stressed the

[1] As a counter to the Ligue de l'Enseignement, a Société générale d'éducation et d'enseignement was founded in 1867 to promote Catholic education.

values of hierarchy, obedience, and discipline. Hence it was preferred by the conservative upper class for their own sons, and by the middle class for their daughters and for the children of the poor. It was one of the differences between the old liberals and the new republicans that the latter were prepared to dispense with the deference-inducing functions of religious instruction and expose the masses to the cold blasts of reason. In our period, however, Catholic educational ideals were accepted in the public primary schools, and the conflict between rival systems which later became general was confined to boys' secondary education.

At the very end of the Empire, and for most of the seventies, the Church was in a position of political strength, and used it as in the 1849–51 period to extract educational concessions—this time on higher education. In general, the fall of the Empire caused a return to the polarization of politics along religious lines, and the sub-ordination of educational policy proper to questions of Church–state relations. Under the Empire, religious conflict had been kept under control. The regime had deferred to Catholic orthodoxy in many ways, and allowed the Church substantial privileges; but the interests of the state had been defended, and many extensions of clerical influence resisted. The fundamental anticlericalism of the regime only emerged openly under Rouland, but the same ten-dencies were apparent even in the fifties. The democratization of education might have to await the arrival of the Republic, but anticlericalism did not. The Second Empire was truly liberal in the anticlerical sense, even if this rested on the Gallican traditions of the bureaucracy as much as on intellectual conviction; here as in other ways the concepts prevalent under the Empire were closer to those of the Orleanist liberals than to either the clerical-conservative or the radical-democratic models.

One of the virtues of strong governments is their ability to over-ride vested interests. The Church was the greatest of these, but the University had in some ways achieved a comparable position. Both Fortoul and Duruy were prepared to impose the reform of education against the teachers' opposition, whereas it was to be a weakness of the Republic that in return for the teachers' loyalty it had to sacrifice on their altars—the militant anticlericalism of the *instituteurs*, the classicism of the *professeurs*. But Fortoul and Duruy also found that the opposition of the teachers could frustrate their designs. The University had a real autonomy which could make it a

refuge from despotism and which mitigated the apparent omni-
potence of the centralized state. The University was a permanent
liberal force in French society, both because its members' social
origins made them support the social principles of 1789, and
because of its commitment to ethical values of a humane and
individualist kind. Its existence helps account for the survival of the
democratic framework of society even under conservative regimes:
like the other great *corps d'État*, the University followed its own
principles over the generations and provided stability and continuity behind the shifting political façade.

The University resembled the other state corporations in its
devotion to duty, cultivation of professional standards, and liability
to succumb to tradition and routine. But as an intellectual
corporation it had a special problem. Unlike the army or the
magistrature, it could not switch allegiance painlessly to an
intolerant and anti-intellectual regime. We teach in the name of the
state, wrote Prévost-Paradol to Taine in December 1851, but how
can we serve a state based on violence and deceit?[1] In France, the
servants of the state included the country's leading philosophers,
scientists, and scholars, and relations between the University and
the Empire were always strained. The events of 1851–2 meant for a
minority a crisis of conscience followed by resignation or expulsion,
for the majority the experience of oppression and stifling orthodoxy.
Even under the liberal Empire, the anomalous position in which
Duruy was often placed shows that the tensions had not been
resolved. Any regime which placed so much emphasis on order and
authority for their own sake was likely to be hampered in dealing
with the teachers, and incapable of evoking their idealism. Only a
liberal regime could allow the teachers to breathe freely and release
their energies. If in the sixties the *instituteurs* were beginning to look
forward to the Republic, the majority of the *professeurs* probably
preferred to look back to the semi-mythical golden age of Orleanist
liberalism.

The general direction of educational change depended on
France's social evolution, but politics and ideology mattered as well.
Each political regime in the nineteenth century represented rather
different social forces, and was better fitted to perform some tasks
than others. Each change of regime opened up some possibilities
for action and development and closed off others. The 1848

[1] O. Gréard, *Prévost-Paradol* (1894), p. 182.

revolution seemed to promise a rapid advance towards universal primary education, and this would surely have come about if the Republic had survived in its first form. The Second Empire, on the other hand, was less well equipped to deal with education than with building railways or developing commerce. Depending on conservative middle-class support, it was unable to act with vigour to expand popular education. Its concern for efficiency was reflected in the reforms of secondary education, but their success was limited. And as a regime based on order rather than liberty, it was incapable of awakening the sympathy and response of the teachers on whom the vitality of education depended, and found difficulty in handling that side of the nation's life concerned with intellectual creativity, free inquiry, and the transmission of humane values.

Appendix

THE ADMINISTRATION OF EDUCATION

The minister of public instruction, sometimes called by the old title Grand-Maître de l'Université, was advised by a central council: Conseil de l'Université or Conseil royal before 1850, Conseil supérieur 1850-3, Conseil impérial 1853-70. As set up in 1850, the Conseil supérieur had a *section permanente* of eight life members appointed from among senior *universitaires*, and representatives of the churches, the Conseil d'État, the Cour de cassation, the Institute, and private education. In 1852 the composition was altered, and eight of the *inspecteurs généraux* replaced the *section permanente*. The *inspecteurs généraux*, for higher, secondary, and primary education, were part of the central administration.

The local administration was based on the local government units of department, *arrondissement*, and commune. France was divided into *académies*, each administered by a *recteur*. There were twenty-seven academies before 1848, nineteen 1848-50; between 1850 and 1854 each academy comprised one department; in 1854 sixteen regional academies were restored. They were Aix, Besançon, Bordeaux, Caen, Clermont, Dijon, Douai, Grenoble, Lyons, Montpellier, Nancy, Paris, Poitiers, Rennes, Strasbourg, and Toulouse. Chambéry was added in 1860. Before and after 1854, each academy had a *conseil académique* including representatives of the churches and public authorities; in 1854 a similar *conseil départemental* was set up in each department. The oversight of private education was among these councils' responsibilities.

Except between 1850 and 1854, the official in charge of a department was the *inspecteur d'académie*. In each *arrondissement* there was an *inspecteur primaire* for primary schools. The educational administration directly supervised the faculties (headed by a *doyen* appointed from among the professors) and the lycées (*collèges royaux* until 1848; headed by a *proviseur*); it shared responsibility for the *collèges communaux* (headed by a *principal*) with the communes.

The *conseil municipal* in each commune had the basic responsibility for primary schools. Under the 1833 law, the supervising authority was the *comité d'arrondissement*, composed chiefly of local notables. In 1850–4, primary education came directly under the rector; in 1852 the actual nomination of teachers was transferred to him from the communes. But in 1854 this last power, and general responsibility for primary education, became the province of the *préfets* of departments. *Inspecteurs d'académie* now had a dual allegiance, to the prefect for primary education and the rector for other matters. The rector and *conseil académique* retained some responsibility for methods and standards.

After 1850, local notables played a minor role in supervising primary education as *délégués cantonaux* in each canton (group of communes). The elected *conseil général* in each department was also involved through its responsibility for *écoles normales*. Yet another body, the *commission d'examen* appointed by the *conseil académique*, awarded *brevets de capacité* to teachers.

Arrangements in the Seine department differed in detail. There was a *vice-recteur* of Paris (the minister being technically rector), and a number of *inspecteurs d'académie* with specialized duties. The title vice-rector was also borne by the *inspecteur d'académie* in Corsica.

Bibliography

In order to make this bibliography as useful as possible, I have laid special emphasis on recent scholarly work, and have selected only what is especially interesting or characteristic from the mass of contemporary publications on education. All books are published at Paris unless otherwise shown.

I. MANUSCRIPT SOURCES

The principal source is the archive of the ministry of public instruction, preserved at the Archives Nationales, Paris, under the classification F^{17}. The Archives Nationales also contain the records of the Academy of Paris for this period, classified AJ 16; among the private papers deposited there are those of Fortoul (246 AP), which are of first-rate importance, and the Duruy–Glachant papers (114 AP), which contain very little.

The footnote references give an idea of the types of document that have been used. It will be observed that I have not used archive sources (or detailed study of the educational press) for the sections on primary education; to have done so would have been to repeat the work of Maurice Gontard.

II. ADMINISTRATIVE PUBLICATIONS

A. The regulations, circulars, etc., of the ministry of education may be found in the periodical *Bulletin administratif de l'instruction publique* (1850–63) and *Bulletin administratif du ministère de l'instruction publique* (from 1864). Those on primary education are collected in O. Gréard, *La Législation de l'instruction primaire en France depuis 1789 jusqu'à nos jours* (2nd edn., 7 vols., 1899–1902). There are also collections, including additional documents, for the ministries of Fortoul and Duruy: *Réforme de l'enseignement* (2 vols. in 3, 1854–6); *L'Administration de l'instruction publique de 1863 à 1869. Ministère de S.E. M. Duruy* (n.d.).

B. Statistics. For primary education, the most valuable source is the retrospective *Statistique de l'enseignement primaire. II. Statistique comparée de l'enseignement primaire (1829–1877)* (1880), with an important methodological introduction. Duruy published the *Statistique de l'instruction primaire. 1863. Situation au 1er janvier 1864* (1865). The reports of his officials in 1864 are in *État de l'instruction primaire en 1864 d'après les rapports officiels des inspecteurs d'académie. Complément de la statistique de 1863* (2 vols., 1866).

On secondary education: *Rapport au roi sur l'instruction secondaire* (1843); *Statistique de l'enseignement secondaire en 1865* (1868); *Statistique de l'enseignement secondaire en 1876* (1878). A report prepared in 1850 but not published is in A.N. F^{17} 6839.

On higher education: *Statistique de l'enseignement supérieur 1865–1868* (1868). Figures for the baccalaureate and other examinations are in *Enquêtes et documents relatifs à l'enseignement supérieur. XXI. État numérique des grades, 1795–1885* (1886).

C. The commission on *enseignement professionnel* published two volumes of evidence and documents, and a report: *Enquête sur l'enseignement professionnel, ou recueil de dépositions faites en 1863 et 1864 devant la commission de l'enseignement professionnel* (2 vols., 1864–5); *Commission de l'enseignement technique. Rapport et notes* (1865).

D. Miscellaneous. On finance, see C. Nicolas, *Les Budgets de la France depuis le commencement du XIXe siècle* (1882); C. Jourdain, *Le Budget de l'instruction publique et des établissements scientifiques et littéraires depuis la fondation de l'Université impériale jusqu'à nos jours* (1857).

Parliamentary debates are usually reported in the educational press, but may also be found from 1861 in *Annales du Sénat et du Corps législatif*.

Relevant reports on international exhibitions: *Exposition universelle de 1851. Travaux de la commission française sur l'industrie des nations*, vol. viii (1856); *Exposition universelle de Londres de 1862. Rapports des membres de la section française du jury international sur l'ensemble de l'Exposition*, vol. vi (1862); *Exposition universelle de 1867 à Paris. Rapports du jury international*, vol. xiii (1868) (on the education exhibits).

E.   Officially-inspired reports on foreign education:

E. Rendu, *De l'état de l'instruction primaire à Londres* (1851);

E. Rendu, *De l'éducation populaire dans l'Allemagne du nord et de ses rapports avec les doctrines philosophiques et religieuses* (1855);

É. Marguerin and J. Motheré, *De l'enseignement des classes moyennes et des classes ouvrières en Angleterre* (1864);

J. M. Baudouin, *Rapport sur l'état actuel de l'enseignement spécial et de l'enseignement primaire en Belgique, en Allemagne et en Suisse* (1865);

L'Instruction secondaire en Prusse, enseignement classique et intermédiaire, d'après les documents les plus récents (1865);

F. Monnier, *L'Instruction populaire en Allemagne, en Suisse et dans les pays scandinaves* (1866);

J. F. Minssen, *Étude sur l'instruction secondaire et supérieure en Allemagne* (1866);

J. Demogeot and H. Montucci, *De l'enseignement secondaire en Angleterre et en Écosse* (1868);

J. Demogeot and H. Montucci, *De l'enseignement supérieur en Angleterre et en Écosse* (1870);

A. Wurtz, *Les Hautes Études pratiques dans les universités allemandes* (1870).

These reports, and similar foreign reports on France, are discussed in H. J. Ody, *Begegnung zwischen Deutschland, England und Frankreich im höheren Schulwesen seit Beginn des 19. Jahrhunderts* (Saarbrücken, 1959).

III. PERIODICALS

The University's leading periodicals were the *Revue de l'instruc-*

I

tion publique and *Journal général de l'instruction publique*. The latter
was officially subsidized until 1863. Both include educational
legislation, parliamentary reports, summaries of press comment,
etc. *L'Enseignement professionnel* appeared 1862–5.

General periodicals which frequently had articles on education
include *Revue des Deux Mondes*; *Journal des Économistes*; *La
Liberté de penser* (1847–51); *Le Correspondant*; *La Philosophie
positive* (from 1867).

Other periodicals cited: *Revue de l'enseignement chrétien*; *Séances
et travaux de l'Académie des sciences morales et politiques*; *Bulletin
de la Société d'encouragement pour l'industrie nationale*; *Mémoires et
compte-rendu des travaux de la Société des Ingénieurs civils*; *Annuaire
de l'Association pour l'encouragement des études grecques*.

IV. GENERAL WORKS

A. The best general introduction is A. Prost, *Histoire de l'enseignement en France 1800–1967* (1968). F. Ponteil, *Histoire de
l'enseignement en France. Les grandes étapes, 1789–1964* (1966) has
a more old-fashioned approach. Both have useful bibliographies.
There are a number of textbook-style histories in French: one
recent one, with a volume of documents, is P. Chevallier, B.
Grosperrin, and J. Maillet, *L'Enseignement français de la Révolution
à nos jours* (2 vols., 1968–71).

Some older histories are still of interest for the attitudes they
reveal: A. F. Théry, *Histoire de l'éducation en France depuis le
cinquième siècle jusqu'à nos jours* (2 vols., 1858); G. Compayré,
*Histoire critique des doctrines de l'éducation en France depuis le
seizième siècle* (2 vols., 1879). Taine's celebrated critique of French
education is in H. Taine, *Les Origines de la France contemporaine.
Le Régime moderne*, vol. ii (1894).

Valuable contemporary surveys are: A. Cournot, *Des institutions
d'instruction publique en France* (1864); C. Jourdain, *Rapport sur
l'organisation et les progrès de l'instruction publique* (1867); and the
writings of Matthew Arnold, reprinted in *Democratic Education*
(Ann Arbor, 1962) and *Schools and Universities on the Continent*
(Ann Arbor, 1964), which are vols. ii and iv of *The Complete Prose
Works of Matthew Arnold*, ed. R. H. Super.

B. For the period 1789–1815: H. C. Barnard, *Education and the
French Revolution* (Cambridge, 1969); L. P. Williams, 'Science,

Education, and the French Revolution', *Isis*, xliv (1953), pp. 311–30, and 'Science, Education, and Napoleon I', *Isis*, xlvii (1956), pp. 369–82; A. Aulard, *Napoléon Ier et le monopole universitaire* (1911); A. Léon, 'Promesses et ambiguités de l'oeuvre d'enseignement technique en France de 1800 à 1815', *Annales historiques de la Révolution française*, xlii (1970), pp. 419–36.

For the period 1815–48: A. Garnier, *Frayssinous, son rôle dans l'Université sous la Restauration (1822–1828)* (1925); D. Johnson, *Guizot. Aspects of French History 1787–1874* (London, 1963); F. Guizot, *Mémoires pour servir à l'histoire de mon temps*, vol. iii (1860); V. Cousin, *Recueil des principaux actes du ministère de l'instruction publique, du 1er mars au 28 octobre 1840* (1841); *Oeuvres de M. Victor Cousin. Cinquième série. Instruction publique* (new edn., 3 vols., 1850); G. Vauthier, *Villemain, 1790–1870. Essai sur sa vie, son rôle, et ses ouvrages* (1913); L. Trénard, *Salvandy en son temps, 1795–1856* (Lille, 1968).

C.   Reference and bibliography. The most useful reference work is F. Buisson, *Dictionnaire de pédagogie et d'instruction primaire*, first part (2 vols., 1882–7). Much material is omitted from the second edition: *Nouveau dictionnaire de pédagogie et d'instruction primaire* (2 vols., 1911). The first edition includes, under 'Bibliographie', a chronological list of books on education published down to 1877, and a similar list of periodicals under 'Périodiques'. For the latter see also A. Beurier, *La Presse pédagogique et les bulletins départementaux. Les périodiques scolaires français de 1789 à 1889* (1889).

For current research, see the *Bibliographie annuelle de l'histoire de France*, which covers work since 1953. The following discuss sources and research opportunities: M. L. Marchand and M. Duchein, 'Les Archives de l'enseignement en France', *La Gazette des Archives*, new series, no. 56 (1967), pp. 89–111; R. Oberlé and P. Leuilliot, 'L'Enseignement au XIXe siècle et l'histoire sociale', *Comité des travaux historiques et scientifiques. Bulletin de la section d'histoire moderne et contemporaine (depuis 1610)*, iv (1962), pp. 25–39; A. Chatelain, 'Une Enquête contemporaine: pour une géographie sociologique de l'éducation et de la laïcité', *Annales. Économies, Sociétés, Civilisations*, vii (1952), pp. 332–6.

D.   Sociological perspectives. A useful work bearing directly on the period is M. Vaughan and M. S. Archer, *Social Conflict and Educational Change in England and France 1789–1848* (Cambridge,

1971). Relevant general ideas may be found in É. Durkheim, *Éducation et sociologie* (1922); M. Crozier, *The Bureaucratic Phenomenon* (London, 1964); P. Bourdieu and J. C. Passeron, *La Reproduction. Éléments pour une théorie du système d'enseignement* (1970); *Niveaux de culture et groupes sociaux. Actes du colloque réuni du 7 au 9 mai 1966 à l'École normale supérieure* (1967); M. Scotford-Morton, 'Some English and French Notions of Democracy in Education', *Archives européennes de sociologie*, viii (1967), pp. 152–61; E. Hopper (ed.), *Readings in the Theory of Educational Systems* (London, 1971); M. F. D. Young (ed.), *Knowledge and Control. New Directions for the Sociology of Education* (London, 1971).

E.   Local studies covering all sectors of education. The model here is R. Oberlé, *L'Enseignement à Mulhouse de 1798 à 1870* (Strasbourg, 1961). Briefer studies of particular areas are: L. Trénard, 'Une Visite à l'Académie de Clermont en 1846', *Revue d'Auvergne*, lxvi (1952), pp. 81–109; L. Bourrilly, 'L'Instruction publique dans la région de Toulon de la Restauration à la Troisième République', *Bulletin de l'Académie du Var*, new series, xviii (1895), pp. 1–120; L. Maggiolo, *Les Écoles en Lorraine (Meurthe—Moselle—Meuse—Vosges) avant et après 1789. Troisième partie. 1802–1890* (Nancy, 1891).

There is usually valuable material in general local histories, e.g.:
M. Bruyère, *Alès, capitale des Cévennes* (Nîmes, 1948);
L. Desgraves and G. Dupeux, *Bordeaux au XIXe siècle* (Bordeaux, 1969);
M. du Camp, *Paris: ses organes, ses fonctions et sa vie dans la seconde moitié du XIXe siècle*, vol. v (1874);
G. Dupeux, *Aspects de l'histoire sociale et politique du Loir-et-Cher 1848–1914* (1962);
M. M. Kahan-Rabecq, *L'Alsace économique et sociale sous le règne de Louis-Philippe. I. La Classe ouvrière en Alsace pendant la monarchie de juillet* (1939);
J. Lovie, *La Savoie dans la vie française de 1860 à 1875* (1963);
C. Marcilhacy, *Le Diocèse d'Orléans sous l'épiscopat de Mgr Dupanloup, 1849–1878. Sociologie religieuse et mentalités collectives* (1962);
P. Pierrard, *La Vie ouvrière à Lille sous le Second Empire* (1965);
J. Vidalenc, *Le Département de l'Eure sous la monarchie constitutionnelle 1814–1848* (1952).

V. MINISTERS AND THEIR POLICIES

A. Second Republic. The documents of Carnot's ministry are in H. Carnot, *Le Ministère de l'instruction publique et des cultes depuis le 24 février jusqu'au 5 juillet 1848* (1848), and there is a brief study of him: P. Carnot, *Hippolyte Carnot et le ministère de l'instruction publique de la IIe République* (1948).

B. Fortoul. There are some biographical articles, but no full study: G. Vauthier, 'La Carrière professorale de Fortoul', *Feuilles d'histoire*, ix (1913), pp. 339–50; M. Gontard, 'La Carrière universitaire d'Hippolyte Fortoul (1848–1849)', *Cahiers d'histoire*, xiii (1968), pp. 115–27; M. Gontard, 'Hippolyte Fortoul, premier doyen de la Faculté des Lettres d'Aix (1846–1849)', *Provence historique*, xx (1970), pp. 375–97; P. Raphaël, 'Fortoul et la Seconde République, d'après des documents inédits', *La Révolution de 1848*, xxvii (1930–1), pp. 185–246; P. Raphaël, 'Fortoul, Sainte-Beuve et Cucheval-Clarigny', *La Révolution de 1848*, xxvii (1930–1), pp. 43–8 (deals with reaction to his 1852 reforms). See also Lange, 'Un Petit Monde d'autrefois: l'Université de M. Fortoul', *Bulletin de la Société des amis de l'Université de Dijon*, xi (1912), pp. 131–64, and speech of du Camp in *Discours prononcés dans la séance publique tenue par l'Académie Française pour la réception de M. Hervé* (1887).

C. Rouland. The only study is F. Dutacq, *Gustave Rouland, ministre de l'instruction publique 1856–1863* (Tulle, 1910). Rouland's speeches are in *Discours et réquisitoires de M. Rouland* (2 vols., 1863).

D. Duruy. V. Duruy, *Notes et souvenirs (1811–1894)* (2nd edn., 2 vols., 1902), is illuminating and well documented, though Duruy tends to exaggerate his own originality. J. Rohr, *Victor Duruy, ministre de Napoléon III* (1967) is an excellent modern study, and E. Lavisse, *Un ministre. Victor Duruy* (1895) is still worth reading for Lavisse's memories of working under Duruy. Other portraits are in E. Legouvé, *Dernier travail, derniers souvenirs* (1898); G. Monod, *Portraits et souvenirs* (1897); Duc de Broglie, *Notice sur la vie et les oeuvres de M. Victor Duruy* (1898).

Some letters illustrating Duruy's anticlericalism are in *La Dépêche* (Toulouse), 31 Oct. 1902, 5–6–7 May 1904. His adoption into the republican pantheon is illustrated in *Institut de France. Inauguration du monument élevé à la mémoire de Victor Duruy à*

Villeneuve-Saint-Georges. Le 27 mai 1900 (1900); *Le Centenaire de Victor Duruy 1811–1911* (Cahors, 1911); M. Schwab, *Victor Duruy et les premiers pas de l'enseignement laïque* (1963).

The political atmosphere during his ministry is described in A. Claveau, *Souvenirs politiques et parlementaires d'un témoin. 1865–1870* (1913).

VI. THE UNIVERSITY AND ITS LIFE

A. General. P. Gerbod, *La Condition universitaire en France au XIXe siècle* (1965) is a major work of scholarship and essential reading; it has an important bibliography. Cf. Gerbod's 'La Vie universitaire à Paris sous la Restauration de 1820 à 1830', *Revue d'histoire moderne et contemporaine*, xiii (1966), pp. 5–48, and 'Associations et syndicalismes universitaires de 1828 à 1928 (dans l'enseignement secondaire public)', *Le Mouvement social*, no. 55 (1966), pp. 3–45.

On opinion within the University, see also: G. Vauthier, 'L'Éducation républicaine, journal des maîtres d'études (1848–1850)', *La Révolution de 1848*, xvii (1920), pp. 29–34; C. Dejob, *Le Réveil de l'opinion dans l'Université sous le Second Empire: la Revue de l'instruction publique et Victor Duruy* (n.d.); L. Lévy-Schneider, *Les Idées politiques des lycéens au siècle dernier* (Lyons, 1904).

On the administrative side: P. Gerbod, 'Les Inspecteurs généraux et l'inspection générale de l'instruction publique de 1802 à 1882', *Revue historique*, ccxxxvi (1966), pp. 79–106; J. Vial, 'L'Administration centrale de l'instruction publique en France de 1792 à 1855', *Paedagogica Historica*, ix (1969), pp. 120–8; P. Raphaël, 'Les Recteurs de 1850', *Revue d'histoire moderne*, x (1935), pp. 448–87.

B. Memoirs, letters, biographies, etc. These may be divided into three categories.

(i) Men involved in educational administration and policy-making: A. Cournot, *Souvenirs (1760–1860)* (1913); *Revue de métaphysique et de morale*, xiii (1905), special no. on Cournot; É. Levasseur, *Octave Gréard* (n.d.); M. P. Bourgain, *Gréard. Un moraliste éducateur* (1907); A. Mourier, *Notes et souvenirs d'un universitaire, 1827–1889* (Orléans, 1889); D. Nisard, *Souvenirs et notes biographiques* (2 vols., 1888); D. Nisard, *Discours académiques et universitaires (1852–1868)* (1884).

(ii) Men who suffered from political oppression, especially the group at the École Normale *c.* 1848–52: É. Gossot, *Arthur Bary 1829–1887* (n.d.); Mme C. Garnier, *Une Famille parisienne universitaire au XIXe siècle* (1911) (the Bary family); E. Grelé, 'Paul Challemel-Lacour. Le professeur, l'insurgé, le proscrit, 1849–1860', *Mémoires de l'Académie nationale des sciences, arts et belles-lettres de Caen*, 1918–20, pp. 3–178; G. Vauthier, 'Le Professeur Jacques-François Denis, disgracié', *La Révolution de 1848*, xxvii (1930), pp. 106–9; O. Gréard, *Prévost-Paradol. Étude suivie d'un choix de lettres* (1894); P. Guiral, *Prévost-Paradol (1829–1870). Pensée et action d'un libéral sous le Second Empire* (1955) (a major study of the intellectual life of the period); F. Sarcey, *Souvenirs de jeunesse* (1885); *Journal de jeunesse de Francisque Sarcey (1839–1857)* (n.d.); H. Taine. *Sa vie et sa correspondance*, vols. i (1902), ii (1904).

(iii) Others, of interest for attitudes in the University or school life: F. Bouillier, *Souvenirs d'un vieil universitaire* (Orléans, 1897); H. Dabot, *Lettres d'un lycéen et d'un étudiant de 1847 à 1854* (n.d.); P. Gerbod, *Paul-François Dubois. Universitaire, journaliste et homme politique 1793–1874* (1967); A. Salles, *L'Abbé Follioley, sa vie et son oeuvre (1836–1902)* (Niort, 1904) (example of a priest in the University); F. Hémon, *Étude d'histoire morale collective. Bersot et ses amis* (1911); E. Lavisse, *Souvenirs* (5th edn., n.d.); A. Mézières, *Au temps passé* (1906); H. Thédenat, *Une Carrière universitaire. Jean-Félix Nourrisson, membre de l'Institut, 1825–1899* (1901); 'Souvenirs de Claude Perroud 1839–1919', *Revue universitaire*, xxxvii.2 (1928), pp. 193–212, xxxviii.1 (1929), pp. 17–26, xxxviii.2 (1929), pp. 118–41; U. Fischer, *Premiers maîtres. Collège de Saint-Claude (1864–1873)* (1931); G. Renard, 'Un Collège sous le Second Empire' and 'Au lycée Napoléon de 1864 à 1867', *La Révolution de 1848*, xxvi (1929), pp. 395–403, 444–55, and xxvii (1930), pp. 65–85, 159–76; P. Allard, *Paul Lamache* (1893).

C. The University's philosophy. There are several studies of Cousin: J. Simon, *Victor Cousin* (1887); P. Janet, *Victor Cousin et son oeuvre* (1885); J. Barthélemy Saint-Hilaire, *M. Victor Cousin, sa vie et sa correspondance* (3 vols., 1895); É. Faguet, *Politiques et moralistes du dix-neuvième siècle. Deuxième série* (n.d.); H. J. Ody, *Victor Cousin. Ein Lebensbild im deutsch-französischen Kulturraum* (Saarbrücken, n.d.). Taine's withering attack on him is in H. Taine, *Les Philosophes classiques du XIXe siècle en France* (7th edn., 1895).

For the development of Cousinism, and other tendencies under the Second Empire: A. F. Gatien-Arnoult, *Victor Cousin, l'école éclectique et l'avenir de la philosophie française* (1867); F. Ravaisson, *La Philosophie en France au XIXe siècle* (1868); P. Janet, 'Une Nouvelle Phase de la philosophie spiritualiste', *Revue des Deux Mondes*, 2nd period, cviii (1873), pp. 363–88; C. Bouglé, 'Spiritualisme et kantisme en France. Jules Lachelier', *La Revue de Paris*, xli.3 (1934), pp. 198–215.

An idea of what philosophy teaching meant in practice may be gained from A. Canivez, *Jules Lagneau, professeur de philosophie. Essai sur la condition du professeur de philosophie jusqu'à la fin du XIXe siècle* (1965) and E. Chauvet, 'L'Enseignement philosophique à Caen depuis 1830. Souvenirs d'un vieux professeur', *Mémoires de l'Académie nationale des sciences, arts et belles-lettres de Caen*, 1891, pp. 105–63.

VII. CHURCH AND STATE

A. General. Histories of Church–state relations tend to be strongly anticlerical, e.g. A. Debidour, *Histoire des rapports de l'Église et de l'État en France de 1789 à 1870* (1898); É. Bourgeois, *La Liberté d'enseignement. Histoire et doctrine* (1902); *La Lutte scolaire en France au dix-neuvième siècle* (1912). More balanced is L. Grimaud, *Histoire de la liberté d'enseignement en France* (Grenoble, 1898). Three essential modern works are G. Weill, *Histoire de l'idée laïque en France au XIXe siècle* (1925); J. Maurain, *La Politique ecclésiastique du Second Empire de 1852 à 1869* (1930); J. B. Duroselle, *Les Débuts du catholicisme social en France (1822–70)* (1951).

On the campaign for liberty of teaching see L. Grimaud, *Histoire de la liberté d'enseignement en France. VI. La monarchie de juillet* (1954) and L. Trénard, 'La Liberté d'enseignement à la veille de 1848', *Revue du Nord*, xlix (1967), pp. 421–81. The fullest account of the *loi Falloux* is H. Michel, *La Loi Falloux* (1906), though it appeared before the publication of *La Commission extraparlementaire de 1849. Texte intégral inédit des procès-verbaux* (1937). Other books are G. Cogniot, *De l'enthousiasme à la conscience enchaînée. La question scolaire en 1848 et la loi Falloux* (1948) and M. Hébert and A. Carnec, *La Loi Falloux et la liberté d'enseignement* (La Rochelle, 1953). The Catholic party's views on the application of the law are in *Rapport au comité de l'enseignement libre sur l'exécution et les effets de la loi organique de l'instruction publique du 15 mars 1850* (1853).

Biographical works with relevant material:

E. Sevrin, *Un Évêque militant et gallican au XIXe siècle, Mgr Clausel de Montals, évêque de Chartres, 1769–1857* (1955);

F. Lagrange, *Vie de Mgr Dupanloup* (3 vols., 1883–4);

N. F. L. Besson, *Vie de Son Éminence Monseigneur le cardinal Mathieu, archevêque de Besançon* (2 vols., 1882);

É. Lecanuet, *Montalembert* (3 vols., 1895–1902);

C. Guillemant, *Pierre-Louis Parisis* (3 vols., 1916–25).

B. Contemporary writings, including examples of anticlerical polemic:

L. E. Bautain, *De l'éducation publique en France au XIXe siècle* (1876);

Du clergé et de l'Université, considérations sur leur situation réciproque (1852);

M. H. de la Garde, *Considérations sur la liberté d'enseignement* (1860);

A. Magnien, *De la liberté d'enseignement et du baccalauréat* (1868);

A. de Margerie, *De la réforme universitaire* (Poitiers, 1850);

L. A. Meunier, *De l'enseignement congréganiste* (1845);

L. A. Meunier, *Lutte du principe clérical et du principe laïque dans l'enseignement* (1861) (a valuable source for Carnot's work in 1848);

C. Sauvestre, *Le Clergé et l'éducation. Question urgente* (1861);

C. Sauvestre, *Les Congrégations religieuses. Enquête par C.S.* (1867);

C. Sauvestre, *On the Knee of the Church. Female Training in Romish Convents and Schools* (2nd edn., London, 1869).

VIII. THE MOVEMENT OF OPINION

A. Studies of educational ideas. The outstanding work here is G. Duveau, *La Pensée ouvrière sur l'éducation pendant la Seconde République et le Second Empire* (n.d.). For other groups on the left, see G. Weill, 'Les Théories Saint-Simoniennes sur l'éducation', *Revue internationale de l'enseignement*, xvi (1896), pp. 237–46; G. Weill, 'Les Saint-Simoniens sous Napoléon III', *Revue des études napoléoniennes*, ii.1 (1913), pp. 391–406; G. Weill, 'Les Républicains et l'enseignement sous Louis-Philippe', *Revue internationale de l'enseignement*, xxxvii (1899), pp. 33–42; R. Pozzi, 'Il problema della scuola nei programmi dei democratici francesi durante la Monarchia di luglio', *Critica Storica*, vii (1968), pp. 169–214. For positivism: P. Arbousse-Bastide, *La Doctrine de l'éducation universelle dans la philosophie d'Auguste Comte* (2 vols., 1957); L. Legrand, *L'Influence du positivisme dans l'oeuvre scolaire de Jules Ferry* (1961); M. Dommanget, *Les Grands Éducateurs socialistes. Paul Robin* (n.d.). Reaction to the German threat, even before 1870, is discussed in C. Digeon, *La Crise allemande de la pensée française (1870–1914)* (1959).

B.   Some contemporary writings on the general problems of education:

T. H. Barrau, *De l'éducation dans la famille et au collège* (1852);

T. H. Barrau, *Du rôle de la famille dans l'éducation ou théorie de l'éducation publique et privée* (1857);

E. Bourdet, *Principes d'éducation positive* (1863);

M. Bréal, *Quelques mots sur l'instruction publique en France* (1872);

L. D. Champeau, *De l'éducation dans la famille, le collège et les institutions* (1868);

E. Chauvet, *L'Éducation* (1868);

A. C. Clavel, *Traité d'éducation physique et morale* (2 vols., 1855);

F. Dupanloup, *De l'éducation* (3 vols., 1850–61);

F. Dupanloup, *De la haute éducation intellectuelle* (3 vols., 1855–66);

J. B. Fonssagrives, *L'Éducation physique des garçons* (1870);

C. Gauthier-Coignet, *De l'enseignement public, au point de vue de l'Université, de la commune et de l'État* (1856);

Gouget, *Essai sur les conditions de l'éducation, envisagée au point de vue social* (Salins, 1853);

M. É. Hubert-Valleroux, *De l'enseignement. Ce qu'il a été, ce qu'il est, ce qu'il devrait être* (1859);

F. Lallemand, *Éducation publique* (2 vols., 1848–52);

A. Lavice, *De l'éducation nationale* (1868);

C. Lenormant, *Essais sur l'instruction publique* (1873);

Malgras, *De l'éducation et de l'instruction publique* (1849);

A. Marais, *L'École et la liberté* (Laon, 1868);

J. Marchef Girard, *Des facultés humaines et de leur développement par l'éducation* (1865);

L. A. Prévost-Paradol, *Du rôle de la famille dans l'éducation* (1857); *Rapport à la Société positiviste par la commission chargée d'examiner la nature et le plan de l'école positive, destinée surtout à régénérer les médecins* (2nd edn., 1850);

P. Robin, *De l'enseignement intégral* (Versailles, 1869).

C.   Books on political and social reform which discuss education:
E. About, *Le Progrès* (1864);
A. Garnier, *Morale sociale* (1850);
É. Laboulaye, *Le Parti libéral, son programme et son avenir* (1863);
F. Le Play, *La Réforme sociale en France* (2 vols., 1864);
É. Vacherot, *La Démocratie* (1860).

IX. PRIMARY EDUCATION

A.   General. The best general histories are those of M. Gontard:
L'Enseignement primaire en France de la Révolution à la loi Guizot
(*1789–1833*) (1959), and *Les Écoles primaires de la France bourgeoise*
(*1833–1875*) (Toulouse, n.d.). On the Catholic side, see G. Rigault,
Histoire générale de l'Institut des Frères des Écoles Chrétiennes,
vol. v (1945). Older histories still worth looking at are E. Deschamps,
*L'Enseignement mutuel. Étude pédagogique et historique sur l'instruc-
tion primaire* (Toulouse, 1883); A. Léaud and É. Glay, *L'École
primaire en France* (2 vols., 1934) (illustrates the official Third
Republic view).

On the content of teaching, there are two excellent recent studies:
H. C. Rulon and P. Friot, *Un Siècle de pédagogie dans les écoles
primaires* (*1820–1940*). *Histoire des méthodes et des manuels scolaires
utilisés dans l'Institut des Frères de l'Instruction chrétienne de
Ploërmel* (1962); P. Zind, *L'Enseignement religieux dans l'instruction
primaire publique en France de 1850 à 1873* (Lyons, 1971) (of wider
scope than the title suggests). For the *salles d'asile*, see É. Gossot,
Les Salles d'asile en France et leur fondateur Denys Cochin (1884)
and *Madame Marie Pape-Carpantier, sa vie et son oeuvre* (1890).

On physical conditions in the schools see C. Robert, *Plaintes et
voeux présentés par les instituteurs publics en 1861 sur la situation des
maisons d'école, du mobilier et du matériel classiques* (1864), which
may be compared with P. Lorain, *Tableau de l'instruction primaire
en France* (1837); see also T. Vacquer, *Bâtiments scolaires récemment
construits en France et propres à servir de types pour les édifices de ce
genre* (n.d.).

O. Gréard, *Éducation et instruction. Enseignement primaire* (1887)
discusses some general questions as well as Gréard's work at Paris,
for which see also his *L'Enseignement primaire à Paris et dans le
département de la Seine de 1867 à 1877* (1878). For the work of

another pioneer, see A. Trombert, *Charles Robert, sa vie, son oeuvre* (2 vols., 1927–31).

B. The teachers. A brief introduction is G. Duveau, *Les Instituteurs* (n.d.). Other recent studies: L. Trénard, 'Les Instituteurs en France à la veille de 1848', *Actes du 90e Congrès National des Sociétés Savantes, Nice 1965. Section d'histoire moderne et contemporaine*, vol. iii (1966), pp. 173–225; H. Dubief, 'Arsène Meunier, instituteur et militant républicain', *Études. Bibliothèque de la Révolution de 1848*, xvi (1954), pp. 17–42; P. Lévêque, 'Sur quelques instituteurs "rouges" de la Seconde République', *Annales de Bourgogne*, xxxvii (1965), pp. 289–300.

On the life of the rural teacher: L. Derome, *L'Église et l'instruction primaire à la campagne* (1861); P. Luiz, *Scènes de la vie d'instituteur* (1868).

Official advice for teachers: E. Rendu, *Manuel de l'enseignement primaire* (5th edn., 1858); E. Rendu, *Conférences de la Sorbonne. Séance du 17 septembre 1867. Pédagogie générale* (1868); A. Théry, *Lettres sur la profession d'instituteur* (1853).

On the *écoles normales*: M. Gontard, *La Question des écoles normales primaires de la Révolution de 1789 à la loi de 1879* (Toulouse, 1962); A. Canivez, *L'École normale d'instituteurs de Douai de 1834 à 1961* (n.d.); É. Reynier and L. Abrial, *Les Écoles normales de l'Ardèche (1831–1944. 1882–1944)* (Privas, 1945).

C. The Ligue de l'Enseignement. The basic source, which reprints Macé's writings of the period, is J. Macé, *La Ligue de l'Enseignement à Beblenheim 1862–1870* (1890). Useful studies of Macé are A. Dessoye, *Jean Macé et la fondation de la Ligue de l'Enseignement* (n.d.) and É. Petit, *Jean Macé. Sa vie, son oeuvre* (n.d.). See also M. Boivin, 'Les Origines de la Ligue de l'Enseignement en Seine-Inférieure 1866–1871', *Revue d'histoire économique et sociale*, xlvi (1968), pp. 203–31.

D. Literacy and school attendance. The literacy figures are conveniently available in C. M. Cipolla, *Literacy and Development in the West* (Harmondsworth, 1969). The question is also discussed in M. Fleury and P. Valmary, 'Les Progrès de l'instruction élémentaire de Louis XIV à Napoléon III d'après l'enquête de Louis Maggiolo (1877–1879)', *Population*, xii (1957), pp. 71–92; É. Levasseur, *L'Enseignement primaire dans les pays civilisés* (1897); G. d'Avenel, 'Le Goût de l'instruction et son prix depuis trois

siècles', *Revue des Deux Mondes*, 7th period, lii (1929), pp. 827–59;
L. Stone, 'Literacy and Education in England 1640–1900', *Past and Present*, no. 42 (1969), pp. 69–139.

For the attendance problem, especially as regards industry, see:
A. Hill (ed.), *Essays upon Educational Subjects* (London, 1857);
A. Audiganne, *Les Populations ouvrières et les industries de la France* (2nd edn., 2 vols., 1860); C. Robert, *De l'ignorance des populations ouvrières et rurales de la France et des causes qui tendent à la perpétuer* (Montbéliard, 1863); É. Levasseur, *Histoire des classes ouvrières en France depuis 1789 jusqu'à nos jours* (2 vols., 1867); G. Duveau, *La Vie ouvrière en France sous le Second Empire* (7th edn., 1946).

E.   Popular culture and libraries. A brief survey of adult education is B. Cacérès, *Histoire de l'éducation populaire* (1964). Other recent studies: C. Jefferson, 'Worker Education in England and France, 1800–1914', *Comparative Studies in Society and History*, vi (1964), pp. 345–66; J. Hassenforder, *Développement comparé des bibliothèques publiques en France, en Grande-Bretagne et aux États-Unis dans la seconde moitié du XIXe siècle (1850–1914)* (1967); R. Bellet, 'Une Bataille culturelle, provinciale et nationale, à propos des bons auteurs pour bibliothèques populaires (janvier–juin 1867)', *Revue des sciences humaines*, xxxiv (1969), pp. 453–73; E. Lefèvre, 'Jules Radu, fondateur des "Bibliothèques Communales", précurseur de Jean Macé', *Bulletin de la Société d'études historiques, géographiques et scientifiques de la région parisienne*, no. 102–3 (1959), pp. 19–37; D. I. Kulstein, 'Economics Instruction for Workers during the Second Empire', *French Historical Studies*, i (1959), pp. 225–34.

Contemporary writing: J. Simon, *Les Bibliothèques populaires* (Lyons, 1865); H. Baudrillart, *Les Bibliothèques et les cours populaires* (1867); L. Maggiolo, *Souvenir des conférences pédagogiques de la Sorbonne. Septembre 1867. Des cours d'adultes—Des bibliothèques scolaires—Du régime disciplinaire et des concours* (Nancy, 1868). Sainte-Beuve's speech in the Saint-Étienne affair is in his *Premiers lundis*, vol. iii (1875).

On *colportage* see J. J. Darmon, *Le Colportage de librairie en France sous le Second Empire. Grands colporteurs et culture populaire* (1972), and some contemporary works: C. Nisard, *Histoire des livres populaires ou de la littérature du colportage* (2 vols., 1854); E. A. de l'Étang, *Des livres utiles et du colportage comme moyen d'avancement moral et intellectuel des classes rurales et ouvrières* (1866); E. A. de l'Étang, *Le Colportage, l'instituteur primaire et les livres utiles dans les campagnes* (1865).

F.   Local studies. Local histories of primary education usually deal with a department, following the pioneering work of R. Lemoine, *La Loi Guizot, 28 juin 1833. Son application dans le département de la Somme* (1933):

É. Anthoine, *L'Instruction primaire dans le département du Nord. 1868–1877* (Lille, 1878);

M. Baudot, 'La Situation de l'enseignement primaire dans le département du Rhône lors de la mise en application de la loi Guizot (1833–1836)', *Actes du 89e Congrès National des Sociétés Savantes. Lyon 1964. Section d'histoire moderne et contemporaine*, vol. ii (1965), pp. 441–50;

P. Bois, 'Dans l'Ouest: politique et enseignement primaire', *Annales. Économies, Sociétés, Civilisations*, ix (1954), pp. 356–67;

G. Bugler, 'Essai sur l'enseignement primaire et le protestantisme dans le pays de Montbéliard entre 1805 et 1880', *Société d'Émulation de Montbéliard. Bulletin et mémoires*, lxvi (1967), pp. 27–66;

A. Chatelain, 'Le Niveau d'éducation des classes laborieuses en Seine-et-Marne en 1848', *Bulletin de la Société d'études historiques, géographiques et scientifiques de la région parisienne*, no. 80 (1953), pp. 1–8;

G. Cholvy, 'Autour de la loi Guizot: état de l'instruction primaire dans l'Hérault vers 1833', *Actes du 89e Congrès National des Sociétés Savantes. Lyon 1964. Section d'histoire moderne et contemporaine*, vol. ii (1965), pp. 485–555;

P. Clémendot, 'L'Enseignement primaire à Nancy de l'ancien régime à 1850', *Annales de l'Est*, 5th series, xxi (1969), pp. 3–53;

É. Coornaert, 'Flamand et français dans l'enseignement en Flandre française des annexions au XIXe siècle', *Revue du Nord*, liii (1971), pp. 217–21;

P. Dauthuile, *L'École primaire dans les Basses-Alpes depuis la Révolution jusqu'à nos jours* (Digne, 1900);

P. Dauthuile, *L'École primaire dans les Deux-Sèvres depuis ses origines jusqu'à nos jours* (Niort 1904);

J. P. David, *L'Établissement de l'enseignement primaire au XIXe siècle dans le département de Maine-et-Loire 1816–1879* (Angers, 1967);

M. Devun, 'La Politique scolaire de la ville de Saint-Étienne du

Premier Empire à la Troisième République', *Actes du 89e Congrès National des Sociétés Savantes. Lyon 1964. Section d'histoire moderne et contemporaine*, vol. ii (1965), pp. 563–88;

P. Gerbod, 'L'Enseignement dans le Puy-de-Dôme de 1848 à 1854', *Revue d'Auvergne*, lxv (1951), pp. 163–223;

M. Gontard, 'Une Bataille scolaire au XIXe siècle: l'affaire des écoles primaires laïques de Lyon (1869–1873)', *Cahiers d'histoire*, iii (1958), pp. 269–94;

J. Gourhand, 'Aperçus sur la situation de l'enseignement primaire dans le Calvados sous le Second Empire', *Bulletin de la Société des Antiquaires de Normandie*, lvii (1963–4), pp. 439–87;

R. Huard, *La Bataille pour l'école primaire dans le Gard (1866–1872)* (Nîmes, n.d.);

M. Leblond, 'La Scolarisation dans le département du Nord au XIXe siècle', *Revue du Nord*, lii (1970), pp. 387–98;

L. Mazoyer, 'Rénovation intellectuelle et problèmes sociaux. La bourgeoisie du Gard et l'instruction au début de la Monarchie de Juillet', *Annales d'histoire économique et sociale*, vi (1934), pp. 20–39;

B. Ménager, *La Laïcisation des écoles communales dans le département du Nord (1879–1899)* (Lille, 1971);

A. Rivet, 'La Loi Falloux: ses antécédents et ses conséquences dans le département de la Haute-Loire', *Actes du 91e Congrès National des Sociétés Savantes. Rennes 1966. Section d'histoire moderne et contemporaine*, vol. iii (1969), pp. 257–79;

C. Robert, *Notice sur l'enseignement donné à Morcenx par la Compagnie des chemins de fer du Midi* (1873);

R. Sancier, 'L'Enseignement primaire en Bretagne de 1815 à 1850', *Mémoires de la Société d'histoire et d'archéologie de Bretagne*, xxxii (1952), pp. 63–89, xxxiii (1953), pp. 151–73;

E. Sayous, *Monographie de l'école primaire supérieure de Pau* (Pau, 1901);

R. Thabault, *Mon village. Ses hommes, ses routes, son école* (8th edn., 1945);

L. de Vaucelles, 'La Querelle scolaire sous la Seconde République à la Guillotière', *Cahiers d'histoire*, x (1965), pp. 365–88;

A. Wolff, *La Loi Falloux et son application en Alsace et Lorraine* (1939);

V. Wright, 'L'Enseignement primaire dans les Basses-Pyrénées de 1848 à 1870', *Bulletin de la Société des Sciences, Lettres et Arts de Pau*, 4th series, iv (1969), pp. 159–73.

G.   Contemporary writings. Works of J. Simon: *L'École* (1865); *La Politique radicale* (3rd edn., 1868) (speeches); *L'Instruction populaire. Conférence faite à Reims, le 25 avril 1869* (n.d.); *L'Ouvrier de huit ans* (1867); *L'Ouvrière* (1861). Speeches of Simon, Carnot, and Havin are in *L'Instruction populaire en France. Débats parlementaires* (n.d.).

Works of C. Robert: *De la nécessité de rendre l'instruction primaire obligatoire en France et des moyens pratiques à employer dans ce but* (Montbéliard, 1861); *Instruction primaire* (Strasbourg, 1863); *De l'ignorance* (1867); *Les Améliorations sociales du Second Empire* (2 vols., 1868); *L'Instruction obligatoire* (1871) (a major source for the campaigns of the 1860s).

Works of J. Michelet: *Le Peuple*, ed. L. Refort (1946); *L'Étudiant* (1899); *Nos fils* (1870).

Others:

T. Assénat, *De la gratuité absolue et de l'obligation de l'instruction primaire* (n.d.);

A. de Caix de Saint-Aymour, *L'Enseignement populaire. Lettres au directeur du Courrier de l'Oise* (Senlis, 1867);

J. V. Daubié, *Du progrès dans l'instruction primaire. Justice et liberté!* (1862);

A. des Michels, *Quelques idées pratiques sur l'instruction universelle* (Draguignan, 1867);

Dommanget, *L'Enseignement élémentaire et l'éducation des filles dans les campagnes* (Strasbourg, 1865);

F. Dupanloup, *Discours prononcé au Congrès de Malines par Mgr l'évêque d'Orléans le 31 août 1864 sur l'enseignement populaire* (1864);

De l'enseignement obligatoire. Discussion entre M. G. de Molinari . . . et M. Frédéric Passy (1859);

L. Fabre, *Nouveau système d'enseignement national considéré surtout au point de vue des intérêts agricoles* (1865);

P. A. Guay, *Une Révolution à faire dans l'enseignement* (1865);

V. Guichard and H. Leneveux, *De l'instruction en France. Études sur les moyens de la propager* (n.d.);

L. Hachette, *L'Instruction populaire et le suffrage universel* (1861);

L. Jubé, *De l'obligatoire en matière d'instruction primaire* (1865);

A. Perdonnet, *De l'utilité de l'instruction pour le peuple* (1867);

S. Popoff, *Du principe de l'instruction obligatoire, au point de vue du droit naturel* (Le Havre, 1867);

E. Quinet, *L'Enseignement du peuple* (1850);

E. Rendu, *De l'enseignement obligatoire. Mémoire présenté à l'Empereur* (1853);

H. Rozy, *L'Instruction primaire obligatoire mais non gratuite* (1870);

J. I. Simonis, *Lettres à M. Jules Simon sur l'instruction primaire* (Strasbourg, 1869);

C. Talbosq and H. F. Delaunay, *A MM. les députés de 1864. Le suffrage universel et l'instruction primaire* (1863).

X. SECONDARY EDUCATION

A.   General history. There are two good introductions: G. Weill, *Histoire de l'enseignement secondaire en France (1802–1920)* (1921) and P. Gerbod, *La Vie quotidienne dans les lycées et collèges au XIXe siècle* (1968).

É. Durkheim, *L'Évolution pédagogique en France* (2 vols., 1938) relates nineteenth-century history to the traditions of the ancien régime, some other books on which are: G. Snyders, *La Pédagogie en France aux XVIIe et XVIIIe siècles* (1965); P. Ariès, *L'Enfant et la vie familiale sous l'ancien régime* (n.d.); F. de Dainville, *Les Jésuites et l'éducation de la société française. La naissance de l'humanisme moderne* (1940); F. de Dainville, 'Effectifs des collèges et scolarité aux XVIIe et XVIIIe siècles dans le Nord-Est de la France', *Population*, x (1955), pp. 455–88; F. de Dainville, 'Collèges et fréquentation scolaire au XVIIe siècle', *Population*, xii (1957), pp. 467–94.

On Catholic schools, see R. Anderson, 'The Conflict in Education. Catholic Secondary Schools (1850–70): a Reappraisal', in T. Zeldin (ed.), *Conflicts in French Society. Anticlericalism, Education and Morals in the Nineteenth Century* (London, 1970) (includes a list of histories of individual schools). On the Jesuits: J. W. Padberg, *Colleges in Controversy. The Jesuit Schools in France from Revival to Suppression, 1815–1880* (Cambridge, Mass., 1969); J. Burnichon, *La Compagnie de Jésus en France. Histoire d'un siècle 1814–1914*, vols. iii–iv (1919–22); F. Charmot, *La Pédagogie des Jésuites. Ses principes, son actualité* (1943).

B.   Social aspects. On the relation of education to class, etc., see E. Goblot, *La Barrière et le niveau. Étude sociologique sur la bourgeoisie française moderne* (new edn., 1967); R. Anderson, 'Secondary Education in Mid Nineteenth-Century France: some

Social Aspects', *Past and Present*, no. 53 (1971), pp. 121–46; L. O'Boyle, 'The Problem of an Excess of Educated Men in Western Europe, 1800–1850', *Journal of Modern History*, xlii (1970), pp. 471–95.

The values of secondary education have been discussed by V. Isambert-Jamati on the basis of a content analysis of prize-giving speeches (which were printed in large numbers): *Crises de la société, crises de l'enseignement. Sociologie de l'enseignement secondaire français* (1970); 'Permanence ou variations des objectifs poursuivis par les lycées depuis cent ans', *Revue française de sociologie*, viii (1967), special no., pp. 57–79; 'Les Objectifs de l'enseignement secondaire français. Esquisse d'une étude diachronique', in *Perspectives de la sociologie contemporaine. Hommage à Georges Gurvitch* (1968). Also on prize-giving speeches, see C. Dejob, 'Les Discours de distributions de prix sous le Second Empire', *Feuilles d'histoire*, ix (1913), pp. 555–63, x (1913), pp. 70–9; A. Théry, *Modèles de discours et allocutions pour les distributions de prix dans les lycées, collèges et autres établissements d'instruction secondaire* (1852); and collections of actual speeches like J. F. C. Peschoud, *Discours sur l'éducation* (1868).

C. The curriculum. The standard history is C. Falcucci, *L'Humanisme dans l'enseignement secondaire en France au XIXe siècle* (Toulouse, 1939). F. Vial, *Trois siècles d'histoire de l'enseignement secondaire* (1936) exaggerates the influence of the *écoles centrales*. J. B. Piobetta, *Le Baccalauréat* (1937) includes full details of the examination programmes; see also P. Meuriot, *Le Baccalauréat. Son évolution historique et statistique des origines (1808) à nos jours* (Nancy, 1919). Curricular and other issues are discussed in O. Gréard, *Éducation et instruction. Enseignement secondaire* (2nd edn., 2 vols., 1889).

Some permanent features of the French classical tradition are discussed in C. Bouglé, *Humanisme, sociologie, philosophie. Remarques sur la conception française de la culture générale* (1938); G. Genette, 'Enseignement et rhétorique au XXe siècle', *Annales. Économies, Sociétés, Civilisations*, xxi (1966), pp. 292–305; P. Bourdieu and J. C. Passeron, 'L'Examen d'une illusion', *Revue française de sociologie*, ix (1968), special no., pp. 227–53.

On particular issues: P. Gerbod, 'La Place de l'histoire dans l'enseignement secondaire de 1802 à 1880', *L'Information historique*, xxvii (1965), pp. 123–30; P. Lévy, *La Langue allemande en France, pénétration et diffusion des origines à nos jours. II. De 1830 à nos jours* (1952) (modern language teaching); L. Trénard, 'L'Enseignement secondaire sous la Monarchie de Juillet: les réformes de Salvandy', *Revue d'histoire moderne et contemporaine*, xii (1965), pp. 81–133; R. D. Anderson, 'French Views of the English Public Schools: Some Nineteenth-Century Episodes', *History of Education*, ii (1973), pp. 159–72 (English influence on Duruy's reforms); A. Duruy, 'La Réforme des études classiques', *Revue des Deux Mondes*, 3rd period, lxi (1884), pp. 845–74 (Duruy's reforms of the classics); E. Zévort, *L'Enseignement secondaire de 1880 à 1890* (1890) (on special secondary education, the subject of much controversy in the years 1870–90).

D.   Duruy's courses for girls. Dupanloup's pamphlets are collected in *Nouvelles oeuvres choisies de Mgr Dupanloup*, vol. iii (1874). Examples of replies to him are I. Amiel, *Réponse à Monseigneur Dupanloup sur l'instruction secondaire des femmes* (1868); L. Audebert, *Réponse d'une mère de famille à Monseigneur l'évêque d'Orléans au sujet de l'enseignement des filles* (1868). See also F. Mayeur, 'Les Évêques français et Victor Duruy: les cours secondaires de jeunes filles', *Revue d'histoire de l'Église de France*, lvii (1971), pp. 267–304.

E.   Local studies. Local histories of secondary education are usually of individual institutions. They are numerous, but of very uneven quality. An outstanding and exhaustive one is G. Dupont-Ferrier, *La Vie quotidienne d'un collège parisien pendant plus de trois cent cinquante ans. Du collège de Clermont au lycée Louis-le-Grand (1563–1920)* (3 vols., 1921–5). For other Paris schools, see:
A. Chatelain, 'Un Collège de la bourgeoisie parisienne aisée au XIXe siècle: le Collège Rollin', *Bulletin de la Société d'études historiques, géographiques et scientifiques de la région parisienne*, no. 88 (1955), pp. 17–36;
A. Chaumeix, *Le Lycée Henri IV* (1936);
V. Chauvin, *Histoire des lycées et collèges de Paris* (1866);
Conseil académique de Paris. Exposés de M. Ad. Mourier, vice-recteur. Sessions 1862–1878 (1879);
C. Lamarre, *Histoire de Sainte-Barbe, avec aperçu sur l'enseignement secondaire en France de 1860 à 1900* (1900);
Louis-le-Grand, 1563–1963. Études, souvenirs, documents (1963);

J. Quicherat, *Histoire de Sainte-Barbe, collège, communauté, institution*, vol. iii (1864).

For the provinces:

A. Anthiaume, *Le Collège du Havre. Contribution à l'histoire de l'enseignement secondaire en France et particulièrement au Havre* (*1579–1865*) (2 vols., Le Havre, 1905);

Le Centenaire du lycée de Bordeaux (*1802–1902*) (Bordeaux, 1905);

M. Chabot and S. Charléty, *Histoire de l'enseignement secondaire dans le Rhône de 1789 à 1900* (1901);

A. Collignon, 'Souvenirs de l'ancien collège de Verdun', *Le Pays lorrain*, iii (1906), pp. 485–92;

E. Corgne, *Le Lycée de Pontivy, 1803–1931* (Pontivy, 1931);

J. Delmas, *Livre d'or. Histoire du lycée de Marseille* (Marseilles, 1898);

H. Duhaut, 'Le Lycée de Versailles (1815–1860)', *Revue de l'histoire de Versailles et de Seine-et-Oise*, xi (1909), pp. 162–76, 228–56, 307–32, xii (1910), pp. 107–30, 210–40, 303–18, xiii (1911), pp. 38–53, 153–76, 234–51, 350–66;

Gaston-Martin, *Le Lycée de Toulouse de 1763 à 1881* (Toulouse, 1930);

L. Gérard-Varet, 'Le Régime Victor Duruy: un collège de province de 1865 à 1880', *Revue universitaire*, xxxvii.2 (1928), pp. 109–15;

J. Godard, *1852–1952. Le lycée Faidherbe de Lille. Ses origines, son histoire* (Lille, 1952);

H. J. Leblanc, *Le Collège communal de Tourcoing pendant les 25 dernières années du régime universitaire* (*1858–1883*) (Lille, 1885);

Lycée Henri-Poincaré. Le livre des centenaires (Nancy, n.d.);

L. Musset, *Le Lycée Malherbe. Notice historique publiée à l'occasion du cent-cinquantenaire* (Caen, 1956);

C. Pouthas, *Le Lycée de Caen sous la Seconde République et le Second Empire 1848–1870* (Caen, 1908);

D. Rebut, 'Histoire du lycée du Mans depuis 1851', *Bulletin de la Société d'agriculture, sciences et arts de la Sarthe*, 2nd series, xxvii (1895–6), pp. 356–410;

A. Rivet, 'L'Enseignement secondaire en Haute-Loire de 1799 à 1850', *Actes du 89e Congrès National des Sociétés Savantes. Lyon 1964. Section d'histoire moderne et contemporaine*, vol. ii (1965), pp. 637–51;

É. Sorin, *Histoire du lycée d'Angers* (Angers, 1873);

L. H. Tranchau, *Le Collège et le lycée d'Orléans* (*1762–1892*) (Orléans, 1893);

F. Xambeu, *Histoire du collège de Saint-Sever* (*Landes*) (Dax, 1884).
For the *école normale spéciale* at Cluny:

F. Roux, *Histoire des six premières années de l'École normale spéciale de Cluny* (Alès, 1889);

J. Lougnon, *L'École normale d'enseignement secondaire spécial de Cluny. Statistique des douze premières promotions* (Cluny, 1880).

F.   Contemporary writings.
(i) Examples of the demand for reform before 1848:
M. Chevalier, *De l'instruction secondaire à l'occasion du rapport au roi de M. Villemain* (1843);

M. Chevalier, *De la nécessité de fonder l'enseignement professionnel* (n.d.);

F. Passy, *De l'instruction secondaire en France, de ses défauts, de leurs causes, et des moyens d'y remédier* (1846);

Saint-Marc Girardin, *De l'instruction intermédiaire et de ses rapports avec l'instruction secondaire* (1847).

(ii) J. Gaume, *Le Ver rongeur des sociétés modernes, ou le paganisme dans l'éducation* (1851) set off a controversy of which other samples are F. Danjou, *Du paganisme dans la société et dans l'éducation* (Montpellier, 1852); J. B. F. Landriot, *Examen critique des lettres de M. l'abbé Gaume sur le paganisme dans l'éducation* (1852);

B. Saint-Bonnet, *De l'affaiblissement de la raison par suite de l'enseignement en Europe depuis le XVIIIe siècle* (1853).

(iii) Some prize-giving speeches, illustrating the orthodox defence of the classics:
Marquis de Belbeuf, *Discours prononcé le 7 août 1866 à la distribution solennelle des prix au lycée impérial de Rouen* (Rouen, 1866);

F. de Bigorie de Laschamps, *De la nécessité des langues mortes comme base de l'éducation littéraire* (1869);

A. Geffroy, *De l'éducation libérale* (1852);

L. Lecuyer, *Du beau et de son rôle dans l'éducation* (Lyons, 1856);

C. Lenient, *Du matérialisme dans l'éducation* (Montpellier, 1852).

(iv) On the teaching of particular subjects:
C. Bénard, *L'Enseignement actuel de la philosophie dans les lycées et les collèges* (1862);

C. Bénard, *De la philosophie dans l'éducation classique* (1862);

Desclozeaux, *Discours prononcé à la distribution des prix du lycée impérial d'Avignon du 12 août 1863* (Avignon, n.d.) (on philosophy);

F. Dübner, *État actuel de notre enseignement public des humanités. Notes et observations sur les projets de réforme* (1863);

J. Duboul, *Du nouveau programme d'histoire contemporaine pour l'enseignement des lycées* (1865);

É. Egger, *La Tradition et les réformes dans l'enseignement universitaire. Souvenirs et conseils* (1883);

É. Levasseur and A. Himly, *Rapport général sur l'enseignement de l'histoire et de la géographie* (1871);

B. Lévy, *De l'enseignement des langues vivantes en France* (1865);

E. Maillet, *Académie d'Aix. Lycée de Marseille. Distribution solennelle des prix, le 9 août 1866. Discours prononcé par M. Maillet, professeur de philosophie* (Marseilles, 1866);

H. Montucci, *Les Langues vivantes dans les lycées* (1863);

H. Montucci, *Les Langues vivantes et la circulaire du 29 septembre* (1864);

H. Montucci, *Les Langues vivantes avant et après la guerre* (1871);

H. Schmidt, *De l'enseignement des langues vivantes en France depuis 1863* (1869);

A. Théry, *Projet d'une réforme dans l'enseignement des langues anciennes* (1872);

J. Tissot, *Du développement de l'esprit philosophique comme objet de l'éducation* (Dijon, 1864).

(v) General and miscellaneous:

F. Bastiat, *Baccalauréat et socialisme* (1850);

E. Bersot, *Questions d'enseignement. Études sur les réformes universitaires* (1880) (includes his criticisms of bifurcation published 1857);

A. Bonnet, *Du décret du dix avril dans ses rapports avec l'éducation du médecin* (Lyons, 1852);

A. Bonnet, *Influence des lettres et des sciences sur l'éducation* (Lyons, 1855);

A. Cahour, *Des études classiques et des études professionnelles* (1852);

C. Clavel, *Lettres sur l'enseignement des collèges en France* (1859);

C. Clavel, *Oeuvres diverses—éducation, morale, politique, littérature* (2 vols., 1871);

A. Ducourneau, *De l'enseignement secondaire spécial au collège d'Alais* (Alès, 1866);

Éducation internationale. Documens du concours provoqué par M. A.

*Barbier, manufacturier à Clermont-Ferrand, en décembre 1861, pour
la fondation d'un collège international* (1862);
C. Fiérville, *De la nécessité de l'enseignement secondaire spécial.
Étude historique* (Bayonne, 1867);
H. Gras, *Famille et collège, leur rôle dans l'éducation* (1861);
C. F. Guibal, *De l'instruction secondaire, et en particulier de l'étude
de la langue latine* (Nancy, 1848);
É. Labbé, *Des réformes dans l'enseignement secondaire* (1865);
V. de Laprade, *De l'enseignement des langues anciennes considéré
comme base des études classiques* (Lyons, 1852);
V. de Laprade, *L'Éducation homicide, plaidoyer pour l'enfance* (2nd
edn., 1868);
V. de Laprade, *Le Baccalauréat et les études classiques, pour faire
suite à l'Éducation homicide* (1869);
J. Simon, *La Réforme de l'enseignement secondaire* (1874) (describes
Simon's own reforms as minister, similar in many respects to
Duruy's);
H. Tabareau, *Sur les avantages du double enseignement littéraire
et scientifique, donné dans les lycées aux élèves de la section des
sciences* (Lyons, 1852).

XI. TECHNICAL EDUCATION

A. General. The best introduction is J. P. Guinot, *Formation
professionnelle et travailleurs qualifiés depuis 1789* (n.d.). See also
A. Prévot, *L'Enseignement technique chez les Frères des Écoles
Chrétiennes au XVIIIe et au XIXe siècles* (n.d.); F. B. Artz, *The
Development of Technical Education in France, 1500–1850* (Cambridge, Mass., 1966); A. Chatelain, 'La Formation de l'enseignement technique populaire à Paris au XIXe siècle', *Bulletin de la
Société d'études historiques, géographiques et scientifiques de la région
parisienne*, no. 85 (1954), pp. 1–10; P. Quef, *Histoire de l'apprentissage, aspects de la formation technique et commerciale* (1964).

Older works still of interest are C. Lucas, *Conférence sur
l'enseignement professionnel en France depuis 1789* (1889); A.
Panthier, *Enquête historique sur l'enseignement manuel dans les
écoles non techniques* (1906); J. B. Paquier, *L'Enseignement professionnel en France. Son histoire, ses différentes formes, ses résultats*
(1908); J. B. Rauber, *De l'influence des expositions universelles sur
l'enseignement des arts du dessin* (n.d.); L. Chateau, *Notice biographique sur Pierre-Philibert Pompée* (1875).

B.   On individual institutions or towns:

J. Bavencove, *Institut agricole de Beauvais (Oise)* (Beauvais, n.d.);

G. Cadoux, *Un Demi-siècle d'enseignement moderne. Le collège Chaptal à Paris* (n.d.);

Cinquantenaire de l'École primaire supérieure et professionnelle de Rouen (24–25 mars 1900). Compte rendu. Notice historique (Rouen, n.d.);

A. Collignon, *L'École Turgot sous l'administration municipale, 1839–1889* (1895);

G. Creveuil, *Un Éducateur français précurseur de l'enseignement technique. Eugène Livet, 1820–1913* (Nantes, n.d.);

1857–1957. École centrale lyonnaise. Un siècle d'une école d'ingénieurs (Lyons, n.d.);

P. de la Garanderie, 'Un Épisode de l'histoire académique d'Angers. L'École préparatoire à l'enseignement supérieur des sciences et des lettres (1855–1885)', *Académie des sciences, belles-lettres et arts, Angers. Mémoires*, 9th series, i (1967), pp. 131–8;

E. Livet, *L'Institution Livet et l'enseignement dans la seconde moitié du XIXe siècle. Histoire de cet établissement. Naissance de l'enseignement technique en France* (Nantes, 1905);

É. Obled, 'L'Enseignement technique à Douai', *Les Amis de Douai*, 5th series, no. 7 (1959), pp. 126–34;

G. Perrin and L. J. Veyron, *Notice historique sur l'École professionnelle Vaucanson* (Grenoble, 1889);

A. Renouard, *Histoire de l'École supérieure de commerce de Paris (1820–1898)* (1898);

R. Robinet, 'L'Institution Rossat de Charleville et la réforme de l'enseignement par Victor Duruy. Enseignement moderne et professionnel', *Actes du 88e Congrès National des Sociétés Savantes. Clermont-Ferrand 1963. Section d'histoire moderne et contemporaine* (1964), pp. 173–80;

C. Saint-Marc, *Collège de Saint-Amour. Distribution solennelle des prix pour l'année 1858. Discours prononcé par M. Corneille Saint-Marc, principal* (Lons-le-Saulnier, 1858).

C.   Contemporary writings:

A. Audiganne, *Les Ouvriers d'à présent et la nouvelle économie du travail* (1865);

C. F. Audley, *De l'enseignement professionnel et de son organisation* (1864);

C. Bertrand, *Lettres sur la fondation d'un véritable enseignement professionnel à créer à Grenoble* (Grenoble, 1857);

C. Bertrand, *Étude sur l'enseignement professionnel* (2nd edn., Brussels, 1864);

Comité central des artistes et des artistes-industriels. Placet et mémoires relatifs à la question des beaux-arts appliqués à l'industrie (1852);

A. Corbon, *De l'enseignement professionnel* (n.d.);

V. Denniée, *De l'enseignement professionnel (1762–1852)* (1852);

V. Denniée, *École professionnelle du Nord. Première année. 1854–1855. Discours prononcé à la distribution solennelle des prix* (Lille, n.d.);

V. Denniée, *École impériale professionnelle du Nord. Deuxième année. Discours prononcé à la distribution solennelle des prix* (Lille, n.d.);

C. Fichet, *Mémoire sur l'apprentissage et sur l'éducation industrielle* (1847);

C. Fichet, *Mémoire sur l'enseignement professionnel, suivi d'un plan d'instruction industrielle rédigé en 1852* (n.d.);

E. Flachat, *Étude sur l'enseignement professionnel* (1864);

J. A. Gentil, *Des syndicats et de l'enseignement professionnel* (1863);

A. Guettier, *De l'organisation de l'enseignement industriel* (1864);

Kula, *L'Apprentissage et l'enseignement technique* (1869);

E. Malet, *De l'enseignement professionnel et de son organisation* (Douai, 1864);

E. Menu de Saint-Mesmin, *L'Enseignement professionnel, étude historique et critique* (1864);

P. P. Pompée, *Études sur l'éducation professionnelle en France* (1863) (an important source for the Second Republic);

F. S. Rossat, *Réformes à introduire dans l'enseignement au profit de l'industrie, du commerce et de l'agriculture* (Charleville, 1862);

F. Roux, *De l'enseignement professionnel en France* (Castres, 1861);

E. Tartaret, *Conférences publiques de la mairie du XIme arrondissement. Enseignement professionnel* (1869).

XII. HIGHER EDUCATION

A. General. The standard history is L. Liard, *L'Enseignement supérieur en France 1789–1893* (2 vols., 1888–94), which also includes much general history of the University. A useful introduction is

T. Zeldin, 'Higher Education in France, 1848–1940', *Journal of Contemporary History*, ii, no. 3 (1967), pp. 53–80. See also O. Gréard, *Éducation et instruction. Enseignement supérieur* (2nd edn., 1889).

B. The *Grandes Écoles*:
J. P. Callot, *Histoire de l'École polytechnique. Ses légendes, ses traditions, sa gloire* (n.d.);
A. Daumard, 'Les Élèves de l'École polytechnique de 1815 à 1848', *Revue d'histoire moderne et contemporaine*, v (1958), pp. 226–34;
L. Guillet, *Cent ans de la vie de l'École centrale des arts et manufactures 1829–1929* (n.d.);
G. Pinet, *Histoire de l'École polytechnique* (1887);
F. Pothier, *Histoire de l'École centrale des arts et manufactures* (1887);
M. Vaughan, 'The *Grandes Écoles*', in R. Wilkinson (ed.), *Governing Elites. Studies in Training and Selection* (New York, 1969).

On the École Normale:
Le Centenaire de l'École normale, 1795–1895 (1895);
R. Fayolle, 'Sainte-Beuve et l'École normale: l'affaire de 1867', *Revue d'histoire littéraire de la France*, lxvii (1967), pp. 557–76;
G. Lanson, 'Nos grandes écoles. I. L'École normale supérieure', *Revue des Deux Mondes*, 7th period, xxxi (1926), pp. 512–41;
A. Peyrefitte (ed.), *Rue d'Ulm. Chroniques de la vie normalienne* (new edn., 1963) (an anthology);
G. Renard, 'L'École Normale de 1867 à 1870', *Revue bleue*, 1919, pp. 196–9, 420–4, 644–7; 1920, pp. 6–11, 513–18, 545–50; 1922, pp. 97–101.

C. The Faculties. Most recent work is on the period before 1848:
L. Trénard, 'Les Facultés des Lettres sous la Monarchie de Juillet', *Actes du 89e Congrès National des Sociétés Savantes. Lyon 1964. Section d'histoire moderne et contemporaine*, vol. ii (1965), pp. 669–715; L. Trénard, 'Salvandy et les études juridiques', *Revue du Nord*, xlviii (1966), pp. 337–79; L. Trénard, 'Les Études médicales sous Louis-Philippe', *Actes du 91e Congrès National des Sociétés Savantes. Rennes 1966. Section d'histoire moderne et contemporaine*, vol. iii (1969), pp. 167–214; J. Léonard, 'Les Études médicales en France entre 1815 et 1848', *Revue d'histoire moderne et contemporaine*, xiii (1966), pp. 87–94.
The career of Pasteur throws some light on the science faculties:

R. Vallery-Radot, *La Vie de Pasteur* (1900); *Pasteur. Correspondance, 1840–1895*, vols. i–ii (1940–51); C. Gernez-Rieux, 'Pasteur, doyen de la Faculté des Sciences de Lille', *Revue générale des sciences pures et appliquées*, lxxii (1965), pp. 29–44; D. Wrotnowska, 'Pasteur, professeur à Strasbourg (1849–1854)', *Comptes rendus du 92e Congrès National des Sociétés Savantes. Strasbourg et Colmar 1967. Section des sciences*, vol. i (1969), pp. 135–44.

On experiments in administrative and economic teaching:

É. Levasseur, *Résumé historique de l'enseignement de l'économie politique et de la statistique en France* (1883); G. Langrod, 'Trois tentatives d'introduction de la science politique dans l'Université française au cours du XIXe siècle', *Revue internationale d'histoire politique et constitutionnelle*, new series, vii (1957), pp. 24–36; C. Tranchant, *Notice sommaire sur l'École nationale d'administration de 1848 et sur les projets ultérieurs d'institutions analogues* (Nancy, 1884); M. Saurin, 'L'École d'administration de 1848', *Politique*, new series, vii–viii (1964–5), pp. 105–95.

There is no history of the faculties at Paris, but some information is in J. Bonnerot, *La Sorbonne. Sa vie, son rôle, son oeuvre à travers les siècles* (1927). The provincial faculties are also neglected, but see: J. Bonnecase, *La Faculté de droit de Strasbourg* (Toulouse, 1916); 'Centenaire de la Faculté des Lettres de Nancy 1854–1954', special no. of *Annales de l'Est*, 5th series, v (1954); A. Gain, 'L'Enseignement supérieur à Nancy de 1789 à 1896', *Annales de l'Est*, 4th series, i (1933), pp. 199–232, ii (1934), pp. 43–92; M. Gontard, 'Une Expérience scolaire au XIXe siècle: l'École normale secondaire d'Aix de 1848', *Provence historique*, xxi (1971), pp. 147–76; P. Janelle, 'Histoire de la Faculté des Lettres de Clermont', *Revue d'Auvergne*, lxviii (1954), pp. 117–56; Y. Laissus, 'L'Université de Strasbourg il y a cent ans d'après les papiers d'Adolphe Brongniart', *Comptes rendus du 92e Congrès National des Sociétés Savantes. Strasbourg et Colmar 1967. Section des sciences*, vol. i (1969), pp. 177–88; A. Logette, *Histoire de la Faculté de Droit de Nancy (1768–1864–1914)* (Nancy, 1964); L. Michon, *Histoire de la Faculté de Droit de Poitiers 1806–1899* (Poitiers, 1900); *Université de Grenoble 1339–1939* (Grenoble, 1939);

G. Versini, 'La Faculté des Lettres de Dijon de sa création à 1939', *Annales de Bourgogne*, xxxviii (1966), pp. 55–63

D. Contemporary writings:

L. Adam, *Réforme et liberté de l'enseignement supérieur* (1870);

F. Dupanloup, *La Liberté de l'enseignement supérieur* (1868);

L'Enseignement supérieur devant le Sénat (1868) (the debates on materialism in the faculties);

P. Guerrier de Dumast, *Sur l'enseignement supérieur tel qu'il est organisé en France, et sur le genre d'extension à y donner* (1865);

K. Hillebrand, *De la réforme de l'enseignement supérieur* (1868);

Lecerf, *De l'enseignement supérieur et des facultés* (Caen, 1852);

É. Lenoël, *Des sciences politiques et administratives et de leur enseignement* (1865);

L. Pasteur, *Pour l'avenir de la science française* (1947);

Oeuvres complètes de Ernest Renan, ed. H. Psichari, vols. i–ii (n.d.);

H. de Riancey, *La Liberté de l'enseignement supérieur à l'ordre du jour* (1868).

XIII. OTHER BOOKS CITED

C. Bénard, *Manuel d'études pour la préparation au baccalauréat ès lettres, rédigé conformément au nouveau programme du 26 novembre 1849. Philosophie* (1850);

C. Bénard, *Manuel d'études pour la préparation au baccalauréat ès lettres, rédigé conformément au nouveau programme du 30 août 1852. Logique* (1852);

Auguste Comte. Oeuvres choisies, ed. H. Gouhier (n.d.);

V. Cousin, *État de l'instruction secondaire dans le royaume de Prusse pendant l'année 1831* (1834);

A. Cuvillier, *Un Journal d'ouvriers: 'L'Atelier' (1840–1850)* (n.d.);

L. Febvre, *Combats pour l'histoire* (1953);

S. Hoffmann and others, *France: Change and Tradition* (London, 1963);

A. Jaume, *Histoire des classes laborieuses* (Toulon, 1852);

L. P. de Lafforest, *Rapport sur l'instruction dans la Loire-Inférieure* (Nantes, 1855);

L. P. de Lafforest, *Rapport sur l'instruction dans la Loire-Inférieure . . . Année scolaire 1855–56* (Nantes, 1856);

P. de la Gorce, *Histoire du Second Empire* (7 vols., 1894–1905);

F. Ravaisson, *Testament philosophique et fragments, précédés de la notice lue en 1904 à l'Académie des sciences morales et politiques par Henri Bergson* (n.d.);

S. Rothblatt, *The Revolution of the Dons. Cambridge and Society in Victorian England* (London, 1968);

Séance d'ouverture des cours gradués pour les jeunes demoiselles protestantes. Discours prononcés à cette occasion (1856);

P. Sorlin, *Waldeck-Rousseau* (1966);

F. Stern (ed.), *The Varieties of History, from Voltaire to the Present* (London, 1957);

H. Taine, *Journeys through France, being impressions of the provinces* (London, 1897).

Index

About, Edmond, writer, 24, 229
academies, 50, 54, 231, 247
Academy of Moral and Political
    Sciences, 121
adults, courses for, 86–7, 95, 115,
    140–2, 144–5, 189, 201–2, 204,
    235–6, 243
agrégation, 25, 74, 105, 175, 177, 181,
    219
agriculture, teaching of, 34, 84, 88–9,
    115, 140, 168, 213, 221, 223
Aisne department, 161 n., 166
Aix-en-Provence, 51, 84, 102
Albi, 102, 173
Alès, 84, 207, 210, 220–1
Allier department, 159, 163 n.
Alsace, 131, 133, 135, 141, 149, 165,
    167, 169–70, 223, 243
Amiens, 101, 173, 204
Angers, 84, 95
anticlericalism, 16, 18–19, 30, 37–8,
    82, 108, 121–8, 132–3, 136,
    143–4, 200, 210–11, 221, 237,
    241, 244
    see also Gallicanism
applied sciences, *see* science
apprenticeship, 34–5, 86–7, 115, 193,
    196, 200–1, 203–4, 243
Arago, François, astronomer, 64
Archer, Margaret S., sociologist, 1–2,
    12 n.
Ardèche department, 168 n., 170 n.
Ardennes department, 161 n., 164
Aristotle, 75
Arlès Dufour, François, industrialist,
    195, 197
army and navy, education for, 11, 26,
    58–9, 61, 74, 99–100, 119, 243
    see also Saint-Cyr
Arnold, Matthew, critic, 174
Arnold, Thomas, headmaster, 120
Arras, diocese of, 110
art education, 77–8, 90, 194, 202
    see also drawing

Artaud, Nicolas-Louis, University
    official, 106 n.
Assemblée nationale, L', legitimist
    newspaper, 68
Association philotechnique, 144
Association polytechnique, 144
Assumptionists, 114
Atelier, L', working-class newspaper,
    133, 195
Aubusson, 213
Audiganne, Alphonse, writer on
    industrial questions, 86–7
Augustine, Saint, 75
Avignon, 100, 173

baccalaureate,
    general, 11, 13, 23, 49, 72–3, 106–7,
        187, 211, 215, 225–6, 228, 230,
        243
    changes in, 23, 68, 70–1, 74, 76,
        99, 105, 107, 174–5, 178, 182,
        220
    taken by girls, 189–90
Baccarat, 167
Bacon, 75
Bader, Léon-Louis, technical teacher,
    92, 197, 203
Balzac, 148
Barrau, Théodore, writer on educa-
    tion, 121–2
Bas-Rhin department, 167
Basses-Alpes department, 159, 169 n.
Bastiat, Frédéric, economist, 64–5,
    132
Bayeux, 206
Bayonne, 223
Beauvais, 115
Beblenheim, 141
Bénard, Charles, philosophy teacher,
    107 n.
Bergson, Henri, philosopher, 75
Bernard, Claude, physiologist, 227,
    232